Heinz A. Richter

Greece 1947-1967
From Civil War to the Putsch of April 21, 1967

Peleus

Studien zur
Geschichte Griechenlands und Zyperns

Herausgegeben von Heinz A. Richter

Band 92

HARRASSOWITZ VERLAG WIESBADEN
IN KOMMISSION

VORMALS VERLAG FRANZ PHILIPP RUTZEN
WWW.RUTZEN-VERLAG.DE

Heinz A. Richter

Greece 1947 - 1967
From Civil War to the Putsch of April 21, 1967

2019

HARRASSOWITZ VERLAG • WIESBADEN
IN KOMMISSION

Peleus
Studien zur Geschichte Griechenlands und Zyperns
Herausgegeben von Heinz A. Richter
Band 92

Umschlagvignetten:
Umschlagbild: Wappen Griechenlands
Gegenüber Titelblatt: Innenbild einer Schale des Peithinosmalers, Berlin, Pergamonmuseum (CVA Berlin 2, Taf. 61).

Bibliografische Information der Deutschen Nationalbibliothek
Die Deutsche Nationalbibliothek verzeichnet diese Publikation in der Deutschen Nationalbibliografie; detaillierte bibliografische Daten sind im Internet über http://dnb.d-nb.de abrufbar.

Bibliographic information published by the Deutsche Nationalbibliothek
The Deutsche Nationalbibliothek lists this publication in the Deutsche Nationalbibliografie; detailed bibliographic data are available in the internet at http://dnb.d-nb.de

Printed in Germany on fade resistant and archival quality paper (PH 7 neutral).
Gesamtherstellung: Beltz Bad Langensalza GmbH, Bad Langensalza

www.harrassowitz-verlag.de

ISBN 978-3-447-11255-0
ISSN 1868-1476

CONTENT

INTRODUCTION

When a few months ago my collection of articles on the decade of Greek history covering the time from the Metaxas' dictatorship to the Peace Treaty of Varkiza was published, which I had translated from their original German text into English, I decided to continue working along this line. The next period covers the civil war years from1946 to 1949 and the preliminary events leading to the dictatorship of the colonels. On the first period I wrote several books. My "British Intervention in Greece" dealt with the origins of the Civil War.[1] The history of the civil war comprised three phases

1) in World War II,
2) the Dekemvriana 1944 and
3) the big "third round" from 1946 to 1949.[2]

The precedent events and the history of the dictatorship from 1967 to 1974 I described in another monograph.[3] The history of KKE is contained in my study describing the history of the Greek left.[4]

All the articles published in this volume are contained in these books, however, only in a very brief form and in German language. Since in recent years German has become an exotic language in modern history and so results published in German are not taken note of in English language publications. Therefore it seems reasonable to present these articles in an English language volume.

The subject of the first chapter is with the Peace Treaty of Varkiza. It was first published in a book edited by John O. Iatrides in 1981. Since the publication date is quite old I considered it reasonable to publish it anew in this volume.[5] The second article deals with violations of the Varkiza agreement that occurred in the Peloponnese. After an overview on the basics of this topic written by me, this article contains a memorandum by C. M. Woodhouse which he wrote in summer 1945. It contains a detailed description of the violations of this treaty in the Peloponnese. Confoundingly Woodhouse didn't take into consideration when he wrote his books on Greek history.[6] Therefore this article will be an important contribution complementing the primary sources of the Greek civil war.

The Second Plenum of the Central Committee of KKE allegedly decided to begin the Civil War; this was written and copied many times and thus it became the "historical truth". My article proved that no such decision was taken. The ominous paragraph empty without a line of dots would have had a totally different content if it had been published, i.e. on the possible participation in the parliamentary elections.[7] KKE was waiting for the advice of Stalin whether

---

1 Heinz A. Richter, *British Intervention in Greece: From Varkiza to Civil War, February 1945 - August 1946* (London: The Merlin Press, 1986), 573 pages; Greek edition: Idem, *Η επέμβαση των Άγγλων στην Ελλάδα. Από τη Βάρκιζα στον Εμφύλιο Πόλεμο* (Athen: Estia, 1997, [2]2003), 669 pages. German edition: Idem, *Griechenland 1945/46: Die britische Intervention* (Ruhpolding: Rutzen, 2016) = Peleus 69.

2 Idem, *Griechenland 1940-1950. Die Zeit der Bürgerkriege* (Ruhpolding: Rutzen, 2012) 548 pages = Peleus 59; second edition in 2018.

3 Idem, *Griechenland 1950-1974: Zwischen Demokratie und Diktatur* (Ruhpolding: Rutzen, 2013) 501 pages = PELEUS 60

4 Idem, *Geschichte der griechischen Linken* (Wiesbaden: Harrassowitz, 2017), 560 pages = Peleus 77

5 Idem, "The Varkiza Agreement and the Origins of the Greek Civil War", in: John O. Iatrides, (ed.), *Greece in the 1940s. A Nation in Crisis* (Hanover, N.H.: University Press of New England, 1981), pp. 167-180. Greek edition: Idem, "Η συμφωνία της Βάρκιζας και τα αίτια του Εμφύλιου Πολέμου", in: John O. Iatrides, ed., *Η Ελλάδα στη δεκαετία 1940-1950. Ένα έθνος σε κρίση* (Athen: Themelio, 1984), pp. 255-306

6 Idem, "Verletzungen des Friedensvertrags von Varkiza auf der Peloponnes im Sommer 1945" *Thetis* 19 (2012), pp. 180-188.

7 Idem, "The Second Plenum of the Central Committee of KKE and the Decision for Civil War: A Reappraisal", in: Lars Baerentzen, et al., eds., *Studies in the History of the Greek Civil War 1945-1949* (Kopenhagen: Museum

to participate in the elections or not. When Partsalidis returned from Moscow with the advice to participate, Zachariadis did not obey... KKE boycotted the elections and hereby gave up any parliamentary presence. Thus they led the party as well as the country into the catastrophe of the Civil War.

The 1948 Polk murder case is the subject of the next chapter.[1] There I proved that Polk was not the victim of the Communists of Salonika but of the same underground right-wing group of the *parakratos* which in May 1963 murdered the left deputy Lambrakis on order of the Athens right-wing leadership.

In literature the attack of the Democratic Army (DSE) on the little town of Konitsa in Epirus is mostly described as one of the many failed military operations during the Greek Civil War.[2] In reality it was the desperate effort of the provisional Communist Government in the mountains to gain international recognition as a government at least from the Eastern Block. Until then the DSE and its provisorial government was not recognized by anyone. There had been a signal from Moscow that recognition might be possible if the DSE conquered a town and made it the seat of their government. When the attack on Konitsa failed, recognition failed as well.

Another most interesting development is that of the Greek Communist Party (KKE) from 1944 to 1947.[3] Before the war it was one of those parties in Greece that would never have a chance in the clientelistic system because they never could distribute *rousfetia*. The Metaxas dictatorship (1936-41) destroyed the traditional big clientelistic parties. Thus when Greece was occupied by the Axis powers a new political system could come into being, the resistance movement of EAM. KKE was one of the founders but EAM never became a creature of KKE. Quite the opposite happened because EAM caused KKE to become a mass party with democratic structures and an ideology which reminded one of Euro-Communism many years later. Had EAM or the KKE of the time been present in postwar Greece the country would have overcome its clientelistic structures and would have become a European country as all other states in Western Europe. But the British intervention in December 1944 ruined this chance and the ensuing counterrevolution stopped this process of democratization. The result was for KKE that it regressed to a cadre party.

In order to enable the reader to understand what Greek clientelism is, I decided to present one of the several articles[4] which I published in German on this topic and translate it into

---

Tusculanum Press, 1987), pp. 179-187. Greek edition: Idem,"Η Δεύτερη Ολομέλεια της ΚΕ του ΚΚΕ και η απόφαση για Εμφύλιο: μια επανεκτίμηση" in: Lars Baerentzen (ed.), *Μελέτες για τον εμφύλιο Πόλεμο* (Athen: Olkos, 1992), pp. 185-193.

1 Idem, "Der Mord an Gorge Polk im Mai 1948 in Thessaloniki" *Thetis* 19 (2012), pp. 189-194

2 Idem, "The Offensive against Konitsa" in: Dimos Konitsas, Pnefmatiko Kentro (ed.) *Η επαρχία Κόνιτσας στο χώρο και το χρόνο* (Konitsa, 1996), pp. 381-87.

3 Idem, "Die griechische kommunistische Partei (KKE) 1944-1947: Von der Massenpartei zur Kaderpartei", in: Dietrich Staritz und Hermann Weber,(eds.), *Einheitsfront Einheitspartei. Kommunisten und Sozialdemokraten in Ost- und Westeuropa 1944-1948* (Köln: Verlag Wissenschaft und Politik, 1989), pp. 453-468.

4 Idem, "Zwischen Tradition und Moderne-Die politische Kultur Griechenlands", in: Armin Kerker, *Griechenland - Entfernungen in die Wirklichkeit. Ein Lesebuch* (Hamburg: Argument, 1988), pp. 100-125: idem, "Gedanken zur politischen Kultur in Griechenland und der Türkei unter Berücksichtigung Zyperns" in: Bernd Rill (ed.), *Griechenland: Politik und Perspektiven* (München: Hans Seidel Stiftung, 1999), pp. 81-90; idem, "Zur politischen Kultur Griechenlands" *Die Politische Meinung* 57;508 (März 2012), pp. 51-58; idem, "Une autre catégorie de démocratie européenne: La culture politique grecque" *Outre Terre. Revue européenne de géopolitique* 31 (2012), pp. 219-226; idem, "Politische Kultur in Griechenland" *APUZ* 35-37 (2012), pp. 30-36; idem, "Turbo-Klientelismus. Zu den Ursachen der Krise in Griechenland seit 1974" *Exantas* 23 (Dezember 2015), pp. 12-15; idem, "Zur politischen Kultur Griechenlands und Zyperns Schlaglichter und Anmerkungen" *Südosteuropa-Mitteilungen* 1 (2018), pp. 38-53.

English. The English language article at hand has a history of its own. When the University of Crete intended to bestow a honorary Ph.D on me I was advised to introduce myself by a scholarly article. I made several proposals and I was told to write another article on the Greek political culture in English. I did so and the University put it on its homepage.[1] Later on, in an attempt to deprive me of this honorary title somebody at the university of Crete blocked the access to this article or even deleted it. As this article is the concentration of all articles on this topic which I have written in German, I decided to publish it again in this volume.

The following three articles describe the developments which led to the dictatorship of the colonels on April 21, 1967. Contained are details not to be found in my book on the three Civil Wars. Thus this collection of articles fills gaps in the contemporary history of Greece and includes interpretations which are not found anywhere else. Thus this book is a contribution to the historiography of Greece in the 20th Century and it opens a window for readers who do not speak the German language or do not have access to German books.

At the same time they present on overview of my scholarly work of 50 years on Greek contemporary history. I hope they will finally contribute to a better understanding between our two countries and their peoples.

As in all other English editions of my books and articles I needed a final control by someone who knows English perfectly well. Many years this controlling work was done by Marion Sarafis and later by Anne Cliadakis. Now this work is done by Hellmut Gernert and I thank him most cordially for his readiness to help me.

1 Idem, "Another Type of European Democracy: The Political Culture of Greece" in: http://www.soc.uoc.gr/political/wp-content/uploads/2012/01/2014-Political-Culture-of-Greece.pdf

THE VARKIZA AGREEMENT AND THE ORIGINS OF THE CIVIL WAR

This paper aims to refute one of the most tenacious myths of Greece's contemporary history: that the Greek Communist party (KKE) began to plan the "Third Round," that is, the civil war of 1946—1949, as early as February 1945 when the peace agreement putting a legal end to the "Second Round" of December 1944 (the so-called Δεκεμβριανά) was signed between the Greek government and the National Liberation Front/'National Peoples' Liberation Army (EAM/ELAS) at Varkiza. Similarly. this is the myth that a democratic state became the victim of premeditated communist aggression.

In this paper I shall try to show, by analysing the actual events, that this myth is a piece of Cold War propaganda based on erroneous facts and improper analogies. In order to refute the myth definitively, it is necessary to examine the full details of both the external and internal affairs of the period. This I have done, in a research study for the *Deutsche Forschungsgemeinschaft*. In this paper I shall confine myself to a summary of the most important internal developments. This method is justified by the fact, during the period under consideration, external factors influenced Greece's history only in a very limited way. Logically, the starting point for the present analysis is the Varkiza Agreement.

The Varkiza Agreement

The Varkiza peace agreement, signed on February 12, 1945,[1] was not a relatively noncommittal agreement like the National Bands Agreement of or the Agreement of Myrofyllo and Plaka of 1944. It was, rather, an official pact between representatives of the Greek state and leaders of leftist resistance organization. Not only the bargaining that led to its signing but also the text itself was closely supervised if not actually dictated by British officials in Athens. In this way the British government shouldered serious responsibilities in Greece. The significance of this agreement is even further corroborated by the fact that on March 13, 1945 not only its text but also the programmatic declarations of Foreign Minister Ioannis Sofianopoulos and of the secretary of the Central Committee of KKE, Georgios Siantos, were published in the *Government Gazette* as *Συντακτική Πράξη* No. 23 [Constitutional Act 23].[2] Such publication made both texts part of the living fundamental law of Greece - not just of ordinary law. The aim of the Varkiza Agreement was twofold: first, to put an end to the civil war that had begun on December 3, 1944, and had temporarily ceased with the truce of January 15, and, second, to establish conditions for the reconciliation of the opposing factions within the country and for peaceful postwar development. The first aim was achieved; the second was not. A little more than one year later, Greece was more split than ever before, a new outbreak of civil strife was slowly building up, and the Varkiza Agreement had proved to be no more than a scrap of paper. The causes for these developments are certainly not to be found in the text; the wording of the Varkiza Agreement was as good as that of any other similar pact of such importance. If both sides had fulfilled their obligations, a peaceful development might have been possible.

This leads to two questions: What were the causes for the failure of the Varkiza Agreement and who was ultimately responsible for its failure Or, to phrase these questions in a different

---

1 English text of the Varkiza Agreement in C. M. *Woodhouse. Appel of Discord: A Survey of Recent Greek Politics in Their International Settmg* (London, 1948), pp. 308—10.

2 Efimeris tis Kyverniseos tou Vasileiou tis Ellados (Government Gazette of the Kingdom of Greece], vol. 1, no. 68 (March 23,1945), pp 235-241..

way: What were the deeper causes of the new civil war and who was responsible for pushing developments beyond the stage where discussion and reconciliation were still possible?

For many years it has been argued that the culprits were the Greek communists. Two main arguments have been advanced to support this one, that the general secretary of the Central Committee of KKE, Nikos Zachariadis, himself said (I quote D. George Kousoulas), *"The Varkiza Agreement was . . . merely the termination of the second round and a respite for the regrouping of the popular democratic forces, in view of the new decisive confrontation which is inevitably coming;"* and, two, that the communists did not give up all the weapons they had in their possession but hid considerable quantities.[1]

To begin with, the latter is an undisputable fact. As we learn from the memoirs of Giorgis Blanas (Kissavos)[2], and from a telegram of Giannis Ioannidis published in KKE's *'Επίσημα Κείμενα* [Official Texts],[3] immediately after the signing of the Varkiza Agreement the KKE Politbureau ordered that part of the weapons should be hidden. The reasoning, however, that because the communists hid some weapons they were therefore preparing the "Third Round" is anachronistic: it explains the communist motives of February 1945 by means of events that occurred more than a year later. The same is true with the argument concerning the words of Zachariadis.[4] He made his statement in 1950, when once again he was trying to justify the party line a posteriori. Both arguments are therefore not valid for 1945. There is not the slightest doubt that KKE, as well as every other party of the country, had the aim of taking over the Greek state. The question, however, is how and when this was to occur. As we shall show later in this paper, in 1945 KKE did not aim at taking over power directly and certainly not by force. The purpose of the above-mentioned arguments was to distract public attention from the true sequence of events.

The Varkiza Agreement consists of nine articles. Of these, only two contained obligations for the Greek left. Article 4 stipulated that EAM/ ELAS was to free its hostages (they were called civil captives); this obligation was fulfilled by the left. Article 6 required the demobilization of the armed forces of the resistance, which was done as well. Thus, except for the fact that not all weapons were handed over to the state, the Greek left fulfilled its obligations. The other seven articles, and to a certain degree even the two articles pertaining specifically to the left, contained obligations for, and guarantees by, the Greek government. By their publication in the *Government Gazette,* these obligations and guarantees became law.

Freedoms

The Greek government promised in Article 1 a full restoration of civil liberties, especially freedom of the press and trade union liberties. Prominent among the government's promises was the pledge to repeal certain illiberal laws of the past, for example, the notorious law of 1929 that made agitation against the existing social order a crime. The government-in-exile had repealed this law, but because this repeal was not published in the *Government Gazette* in Athens, the law remained in force and judges continued to apply it.[5] In addition, notoriously illiberal laws of the Metaxas period continued to be valid.[6] Only a few of the more than four thousand laws of the various collaboration governments were repealed, and many of them

1 D. George Kousoulas, *Revolution and Defeat: The Story of the Communist Party* (London, 1965), p. 217.
2 Giorgios Blanas (Kissavos), *'Emfylios polemos 1946—1949: Opos to ezisa* (Athens, 1976), pp. 35ff.
3 KKE, *Episima keimena*, vol. V, (Athens: KKE Interior, 1974), p. 357.
4 Nikos Zachariadis, *Ta provlimata kathodigisis sto KKE* (1952), p. 87.
5 Politikos Synaspismos ton Tmimaton tou EAM, *Lefki Vivlos: Paravseis tis Varkizas* (Athens, 1945), p. 11.
6 *Ibidem*, p. 10f

remain in force to this day.[1] This meant that the antidemocratic legal system of the Metaxas dictatorship and of the occupation still existed and was applied by a supposedly democratic government.

The provisions of the Varkiza Agreement guaranteeing freedom of the press were applied in a "tricky" way. It is true that until 1947 not one newspaper of the left was prohibited or officially suppressed. The methods used to hamper the freedom of the leftist press were more subtle. At the time of the country's liberation there had been EAM newspapers in almost every provincial town of reasonable size. In 1946 only *Ριζοσπάστης* and *'Ελευθερη Ελλάδα* still appeared on a few newsstands. In the provinces national guardsmen, gendarmerie and other sympathizers with the extreme right had smashed the printing presses and had "convinced" leftist editors by intimidation that it was better to have only two newspapers that were printed in Athens.[2] Moreover, readers were threatened even if caught reading liberal newspapers such as "*Ελευθερία*".[3] Thus circulation of the leftist press was considerably reduced, if not halted altogether. Another method of suppressing leftist newspapers in the provinces was to hamper transport from Athens to the provinces; the buses that were to take the leftist newspapers to the provincial towns had "unfortunately" departed already. To reduce the circulation of the leftist press even in Athens, the government supplied leftist newspapers with only the "correct" quota of the rationed newsprint. Progovernment newspapers, on the other hand, were amply supplied by the "gray market."[4] Thus the various Greek governments could prove to the world that freedom of the press existed in the country even though freedom of reading and freedom of newspaper circulation were almost nonexistent.

Trade Union Liberties

Similarly, the restoration of trade union liberties proved to be an equal farce. Since details of the Greek trade union movement are not generally known, we must supply some background information.[5] Before the Metaxas dictatorship, the General Federation of Greek Labour (GSEE) had been a feeble movement of more than fifteen hundred small unions engulfed in party disputes and open to constant governmental interference. Under Metaxas, the GSEE was "welded" into one organism modelled after the German *Arbeitsfront*. During the occupation, a new syndicalist organization, the National Workers' Liberation Front (EEAM), came into being. EEAM, the workers' EAM, attracted the overwhelming majority of the Greek working class and efficiently frustrated plans by Fritz Saukel, Hitler's minister of Labour, to conscript forced Labour in Greece. After the creation of the Political Committee of National Liberation early in 1944, the EEAM Central Committee declared the extant official (and collaborationist) GSEE leadership under Hatzidimitriou deposed and constituted itself as the new provisional

---

1 Foreign Office Archives, Public Record Office, London (hereafter - FO. R12.370/4/19, "Summary of principal events during the week ending 22 July 1945".

2 William H. McNeill, *The Greek Dilemma, War and Aftermath* (New York, 1947), p. 199.

3 Frank Smothers, W. H. McNeill, E.D. McNeill, *Report on the Greeks. Findings of a Twentieth Century Fund Team which Surveyed Conditions m Greece in 1947* (New York, 1948), p. 130.

4 *Ibidem.* "Grey market:" a market sponsored and controlled by the government for partisan purposes.

5 On the Greek trade union movement, see Christos Jecchinis. *Trade Unionism in Greece: A Study in Political Paternalism* (Chicago, 1967); Basil P Mathiopoulos, *Die Geschichte der sozialen Frage und des Sozialismus in Griechenland (1921—1961)* (Hannover, 1961); Nikolaos Stavrou, "Pressure Groups the Greek Political Setting" Diss. (The George Washington University, 1970); Kostas Sepheris, *Elliniko syndikalistiko kinima,* 1880-1975(Athens, 1976); Kostas Theos, *Ta ellinika syndikata stin pali enantia sto fasismo kai gia tin anexartisia tous* (Athens, 1947), and International Labour Office, Labour Problemsin Greece: Report of the Mission of the International Labour Office to Greece (October—November 1947) (Geneva, 1949).

executive of the GSEE. After the liberation, the minister of Labour in the Papandreou cabinet, Miltiadesi, officially recognized the new executive by virtue of a 1942. law of the Tsouderos government,[1] which had repealed the illiberal, antisyndicalist legislation of Metaxas and had obliged the minister of labour to help in the reorganization of the GSEE. The officially recognized GSEE executive began to prepare union elections for a national congress. A few days later, however, the "Second Round" broke out in Athens and the GSEE leadership found themselves on the wrong side, that is, on the EAM side. Hatzidimitriou[2] and a few other collaborationist union leaders of former days (nineteen altogether) who had stayed in Athens took advantage of this opportunity and induced the new minister of labour to recognize them as the real GSEE executive. Hatzidimitriou became general secretary.

Thus at the time of the truce in January 1945 there were two GSEE executives: one representing the majority of the Greek workers - as even C. M. Woodhouse, no friend of the Greek left, has stated in his book *Apple of Discord*[3] - and the other representing no one, yet having the authority of the government behind it. Both claimed to be the official leadership. The rivalry was ended by Sir Walter Citrine of the British Trades Union Congress (TUC). Though he knew that the law on the basis of which both leaderships had been appointed was not valid because it had not been republished in Athens in the *Government Gazette*, out of anticommunist motives he accepted the Chatzidimitriou group as the acting GSEE leadership. In the so-called Citrine Agreement,[4] he sanctioned state intervention into trade union affairs and artificially revived the old system of tiny competing unions by obliging the union leaders to accept a new GSEE executive in which *all* fractions of the Greek trade union movement would be represented. At the same time he destroyed the unity of the working class and rehabilitated the small clique of collaboration's and former adherents of Metaxas.

The following months were characterized by repeated state interventions in favour of these right-wing union leaders. In the union elections the former EAM unions, which had created a new organization, the Workers' Antifascist League (ERGAS), always won a majority. The right-wing unions, however, had the help of the state and of the courts, and by constant intrigues their new leader, Fotis Makris, was able to stay in power. In the end, the left succeeded in gaining the majority of the representatives to the National Congress of Labour in March 1946, and a new leadership of GSEE emerged that had the official blessing of the World Federation of Trade Unions. But again the state intervened. The Council of State ruled that the legal basis of the elections had been contrary to the constitution and the new minister of labour appointed a new GSEE executive giving the Makris clique a majority. From then until the 1960s, Makris remained the uncontested leader of the Greek trade union movement.

Amnesty Misapplied

Under Article 3 of the Varkiza Agreement the government had promised a far-reaching amnesty for crimes committed during the "Second Round," excluding common-law crimes against life and property which were not absolutely necessary for the achievement of the political crime concerned.[5] However, the courts made a travesty of justice out of this clause. The judges, most of whom had served under Metaxas and the occupation, did not confine

---

1 Law no. 3127, of October 31, 1942.

2 The Labour Attache of the British Embassy in Athens characterized Hatzidimitriou as "a corrupt and incompetent placeseeker." "Internal situation of Greece, September 1945. Labour and Trade Unions in Greece." FO R 18.945/4/19.

3 Woodhouse, *op. cit.*, p. 32f

4 Trade Union Congress, *What We Saw in Greece: Report of the TUC Delegation* (London: TUC, 1945), p. 22f.

5 *Report of the British Legal Mission to Greece*, Cmd 6838, (London, 1946).

themselves to trying those charged with a crime during the "Second Round," but extended their charges to crimes committed at the time of the occupation as well. Thus, persons who had collected taxes for the wartime PEEA (that is, suppliers for ELAS) were charged with robbery and looting. Others who had executed collaborators, following trials by courts set up by EAM, were now charged with murder. Former judges of such courts were also charged with murder on the grounds of moral responsibility. Former ELAS commanders - Stefanos Sarafis was not exempted[1] - were held morally responsible for all sorts of crimes. Even the killing of a German or Bulgarian by a member of the leftist resistance movement was considered a crime. The jurors who passed the sentences belonged exclusively to the propertied class. In December 1945 the British Legal Mission stated that the courts were in fact disregarding certain laws. Between January and April 1945, more than forty thousand people were put in jail; by April, twenty-nine thousand had been set free again.

In August the Greek government passed a law that prohibited arrest without a warrant and that ordered the release of those who had been in jail for more than six months without having had their cases examined.[2] Accordingly, between September and November some six thousand people were released, but the number of the newly arrested still surpassed that of the released. In November 1945 more than eighteen thousand people were incarcerated, of whom fewer than three thousand served a sentence. Warrants had been issued against eighty thousand persons.[3] Before the war the normal population of the Greek prisons had been less than eight thousand. Moreover, conditions in the prisons were far from satisfactory. By November the overcrowding had assumed such serious proportions that the government was forced to publish a law for the decongestion of the prisons, by virtue of which the prison population was reduced by March 1946 to fourteen thousand[4]—the lowest number in many years. A general amnesty, which would have been the only practical remedy, however was not considered.

Creation of a New National Army

In Article 5 of the Varkiza Agreement the Greek government had promised to create a national army to which even former ELAS members would be admitted. Instead of this, the army was welded into an anticommunist weapon. From the lower ranks to the top commands, the army was filled with royalists, anticommunists, and former members of the wartime Security Battalions.[5] The General Staff was controlled by a secret, extreme right-wing organization called League of Young Officers SAN), which had come into being in the Middle East and which, after the liberation, changed its name to the Sacred League of Greek Officers (IDEA).[6] The purge of the armed forces, which the Varkiza Agreement had called for, did not take place: they were purged of all democratic elements.

Purge of Fascists and Collaborators

The same thing happened with the provisions of Article 7 (purge of civil service) and Article 8 (purge of security services, gendarmerie, and city police). Instead of purging the civil ser-

1 Ambassador Reginald Leeper to FO, May 7, 1945, FO R 478/4/19. Leeper reported: *"the Crown Prosecutor of Tripoli has caused a small-scale flutter by issuing warrants for the arrest of Aris (which is understandable), General Saraphis, and two former ELAS commanders ... as being morally responsible for atrocities. This runs counter to the spirit of the Varkiza agreement."*

2 *Efimeris tis Kyverniseos* [Government Gazette] vol. I, no. 213 (August 25, 1945), p. 1044ff.

3 *Eleftheria*, (December 11, 1945)..

4 Ambassador Clifford V. Norton to FO, March 21, 1946, FO R 4.702/1/19.

5 Hal Lehrman, "Athens Calling," Nation, 160 (May 5, 1945), p. 515.

6 Ieros Desmos Ellinikon Axiomatikon (IDEA) 'Apokalipseis tou tipou, 1951-1952 (Athens, 1975), p. 65.

vice of former fascists and collaborators, the government applied one of Metaxas's laws and purged thousands of civil servants who had joined the resistance, on the ground that they were members of "anti-national organizations."[1] Men of the gendarmerie who had joined ELAS during the occupation were prosecuted for desertion.[2] Former agents of Konstantinos Maniadakis, Metaxas's Minister of security, continued to serve in the 'Ασφάλεια ("secret police"). University professors were fired because of their membership in EAM.[3] Even the church got rid of its "undesirable elements." In March 1945, at a meeting of the Holy Synod presided over by the notorious wartime collaborator Bishop Spyridonos of Ioannina, former EAM-connected bishops were removed from their sees.[4]

Treatment of Collaborators

In his opening speech at the Varkiza conference, Foreign Minister Ioannis Sofianopoulos promised that the government would bring the collaborators to trial. There were three distinct categories of collaborators: one, former ministers of the quisling cabinets, two, members of the police, gendarmerie, and the Security Battalions, and three, common criminals such as black marketeers, speculators, agents of the Gestapo, informers, and Greek Nazis. Only the last category was prosecuted seriously, some of them were sentenced to death (but only a few being executed). In the second category only a few notorious torturers were prosecuted. The others were left unmolested when they argued that they had not collaborated with the enemy but had fought communism. There was even a tendency to reward them, as is shown by the posthumous promotion of one of the main organizers of the Security Battalions.[5] Many prominent figures of these battalions found their way back into the armed forces.

The great trial of the occupation ministers was a farce.[6] On the very first day of the trial the court decided that any sentences imposed would be subject to ratification by the future parliament, which was expected - by fraud and intimidation - to be controlled by extreme rightists.[7] Quisling Prime Minister Ioannis's Rallis comment on this decision was characteristic: *"He was now confident that the Good God had granted him several more years to live."*[8]Another decision of the court was equally "delicate:" it ruled that there would be no official minutes of the trial and that the unofficial stenographic ones were to be destroyed after six months - a clear travesty of justice.[9] The trial itself was strange indeed. Almost all of the prosecution witnesses, even the liberals, tended to minimize the guilt of the accused.[10] The defence witnesses tried to prove that practically the whole political world of Athens had been accomplices of the accused, who, it was alleged, had not collaborated, primarily, but had fought against communism.[11] This strategy of the defence was successful. The sentences were relatively mild and the prison in which the convicted served their sentences until they were pardoned soon afterwards was a kind of gentlemen's prison. Thus Greece was the only coun-

1 *Lefki Vivlos*, p. 33.
2 *Ibidem*, p. 43. Also, Leeper to FO, November 30, 1945, FO R 20.2624 19.
3 EAM memorandum, March 12, 1945, in FO R 5.617/4/19.
4 *Lefki Vivlos,* p.39. Also, Leeper to FO, April 17,1945, FO R 7.363/4 19.
5 Woodhouse, *op. cit.* .p. 97.
6 On the trial of the collaborators, see Leeper to FO, March 19,1945, FO R 5.857/4/19; Leeper to FO, June 5, 1945, FO R 10.14/4/19, and Lefteris Apostolou, *I Parodia ris dikis ton dosilogon kai i aftokatadiki tis dexias* (Athens, 1945).
7 FO R 5.857/4/19.
8 *Ibidem.*
9 FO R 10.144/4/19.
10 FO R 5.857/4/19.
11 FO R 10.144/4/19.

try in Europe where collaborators were practically exempt from punishment and where communism was a worse "crime" than collaboration.[1]

Reasons for the Violations of Varkiza

These few examples of violations of the Varkiza Agreement show that the obligations that the government had assumed were not fulfilled at all. To explain and interpret the reasons for these violations, together with all the necessary background, is sufficiently complicated, since so many factors contributed to them. The simplest explanation for the actions of the various postwar governments of Greece is their irreconcilably anticommunist character, which made them relatively insensitive toward infringements against the left by subordinate authorities. They considered such illegal actions to be the natural aftermath of what they called a "red conspiracy." Some ministers deliberately closed their eyes towards these infringements; others openly encouraged them; only few tried to stop them. Another explanation is the government's lack of control over subordinate authorities. None of the postwar governments succeeded in establishing full authority over the secondary governmental organs, which were still in the hands of former Metaxists and collaborators. Only by a thorough purge could adequate control have been reestablished. But to initiate such a purge would have exposed the various governments to the accusation of being procommunist, a thing that they abhorred. Anticommunism and executive weakness are thus the main contributing factors, on the government side, for the violations of the Varkiza Agreement.

The Emergence of the παρακράτος ("Parastate")

To make matters worse, the lack of control favoured the development of an independent power apparatus of the extreme right which successfully competed with the authority of the state. The nuclei of these new power centres had already existed during the occupation. So-called nationalist organizations had been created in direct opposition to EAM. As early as the autumn of 1943, these organizations had been united in the Panhellenic Liberation League (PAS). In 1944, close contacts with the extreme right-wing organization in the armed forces, SAN (which, after liberation, became IDEA), were established. After the unrest in the Greek armed forces in the Middle East in the spring of 1944, a leading figure of SAN became commander-in chief of the Greek army, as well as Chief of the General Staff. The armed forces were purged of all "antinational" elements, and members of SAN were eased into key posts. Meanwhile, in occupied Greece, Colonel George Grivas created another rightist anti-EAM organization, the notorious "X." After the "Second Round," these right-wing organizations succeeded in packing the army, gendarmerie, and police with their members. In addition, they created armed bands which, in close cooperation with the National Guard and later under the benevolent eyes of the gendarmerie, began at a constantly increasing rate to terrorize their political opponents.

All this leads us to conclude that the communists were not entirely wrong when they spoke of a unilateral civil war. Toward the end of 1945 these right-wing organizations controlled large parts of the state and were able successfully to frustrate any attempt of liberal politicians to improve the political climate. The country was no longer controlled by its constitutional authorities but by this competing power apparatus which the Greeks call *παρακράτος* ("parastate").

---

1 Woodhouse, *op. cit.*, p. 241; also "Greek Balance Sheet," *New Statesman and Nation,* XXXV:901 (June 12, 1948), 475.

Economic Crisis

The political climate was further worsened by a rapidly deteriorating economic and financial situation. In October 1944 there had been general enthusiasm among workers and peasants, who were ready to undertake the reconstruction of their country with their own hands. Thousands of young men voluntarily repaired roads and rebuilt demolished bridges.[1] EAM, which had been the soul of the resistance against the Axis occupiers, became the promoter of reconstruction; the majority of the population was ready to join in the reconstruction efforts. But this initiative from the grassroots was destroyed by the "Second Round", which restored the old economic and financial oligarchy that was closely connected with the political oligarchy. From now on, reconstruction was the responsibility of this oligarchy and the majority of the population became indifferent and apathetic. The result was complete chaos. The industrialists did not open their factories. The government had no revenues. Speculators earned fortunes on the black market. Inflation ruined everyone who had no gold sovereigns. Corruption was omnipresent.[2] Tens of thousands were out of work and the United Nations Relief and Rehabilitation Administration (UNRRA) was able only to keep people alive. When, as in the case of Kyriakos Varvaressos, deputy prime minister and minister of supply, there was an effort to improve the situation, the oligarchy in power sabotaged this effort. Strikes were numerous. Slowly, when the mass of the population was almost starving, apathy turned into .hatred. Thus at the beginning of 1946 the political climate was characterized by fear, oppression, hopelessness, want, desperation, and demoralization.

British Policy

Although responsibility for these developments rests to a great extent with the Greek government, British policy makers were equally responsible for the outcome.[3] In December 1944 they had intervened to save Greece from an alleged communist danger. In 1945, when a counter-revolutionary tide hit Greece, sweeping away everything the resistance had built up and bringing back the old structures, the British reacted with great hesitation. The trouble with British policy toward Greece in 1945 was not so much intervention as inconsistency. There were political spheres under total British control and others where the British were totally uninterested. There were inconsistencies between the two different levels of British policy making, one centre being in Athens and the other in London. Within a single year British policy changed from total penetration to hands off, and then back again to intervention. At one time British policy makers actively overthrew a government (Nikolaos Plastiras's) and at another time they passively watched the petering out of another (Petros Voulgaris's). In October they rejected the economic program of the government of Panagiotis Kanellopoulos only to accept this same program in slightly modified form two months later. On the one hand they intervened in the tiniest details of internal affairs while on the other hand they failed to ensure the Greek government's compliance with its obligations under the Varkiza Agreement. At one moment they were depriving one Greek government of its authority and at another moment expecting another government to act responsibly. No wonder, then, that the Παρακράτος was able to assume actual control. In short, British foreign policy toward Greece in 1945 showed the same symptoms of incoherence as it had during World War II. There was, however, a decisive difference. Whereas until the end of 1944 the various British interventions had influenced,

---

1 Constantine Poulos, "Greek Tragedy, 1945," *Nation*, no. 161 (November 3, 1945), p. 452.

2 *Ibidem*.

3 This section is based on a very large number of British documents and it is therefore impossible to quote them specifically and in detail.

but not totally altered, the course of Greek history, by their intervention in December 1944 British policy makers brought a line of development to an abrupt end. From then on they were responsible for the course of events. Unfortunately this was not understood in London. Ultimately, therefore, British policy makers - Tories as well as Laborites - were responsible for the rapid deterioration of the situation in Greece.

Policy of KKE

To complete this review of the origins of the Greek civil war, we must add a few remarks about the policy of KKE during this period. Immediately after signing the Varkiza Agreement, Georgios Siantos, secretary of KKE's Central Committee, answered questions put to him by foreign correspondents. Among many other things, he said that KKE's aim was now to become a legal party and to pursue a policy within the constitutional framework.[1] In other words, after Varkiza, KKE's aim was integration into the country's parliamentary system. The decision of the KKE Politburo to hide some weapons does not contradict this policy. It was a defensive measure against unforeseen eventualities, not a strategic move for the preparation of the "Third Round." For KKE the Varkiza Agreement meant the end of the armed struggle and the beginning of its integration into the parliamentary system. This is further proved by a series of theoretical articles published in *Κομμουνιστικό 'Επιθεόριθηση* [*Communist Review*] after Varkiza, all of which show KKE's readiness for reconciliation. Flow serious the communists' desire for reconciliation and integration was is shown by their treatment of the opponents to this policy within their own ranks, as for example the wartime ELAS leader Aris Velouchiotis. The 11th Plenum of the Central Committee, which met early in April 1945, emphasized that the KKE had fought for national liberation, not for power. A development analogous to that in Yugoslavia was excluded in express terms: Greece's geographical position prohibited such a development. The only mistake of the past, it was argued, had been that KKE had not tried hard enough to arrive at an understanding with Great Britain. The "Second Round" had been the tragic result of a misunderstanding.[2]

This course was not changed even when General Secretary Nikos Zachariadis returned from Dachau. On June 1, he flatly denied that KKE had ever fought for a social revolution out of a minority position, claiming instead that the aim of the party was to win over the majority of the people. Only Trotskyites, anarchists, and idiots, as he put it, believed in a forced transition to socialism against the will of the majority of the people. Moreover, since 1934 KKE had striven for the erection of a bourgeois democratic republic. Zachariadis then stated that KKE's course was identical with the line taken by the French communists,[3] a line which was later criticized by the Cominform as "revisionist." In other words, KKE still stuck to the line of the Seventh World Congress of the Comintern (1934).

A few days later Zachariadis analysed Anglo-Greek relations. In his famous "two poles theory" he officially recognized British hegemony in Greece and implicitly accepted the view that any social change in Greece would need the prior blessing of Britain[4]- a theory shared by the Italian Communist party. In other words, Zachariadis continued the Anglophile course that KKE had pursued during the war. His words and acts had two aims: one, to signal to the bourgeois parties that there was no danger of a communist revolution; and, two, to make Britain understand that KKE accepted her leading role in Greece. But neither of the two groups to

1 KKE, *Episima keimena*, vol. V, pp. 350-352.
2 Zisis Zographos, "Merika zitimata tis politikis mas grammis" Neos Kosmos (September 1950), p. 642ff
3 *Rizospastis* (June 4, 1945).
4 *Ibidem* (June 5, 1945).

whom Zachariadis had addressed his speeches was interested in his offers; both gave him the cold shoulder. The 12th Plenum, which took place during the last days of June, brought no change in KKE's political line, which continued to be "revisionist." The only new item was the decision to offer resistance to the constant persecutions by the right by organizing a mass "self-defence movement" (*μαζική αυτοάμυνα)*. The weapons of this self-defence were to be mass strikes and demonstrations, but *not* armed resistance.[1] A few days later KKE's newpaper *Ριζοσπάστης*[2] spoke for the first time of the "new occupation"—that is, the British occupation—but even this was not the sign of a radical change in the party line. This verbal radicalism echoed similar excesses on the part of the bourgeois parties against the worsening political situation. Even when, in an outburst on August 24th, Zachariadis spoke of a possible civil war, this too was not a sign of a new course.[3] It was again a verbal excess provoked by the frustration of his offers for reconciliation.

However, the Seventh Party Congress (October 1945) did bring about a shift in the party line. From then on the party's ideological orientation would no longer follow the ideological conceptions of the French and Italian communist parties. It would, instead, be modelled on that of the eastern European communist parties. The term "people's democracy" now meant a regime in the Soviet sphere of influence. It was hinted that a violent transition to socialism could not be excluded.[4] A Panhellenic military committee was established to study a possible armed clash.[5] But even this did not mean that Zachariadis had decided to lead the party toward an armed uprising. The new development was once more a measure taken against unforeseen eventualities, and it served far more to calm the more militant members of KKE than to prepare for the civil war, as is shown by the fact that the Panhellenic military committee only met twice.[6] What happened was simply that the course of the party became tougher and more militant, that the party was no longer ready to be passive in its acceptance of the persecutions by the right, and that it was preparing for all eventualities. But Zachariadis still tried to leave all options open. Just as during the occupation and throughout the year 1945, KKE did not act but instead reacted to the persecutions by its opponents. The initiative rested with the government. Not even in 1946 was there a decision to start a full-scale civil war. The 2nd Plenum in February of that year did not decide to begin an armed uprising; it merely permitted armed resistance against the rightist terror in the countryside.[7] The civil war did not come as a result of the decision or the acts of KKE; it was rather the outcome of a process set in motion by the terrorist acts of the extreme right.

Conclusions

At the beginning of this paper I stated that its aim was to refute the myth that from the time of the Varkiza Agreement KKE was planning the "Third Round," the myth that the democratic state of Greece became the victim of communist aggression. I hope that I have succeeded in showing, one, that there was no such plan, and, two, that Greek society was far rom being

---

1 *Apofasi ris 12^{is} olomeleias tis Kentrikis Epitropis tou KKE* (Athens, 1945), p. 5f.
2 *Pizospastis*, (July 5, 1945)..
3 Consul General Rapp (Thessaloniki) to British Embassy, Athens, August 25, 1945, FO R 14.411/8001/19; *Manchester Guardian*, (August 28, 1945); Consul General Rapp to British Embassy, Athens, August 27, 1945, FO 14.520/2001/19; *Pizospastis* (August 28, 1945)
4 To 7° Synedrio tou KKE ,vol. V (Athens. 1945), p. 16.
5 *Ibidem*, vol. I, p. 10
6 Blanas, *op. cit.*, p. 75.
7 Speech of Markos Vapheiadis at the 7th Plenum of the Central Committee (1957), Neos Kosmos, (April-May 1957P, pp., 47, 50.

democratic. But if the communists did not aim at civil war, who then wanted the civil war? The various Greek governments? Certainly not. The British? Not at all. Who then? It is my firm conviction that except for former fascists and collaborators, and other die-hard rightists, no one directly wanted the civil war. But fear of the communist danger was omnipresent and was played up by the extreme right. The nation's politicians suffered from a pathological hatred of communism, and this made them incapable of offering a conciliatory alternative to the left. They were afraid that each conciliatory move would be interpreted by the communists, as well as by the right, as a weakness. Thus they opened the field to the extreme right, which offered nothing but the alternatives of unconditional submission or armed clash. The origins of the civil war are thus to be found primarily in the political climate, in factors such as the terrorism, want, desperation, and hopelessness, which were he result of the past and of the rule of the parakratos. In order to have broken this rule a major effort to purge the state of all its extreme right-wing elements would have been necessary. But not one of the postwar Greek governments was ready or able to undertake such a purge, which could only have been done with the help of Britain—and Britain did not offer this help. Thus ultimately the responsibility for the creation of this climate rests with Britain's *laissez faire* policy.

I also argued in the introduction that I considered this myth to be part of the Cold War propaganda. Within the Soviet sphere of influence in Eastern Europe the communist parties of these countries successively took over control of the respective states with the help of the Red Army and subsequently purged their opponents. In Greece things happened the other way around. There is no doubt that these parties acted on orders from the Kremlin. But it would be wrong to assume that the parties outside the Soviet sphere of influence had received similar orders. In 1945 the communist world was on its way toward becoming polycentric. and the various parties outside the Soviet sphere had started to follow lines of their own. The Kremlin, uninterested in their fate, preferred that they not create any trouble for the Soviet Union. The result was the "revisionist" line of the French, of the Italian, and, originally, of the Greek communists. We have shown how and why the Greek communists abandoned this line and followed a tougher course. But there was a decisive difference between the conditions in France and Italy and those in Greece. In France and to a lesser extent in Italy, fascism and collaborationism had been uprooted or at least had lost all influence. In Greece it was the other way round. Greece became the living proof that Bertholt Brecht's warning was only too true—the warning that the womb from which this monster, fascism, had crept was still fertile. However, according to the propaganda of that time, fascism had been defeated and the new danger to freedom was now communism.

VIOLATIONS OF VARKIZA IN THE PELOPONNESE IN SUMMER 1945

On 12 February 1945 the Peace Treaty of Varkiza ended the *Dekemvriana* which on the one side was a civil war between the Greek Right and Left but on the other side an armed intervention by the British in this civil war. The fighting had begun on 3 December when the police fired on a proven unarmed demonstration of the Left resistance organization EAM in Syntagma Square in Athens, on a demonstration which intended nothing except doing what all demonstrations do, move from Syntagma to Omonia Square, waving banners and shouting slogans. The leadership of the Left did not want a clash, but a change of government. However, there were 28 dead and 148 wounded.[1] The correspondent of the London *Times*, Geoffrey Hoare, called this massacre a Fascist action.[2]

Consequently the Left attacked the Athens police stations. In this internal Greek conflict Churchill intervened. He had been informed of the events of 3 December and had learned that ELAS was attacking police stations. He defined these events as an all-out attack on the centre of the town. He telegraphed to Ambassador Leeper that a change of government was excluded and he should take care that G. Papandreou remained in office. To general Scobie he sent the following order: He had to keep Athens quiet and destroy ELAS units marching on Athens: *"Naturally E.L.A.S. will try to put women and children in the van where shooting may occur. You must be clever about this and avoid mistakes. But do not hesitate to fire at any armed male in Athens who assails the British authority or Greek authority [...]. Do not however hesitate to act as if you were in a conquered city where a local rebellion is in progress. [...] You may count upon my support in all reasonable and sensible action taken on this basis. We have to hold and dominate Athens. It would be a great thing for you to succeed in this without bloodshed if possible, but also with bloodshed if necessary."*[3]

As Churchill himself admits he took the position of Arthur Balfour who in the late 1880s telegraphed to the British authorities in Ireland in the same sense. Churchill wanted an armed clash. A political solution was no longer acceptable for him. His aim was the restoration of the Greek monarchy. In order to achieve this he had concluded the notorious percentage agreement with Stalin which left the latter free hand in Bulgaria and Rumania and to him in Greece. Since 6 December British troops participated in the fighting in Athens. Churchill justified the intervention with the claim that a Communist take-over was threatening in Athens.

In London Churchill had to face a heated debate in the House of Commons. Labour MPs attacked him massively. Finally Churchill threatened that would demand a vote of confidence. If he did not lose it he would continue his policy and purge Athens and its surroundings from all rebels. Of the 680 deputies only 279 voted for him. 30 deputies voted against him, and an overwhelming majority (371) abstained from voting. Churchill, however, considered this a a parliamentary victory. American criticism on Churchill's action was massive. By an indiscretion Churchill's "don't hesitate to shoot" telegram was published in the US and triggered a storm of protest on both sides of the Atlantic. The only direction from where not protest was heard was Moscow. Stalin stuck to the percentage agreement and remained silent and abandoned his Greek comrades. In mid-December he informed them that KKE could not expect any support from Moscow. The representative of the Soviet Union stayed in the area control-

---

1 The narrative follows if not mentioned otherwise Heinz Richter, *British Intervention in Greece. From Varkiza to Civil War February 1945 to August 1946* (London: Merlin Press, 1986).

2 *The Times* (London, 4 December 1944).

3 Richter, *op.cit*, p. 252.

led by the British all the time. Churchill permitted Stalin's game by talking of a Trotzkyte rebellion in Athens.

By Christmas 1944 the pressure of Churchill became so strong that he felt obliged to travel to Athens to find a compromise. It was found in the person of Archbishop Damaskinos who became regent and a new government was formed. On 11 January an armistice was concluded and on 2 February 1945 peace negotiations began in the village of Varkiza situated on the Saronic Gulf which ended on 12 February wit the signing of the Peace Treaty of Varkiza, as it was called from now on. On 23 February the text was published in the *Efimeris tis Kyverniseos* (Government Gazette) as constitutional act no. 23 thus making it direct law.

The Peace Treaty of Varkiza was a fair compromise and had it been fulfilled according to the wording and ist spirit there would have been a peaceful postwar development in Greece. The aim of the chief of KKE, Siantos, was the loyalty of his to the constitution similar to what Maurice Thorez was aiming at in France. Siantos did not have any other option. Of course he could have insisted on a broad amnesty, but who could imagine at that time what would happen during the next 18 months? To a certain degree Siantos trusted the left-liberal Sofianopoulos and his guarantees and even he did not have an idea that the Peace Treaty would become an instrument of repression par excellence.

From April on Greece was under total British control. Ambassador Leeper became the High Commissioner and Greece became a British protectorate.[1] The regent Damaskinos took over the role which the Greek Kings had played since the 1860s, that of a British viceroy. In the beginning Leeper did his best to fulfill the conditions of the Varkiza Peace Treaty. But on 22 April Churchill intervened again and recommended to Leeper to keep outside the details of Greek politics. When Orme Sargent of the Foreign Office criticised that Leeper considered membership in EAM a greater crime than collaboration with the Germans and demanded that he did something against the collaborators Churchill intervened: *"I do not agree at all [...] It seems to me that the collaborators in Greece in many cases did the best they could to shelter the Greek population from German oppression. Anyhow they did nothing to stop the entry of liberating forces, nor did they give any support to the EAM designs. The Communists are the main foe, though the punishment of notorious pro-German collaborators [...] should proceed in a regular and strict manner. There should be no question of increasing the severities against collaborationists opinions, in order to win Communist approval. [...] Our policy is the plebiscite within three or four months, and implacable hostility to the Communists."* In the Foreign Office they were shocked about Churchill's order.[2]

With this order to keep away from the details of Greek politics Churchill wanted to return to the traditional means of British policy, i.e. the indirect control via the monarch in this case the regent which had functioned for decades but in 1945 would lead to a catastrophe because neither the Greek Government nor the regent controlled th development. Only High Commissioner Leeper might have been able to stop the beginning violations of the Varkiza Peace Treaty with the help of various British missions. But Churchill's *ukase* made Leeper steer a laissez-faire course.

---

1 The denomination "protectorate" stems from "Relations between HMG and the Greek Government. Minutes", (PRO F.O. 371 R 4385/4/19).

2 Churchill to Sir Orme Sargent 22nd April, 1945. Prime Minister's Personal Minute Serial No. M 382/5 (PRO F.O. 371 R 7423/4/19).

Freedoms

Article 1 of the Varkiza Peace Treaty read: *"The Government will secure in accordance with the Constitution and the democratic principles everywhere recognised, the free expression of the political and social opinions of the citizens, repealing any existing illiberal law. It will also secure the unhindered functioning of individual liberties such as those of assembly, association and expression of views in the Press. More especially, the government will fully restore trade union liberties."*

The trade union liberties guaranteed by the Peace Treaty were trampled under foot. The trade union leaders of the Metaxas time managed - with the help of the government - to recreat their state controlled unions. The second TUC-delegation helped them and so did he right wing underground organizations. If the trade unions had not fully returned to fascism the reason was that the members of the former EEAM (worker EAM) had joined ERGAS and fought against it.

The promise to annul illiberal laws was not kept. Not even the infamous idionymo law of 1929 which penalized agitation against the existing system was removed. Laws of Metaxas dictatorship and those of the Quisling Governments remained in power and justice continued to apply them against the left.

The peace treaty had hardly been signed when the attack against the freedom of the press began. In Athens CHI-members destroyed the editorial office of the newspapers *Eleftheri Ellada* (EAM) and *Rizospastis* (KKE). Since this was registered by the international press a new technic was used. The police confiscated papers, forbade the sale at newspaper kiosks, beat up news-vendors and threatened the buyers. Only in the working class suburbs the left press could circulate freely, When the National Guard entered the areas which had been under the control of the ELAS it became an enjoyable game after service hours to destroy the rooms the local left papers. The local commanders began to censor the press. Others simply forbade the printing. In autumn 1945 there were almost no leftist newspapers in the provinces. Alleged shortage of paper hindered the appearance of leftist papers. The transport of papers to the provinces was hindered.

Reading of liberal or leftist newspapers in a coffee house was dangerous because it could lead to a police intervention or attacks by political opponents. That the two leftist papers could appear in Athens was described as a proof of the freedom of the press. In reality the freedom of the press was systematically suppressed. The final point was reached when *Rizospastis* was forbidden in October 1947 but then the civil war was in full swing.

Treatment of the Collaborators

In Varkiza Sofianopoulos had guaranteed that the collaborators would be brought to court and in the text of the Peace Treaty this was written down as a judicial obligation. There existed three groups of collaborators: The members of the collaborating governments, members of the police and the gendarmerie and the *Tagmata Asfalias* and finally profiteers, Gestapo agents informers and Greek Nazis. The legal foundation for their legal treatment had been formulated by the Papandreou Government. The trial against the first group began on 21 February 1945.

At first the defence tried to doubt the legality of the tribunals and refused the right to bring in actions - according to the principle of *sine lege nulla poena*. The court rejected this, but curtailed its own competence by stating that the judgement would be finalised by the future parliament, This provoked the collaboration PM, Rallis, to state that he was sure now the the Good God would give him many years to live. Another typical fact was that the courts did not write protocols and had the stenographical notes destroyed after six months. The witnesses of the persecution remained vague and avoided to burden the accused and mention facts. They all belonged to the same group, leftist witnesses did not exist.

The witnesses of the defence all praised the noble character of the defendant. A royalist praised the deployment of the *Tagmata Asfalias* (security battalions) which had proved their usefulness during the Dekemvriana. Statements that the ministers of the collaboration government had close contacts to the British secret services turned out to be embarrassing for the British were . Rallis was proud that he had influenced the Germans when taking of hostages so that only Communists and Leftists were arrested as hostage. The verdict stated that the putting up of the *Tagmata Asfaleias* had contributed to keep law and order in the country which had been threatened by the criminals of the resistance. There were some death sentences but the court recommended to the future parliament to convert these into prison sentences. Not one death sentence was executed and in 1948 all convicts were pardoned. The only collaborator who had died in prison until then was Ioannis Rallis.

Not even the Athenian police chief who had collaborated with the Gestapo was executed. Greece was the only country in Europe in which collaborators were not punished. In contrast the trials against the EAM/ELAS members ended almost regularly with death sentences and when the civil war broke out they were executed in great numbers. Prison sentences had to be served. It was a typical example of class justice.

The National Army

Article 7 of the Peace Treaty had fixed the details of the formation of the new army and the demobilization of the ELAS. In this case the regulations were disregarded as well. During the fighting in December 1944 36 battalions of the so-called National Guard had been created. These consisted almost exclusively of adherents of the Right. Among them were gendarmes who had been brought to Athens to have their behaviour during the occupation examined, as well as former members of the *Tagmata Asfaleias* and militant anti-Communists. These battalions followed the British troops when these extended their control in the areas which been controlled by ELAS so far. ELAS handed over their weapons but kept a small number and hid them because it didn't rust the development. These were the first weapons of the future DSE (Dimokratikos Stratos Elladas - Democratic Army of Greece) when the civil war began 15 months later.

The National Guard was to take care of quietness and order and create new battalions. On 1 April the British had finished their task. Until the end of April another 22 battalions were deployed. On 15 May the National Guard controlled the whole of Greece. The new battalions consisted of the same people as those from Athens. So that he new army consisted exclusively out of followers of the Right. The temporary call-up as guaranteed by the Varkiza treaty did not take place. Until summer 1945 the members of the National Guard managed that the political power on the level of the nomarchies and villages was conferred to the Right. The adherents of the Right denounced former resistance fighters who were then promptly imprisoned. As the courts in the provinces did not function the arrested remained in jail for months. At the end of summer the jails were so overcrowded that the Government felt obliged to issue partial-amnesties.

When in April the conscription for the new army began it became quickly clear that the future army would consist of "national thinking persons" only. Former EAM members were rejected for "health reasons". Of the 800 officers who had served in ELAS only 50 were considered worthy to be accepted in the new army. The regular officers among them were transferred to the reserve. Officers who had served in EDES, CHI or the *Tagmata Asfaleias* were taken over. Promotions of the latter which had been made during the occupation by Rallis were confirmed. But when the commander of the Peloponnesian *Tagmata Asfalias*, colonel Papadongonas, was advanced by two ranks for his merits this triggered such a scandal that the promotion was taken back. However, other cases which were executed in a more discreet way were successful.

In the high command of the army there were a few republicans but like royalist comrades were fanatic anti-Communists. Decisive, however, was that officers were in the important positions who during the war had served in the right-wing underground organizations or in the rightwing secret organization in the Near East of which the IDEA *(Ieros Desmos Ellinon Axiomatikon* - Holy League of Greek Officers) was the most important. There was an effort to disempower the IDEA Clique which failed because the British opposed it. Thus the character of the Greek armed forces was fixed for decades: They were fanatically anti-Communist and royalist. Whenever they saw the state endangered by Communism they were ready to interfere and in 1967 to instigate a putsch. Thus also in the case of the armed forces the Peace Treaty of Varkiza was disregarded.

The Genesis of the Parakratos

Wherever the National Guard took over a little later rightwing organizations came into being; they often were given the weapons which ELAS had surrendered. If there were no British officers who could moderate the Greek officers the Right attacked the Left in the most brutal manner. The biggest of these organization was that of colonel Grivas which allegedly had 200,000 members in autumn 1945. At the same time these organizations organized the groups and formed networks which penetrated all parts of Greece. The cooperated closely with the Gendarmerie and National Guard and later with the army as well as with the secret services and the General Staff which controlled them. A power structure came into being which existed parallel to that of the state. The state had no influence over it, it was a state within the state. Quite the contrary with this structure the Greek Right influenced the Greek state, there were times when the Right thus controlled the state. The Greeks call this type of a power structure parakratos (para-state). If someone dared to thwart the parakratos he was killed. There even existed groups which reminded one of notorious Southamerican death squadrons. Since summer 1945 the parakratos was fixed ingredient of the Greek political system.

In the course of the summer 1945 the police aided by CHI cleansed the red suburbs of Athens of all leftists. The methods applied reminded fatally of those used during the German occupation: Encircling of quarters and searching of all houses. Thousands were arrested with the accusation that they had been members of OPLA. There were murders and the killers remained free despite the fact that they were known. But they belonged to CHI. In the provinces terror was even worse. Without any orders the National Guard arrested people on account of crimes committed during the occupation, i.e. membership in EAM/ELAS. The prisons were filled by EAM members who were made responsible for unspecified crimes during the occupation. In the Peloponnese 90 percent of the inmates of the prisons were former EAM members. Not one collaborator was arrested and brought to court. Quite the opposite, collaborators were often those who now commanded the National Guard. Well known bandits discovered their love for the monarchy and could follow their craft legally and terrorize, and rob the Left.

From spring to summer 1945 a wave of terror swept over Greece performed first by the National Guard and then by the local parakratos. At the end of the summer the gendarmerie took over but not much changed. Now the arrests were made on the basis of well grounded orders but the parakratos saw to it under the benevolent eyes of the gendarmerie that those leftists who could not be accused of anything could not enjoy their lives.

The British were informed about this but looked the other way. When the American journalist Hal Lehrman wrote about it Leeper's deputy Caccia stated angrily that Lehrman was one of those journalists who could not be controlled. He advised a certain journalist of the *New*

York Times to write against this and to praise the work of the government. Indeed the British Embassy considered the whole Greek Left as Communists and enemies against whose suppression nothing could be said provided it did not bother British interests. Leeper as High Commissioner might have stopped this development but he looked to the other way. In his reports to the Foreign Office he described the justified complaints of the Greek Left as propaganda. The Embassy steered a laissez-faire course and did not say one word against the taking over of power by the Greek Right. The persecution of the Greek Left was of no interest for the British, to stop the white terror was unthinkable for them.

The Cleansing of the State Apparatus

Articles 7 and 8 of the Varkiza Peace Treaty had guaranteed a cleansing of the state administration and the security apparatus. This, too, was neglected. The cleansing hit the Left. Civil servants and employees of the state, even those working for the health insurance (IKA),and who had belonged to the "anti-national organizations" (meaning EAM/ELAS) were fired or forced in retirement. The police and the gendarmerie were cleansed from all Leftists. A typical case from the gendarmerie illustrates the methods of the Right: In August 1943 BBC praised in its Greek service the gendarmerie lieutenant, Thomas Venetsanopoulos and lauded him as an example because he had gone over to ELAS with his whole unit. At the end of April 1945 he was arrested and on 15 May brought to court because in February 1943 he had left his post without permission. He was discharged but re-arrested immediately and accused of an alleged murder. Gendarmes which had hunted members of the resistance on German orders remained free.

The British police restricted itself to training of the police and look the other way. The gendarmerie developed into a fighting group of the Right and was closely linked to the parakratos. On October 1945 it became known that about 500 gendarmes had joined the parakratos in Macedonia. In the Athenian police also there was continuity on all levels: Angelos Evert who had been chief of the police under Metaxas and the Germans remained in office. The cleansing even hit the church. Clerics who had sympathized with EAM were fired. In the universities all professors who had been in EAM were thrown out, among them Alexandros Svolos, Angelos Angelopoulos and Petros Kokkalis who had been ministers in the Papandreou Government. All over the country EAM-leader were arrested because of moral responsibility for alleged crimes. The majority of the judges persecuted the Left fanatically. Any excuse was appreciated to return a verdict.

The special courts which were to deal with the Tagmata Asfaleias consisted out of royalists and members of the extreme Right. For them the killing of a member of the collaborating units by the resistance was murder. In June 1945 these excesses became so extreme that the Greek liberals of Sofoulis protested cautiously. At the end of June the EAM sent a memorandum to Potsdam to the big Three reporting that about 30,000 EAM members were in jail. However, the Greek government denied this and spoke of 12,000 and claimed 1,000 were convicted collaborators.

Change of Government in Britain

On 28 July 1945 general elections took place in Britain and the Labour Party won. In his first message to Damaskinos the new Prime Minister Clement Attlee stressed the necessity to observe the Varkiza agreement. Damaskinos agreed ostensibly but when the Labour Government suggested a general amnesty for prosecuted in the Dekemvriana context Damaskinos rejected this together with Prime Minister Voulgaris giving reasons for rejection: It would lead to renewed unrests. But the were ready to release all who were not accused of murder. Consequently several laws were passed and several times a few thousand of prisoners were set free.

But Damaskinos had to admit to the new Foreign Secretary Ernest Bevin in September that in spite of these measures 18,000 EAM members still were in prison. If more prisoners were released this could lead to new unrests.

When the new leadership of the Foreign Office urged Leeper to do something he blocked: The prisons could only be emptied by the decreeing a general amnesty. If this was done there would be another upheaval with which the weak Greek security forces could not cope. There would acts of revenge. The majority of the Greeks rejected an amnesty. Besides a resignation of the government threatened. But the government did not give in and Leeper had to put pressure on Damaskinos. Thus in autumn another 3,000 prisoners were released. Finally it was suggested to send a British Legal Mission to Greece, which might submit proposals for a solution of the problem.

But this proposal came too late. With Churchill's *ukase* of 22 March that Leeper should not mingle in the details of Greek politics the decisive switch had been moved to a total change of the power structure. On the basis as the High Commissioner Leeper could have changed the development into democratic course respecting the Varkiza Peace Treaty. But with his *ukase* had intervened a second time into the inner Greek developments, both times with catastrophic consequences: the first time the Dekemvriana had been the result and the second led to the Civil War.

Sources on the events in summer 1945 are scarce and the only published ones are the two EAM-white books on the violations of the Varkiza Treaty.[1] The text by C. M. Woodhouse published hereafter is unique. It is the only objective account describing events in summer 1945 on the Peloponnese.

Woodhouse had been chief of the BMM (British Military Mission) with the Greek partisans. Politically he was a conservative and had no sympathies for the Left as such. EAM-members, in his eyes, were Communists. But he also had a sense for political fair play. The political excesses in summer 1945 of the Greek Right in the Peloponnese enraged him extremely. His descriptions are beyond any doubt. They are a true account. The text was not written by a partisan of the Left but by a British conservative. His descriptions confirm everything that was published in the EAM white book of 1945 but this was denounced as a piece of Communist propaganda. If the British had followed Woodhouse's advice and had insisted on the decree of the general amnesty almost certainly the Greek Civil War would have been avoided. As this was not done the persecuted Left began to fight back in summer 1946.

Regrettably Woodhouse did not integrate this report neither in his book on the developments in Greece between 1939 and 1949 nor in his memoirs.[2] In both volumes he trivializes the White Terror and does not mention the EAM white books, not even in his bibliography. But both accounts were written during the time of the Cold War.

1 EAM, Lefki Vivlos: *Parvaseis tis Varkizas Flevaris - Iounis 1945* (Athen, Juni 1945); Reprint edition (Athen: Ellinika Themata,1975); EAM, *Dimokratikos neofasismos Ioulis-Oktovris 1945* (Athen, Oktober 1945).

2 C. M. Woodhouse, *The Struggle for Greece* (London: Hart Davis, 1976) und idem, *Something Ventured* (London: Grenada, 1982).

Subject: Situation in the PELOPONNESE
To: H. M. Minister, ATHENS 11th August, 1945
From: Col. C.M. WOODHOUSE

PART I: GENERAL SUMMARY

1. There is some cause for alarm in the PELOPONNESE, though no fear of an organised revolt in arms against the government.

2. The situation has been created by the reprehensible behaviour of both left and right wings, but very much more by the latter in virtue of their complete control of power.

3. The case against both is stated here on the most unbiased evidence available. (Sources are given in part II). In no case have I accepted one side's accusations against the other. Much evidence was given me in the strictest confidence.

4. The case against the left, which is stated in detail in part II can be summed up as follows:-

(a) Illegal left-wing activity persists both underground in the towns and openly in the hills.

(b) No effort is spared to hamper the authorities by wasting their time in order to make government impossible.

(c) Left-wing policy continually shifts and veers to new directions when the authorities sincerely try to meet complaints.

(d) The left-wing is still completely dominated by the Communists, who direct even the most moderate into subversion.

5. The case against the right, which is identical with the government authority, can be summed up as follows:-

(a) Arrest without warrant is enforced exclusively against the left wing, never against "nationalists" or collaborators.

(b) Discrimination against the left is fanatically exercised by the National Guard and condoned by most officers and officials.

(c) Lack of control on the part of the authorities is obvious, not only over the enemies of justice but over their own forces. The National Guard are far worse than the Gendarmerie in this respect.

(d) Arming of right-wing civilians to help break up the left is openly practised.

6. The above remarks suggest, as part II will confirm, that the case against the left is slight in comparison with that against the right. A most determined effort is needed to rectify the latter.

7. The following steps are already being taken:-

(a) A partial and local redistribution of the National Guard. It Is intended that units shall not serve in their own villages, but the measures taken are insufficient. For instance, all units in the PELOPONNESE are still Peloponnesians, though they are now located further from their homes.

(b) The replacement of the National Guard by the gendarmerie. This is expected to be complete by mid-September. Our savingram 156 of 10 August refers.

(c) Some disciplinary action against offenders, e.g. the military commander of MEJOLONGI was recently removed for personally taking part in beating a left-wing prisoner. This has not yet been applied in the PELOPONNESE.

8. The following additional steps are called for:

(a) Complete re-shuffle of the National Guard to prevent them carrying on private vendettas. The PELOPONNESE should be garrisoned by e.g. Macedonians.

(b) Application of identical standards of justice towards right-wing collaborators and towards EAM criminals.
(c) Tightening up of discipline at all levels, e.g, subordinates not to act without orders and without reporting, superiors to spend less time in ATHENS. Half a dozen ruthless disciplinary actions, well publicised and exemplary, would do much to destroy the belief (almost universal in Greece) that the government and ourselves condone right-wing illegalities.
(d) General amnesty of all prisoners except those already convicted or charged with murder. This bears out the suggestion in your 1376 of 8 August and our 1664 of 8 August.
(e) Considerable increase of M.T. [Motor Transport] allotment. Without this neither (a) nor (c) above will be possible, and the eventual position of the gendarmerie will be as bad as that of the National Guard at present. Our 1642 of 4 August shows the desperate nature of the present position. Motor Boats are also needed in coastal areas.
(f) Restoration of Article 5 of the Constitution, forbidding arrest without warrant, which was suspended after Varkiza. This suspension has been gravely abused.

Part II -SUPPLEMENTARY NARRATIVE

1. My tour of the PELOPONNESE was not occasioned by (though it coincided with) the renewal of a state of alarm, which brought Brigadier ARKWRIGHT down there at the same time on a wild-goose chase. I found, however, causes for alarm of a different sort: not from the danger of a left uprising, but from the danger of an obliteration of justice by the right. My route was CORINTH-PATRAS-PYRGOS-TRIPOLIS: then TRIPOLIS-SPARTA-YITHION and back: then TRIPOLIS-MELIGALA-KALAMATA and back: then TRIPOLIS-ARGOS-CORINTH. I tried to meet the principal authorities in every town, as well as the BLOS, [British Liaison Officers] and to base my report on authoritative and confidential information given by them alone. I was often also visited by representatives of EAM, and I saw certain prisons. But I have tried to exclude their biased and irresponsible complaints. The following supplement to part I should be read in this light.
2. The case against the left is put with prodigious emphasis and complete lack of logic by those in authority and respectable citizens generally. It is worst put, as usual, by the representatives of EAM itself, who continue to antagonise the dispassionate enquirer by their alternations of smugly injured innocence and cantankerous invective. I shall try to ignore the disagreeable impressions created by both, and present the relevant facts against the left on their merits.

(a) Illegal left-wing activity continues both the hills and the towns. In the hills there are undoubtedly considerable stores of weapons, especially of the modern British equipment seized from the National Guard in PATRAS and SPARTA last year. In the towns, there is some overt activity, especially the publication of newspapers, which appear in PATRAS, TRIPOLIS, CORINTH and KALAMATA, All accounts agree that there is a good deal more covert activity. One symptom of this is their effort to prevent a diminution of the armed bands in the mountains by warning people in the towns that they are about to be arrested, and by warning those in the hills that they will be beaten up if they surrender. Another symptom is the occasional calling of rather ineffectual strikes, as happened among the dock-workers in KALAMATA shortly before my arrival.
(b) Time-wasting tactics are employed to make the work of government as difficult as possible. The ideal is to present the authorities with more deputations than they can possibly receive and more complaints than they can possibly investigate. Mr. KALKA-

NDIS, Nomarch of KALAMATA, had to deal personally with 7 telephone calls and 2 visitors during the half-hour in which I was trying to talk to him in his office. MR. NOMAS, Nomarch of PATRAS, quoted a typical case of a woman in black who persistently badgered him with a story that her son had been murdered and herself seriously wounded in the head by X-ites, until investigation proved that she was a notorious prostitute who had never had a son, and had received the wound as a present from an admirer.

(c) Inconsistencies of policy are persistently made to annoy the government authorities as soon as complaints ore dealt with. For instance, prisoners in PATRAS gaol clamoured to be tried, until a sufficient number of judges became available. They then clamoured to have the trials postponed, on the grounds that the present political situation created an unfair bias against them. Another example is the EAM attitude towards their armed adherents in the hills. They have officially denounced them in their local press, of which I have seen copies, but they continue to castigate the local authorities for persecuting them.

(d) Communist control of all left-wing activities is still complete and dangerous. All local authorities agreed that the bandits in the hills are directed by communist cells in the towns, This is corroborated by the known fact that most telephone operators belong to EAM; and outlying villages appear to get warning of raids well in advance. The Communists even contrive to organise the prisons. I visited several, where I formed the impression that those inside looked more intelligent and talked more reasonably than those outside. But unfortunately for official purposes they allowed themselves to be represented by the most loathsome type of ex-OPLA Communists.

5. The case against the right, which is identical for most practical purposes with the governing authorities, is very much worse. The following principal faults are noted from the reports of BLOs and the authorities themselves. All testimony from the left-wing, which is naturally more damaging still, has been excluded. What remains is bad enough

.

(i) Arrests without warrant

(a) The public prosecutor of KALAMATA (Mr. KARDARAS) pointed out that the National Guard have the right to arrest without warrant. He admitted that this practice is enforced solely against "'those accused of crimes during the occupation". (By these he meant EAM-ELAS). Those accused of collaboration with the Germans are not so arrested, on two grounds. One is that it is unsafe to put them in the same prison with EAM-ites for fear of violence: the other is that EAM-ites, if not arrested, might take to the hills as bandits, whereas collaborationists would not. Both arguments are nonsense. In KALAMATA, as in most towns in the PELOPONNESE, there are two goals as well as police-lock-up. The second argument is an obvious confusion of cause and effect, which refutes itself.

(b) the public prosecutor of YITHION (Mr, KRITIKOS), a well-meaning and simple-minded reactionary, agreed that arrest without warrant had long been practised. I expressed surprise that it was enforced only against EAM, who compose almost the whole of his 290 prisoners. He indignantly replied that they aid also arrest collaborationists (though not without warrant}, and claimed to have at least 5 under lock and key already.

(c) The BLO at TRIPOLIS (Major ORR) reported finding 7 men arrested in a nearby village by the local National Guard sergeant, not only without warrant, but without even a report to his superiors. They would have been held indefinitely if Major ORR had not intervened. No charge was ever brought against any of them.

(d) Sergeant ZLATANIS of AGIS, KALAMATA, saw a man arrested by the National Guard in the street on the prompting of a woman who stated that he had killed her son. No war-

rant was shown, and obviously none had ever been issued. The Nomarch of KALAMATA has ordered the gradual, unostentatious release of such cases, to reduce overcrowding in the prisons. But the prisons continue to fill up daily,

(ii) Discrimination against the left.

(a) Most National Guard lower ranks are using their position to work out local vendettas. They are drawn almost exclusively from the enemies of EAM, their officers in most cases either sympathise with them or have no control over them. Every National Guard commander whom I interviewed (in PATRAS, PYRGOS, KALMATA, SPARTA, YITHION) assured me in identical terms that the situation was satisfactory throughout his area. It was obvious that none of them had any acquaintance whatever with his area outside his H.Q., nor with the contents of the local gaol. A few instances will show the injustice of the resulting discrimination against the Left.

(b) In PYRGOS gaol there is a man called DHROMEZIS who carries in his pocket a certificate signed by Field Marshal ALEXANDER in recognition of his services during the occupation. He is held for (unspecified) crimes committed during the occupation as a member of .ELAS. There is another man there for the same reason who was actually "executed" and left for dead by the Germans: he still has three bullet holes in him. There is a lawyer called MARAS, a member of EAM, who was appointed prefect of PYRGOS by the PAPANDREOU Government. In order to save the people from starving, he distributed the wine crop free so that it could be used for barter; a measure which was, and still is, universally applauded by all classes. He was arrested on the ground that this was illegal. In fact, he is held for belonging to EAM.

(c) These are rot isolated instances. Wherever one member of EAM is accused of a crime, all the local members of the organisation are liable to be arrested as "morally responsible". I was informed by British officers stationed in PYRGOS that the 270 prisoners held there are divided as follows:-

Convicted felons 36
Criminal charges ¡34
Nationalist 1
EAM-ites hold as "morally responsible" 199

These figures were confirmed by the Nomarch, Mr. PAPADIPOULOS, an ex-adherent of ZERVAS who was as disgusted as myself.

(d) Until very recently, warrants against men charged with collaboration against the Germans could only be issued by the two senior Public Prosecutors in the PELOPONNESE at NAFPLION and PATRAS. Other warrants could be issued by all Public Prosecutors, of whom there are nine in the PELOPONNESE. Obviously, then, the chances of a collaborator are much rosier than those of a communist, quite apart from the fanatical bias of the National Guard. An order has now been made permitting all Public Prosecutors to issue warrants against collaborators. But the papers referring to those cases which have already been submitted continue to be held at PATRAS and NAVPLION, so that for the present it is still impossible to proceed. Mr. CHRONAIOS deputy Public Prosecutor of TPIPOLIS, informed me that he had been trying in vain ever since his appointment to obtain warrants against two collaborationists, BEKHLOS and THODOROPOULOS, of LEONDARI. They are known by the entire neighbourhood to have handed over to the Italians a Greek officer of Force 133, Lieutenant KOURKOUTAS, who parachuted into the PELOPONNESE under my command in 1943.

(e) The gaols of the PELOPONNESE, which are inhumanly overcrowded, contain about 6,000 prisoners, of whom probably over 90% are held on charges which amount to no more than having been members of EAM-ELAS. "Moral responsibility" for EAM crimes is the basic charge. It is quite impossible to dispose of their cases this year. It follows that a very large number of men who may eventually be acquitted will be disfranchised at the elections if they are held this year. This handicap will operate exclusively to the detriment of one side. The relatives and friends of these men dare not present themselves for enrolment on the electoral lists for fear of being arrested themselves. Obviously, this makes the prospects of the left wing at the elections hopeless. They will therefore persist in their intention to boycott the elections unless radical reforms are made. This was stated categorically to me by the official representatives of EAM in PYPGOS, TRIPOLIS and KALAMATA.

(f) The EAM papers are prevented by the National Guard from circulating freely outside the towns where they are published. Even in the towns, as elsewhere in Greece, their presses are occasionally attacked. I saw their press at KALAMATA, which had recently been destroyed. Nevertheless, it is surprising how quickly the papers start coming out again.

(g) Mr. PAPADOPOULOS, Nomarch of PYRGOS, was outspoken in his criticism of the Government and National Guard for discriminating against the left. He regarded the collaborationists, especially TAVOULARIS, as responsible for the whole of the present situation. He deplored the fact that so few had been arrested, and quoted the case of Major MITROPOULOS, formerly an officer of the local security battalion, who had just been promoted Lieutenant-Colonel in the National Guard. Mr, CHRONAIOS, deputy Public Prosecutor of TRIPOLIS, spoke in confidence to me in strikingly similar terms, and accused even the Gendarmerie of discriminating against the left.

(h) Colonel BALINGRATIS, O.C. Gendarmerie at TRIPOLIS quoted to me a case of armed civilians arresting communists and keeping them under lock and key at the neighbouring village of PARTHENI. Against the protests of several other officials present, he insisted heatedly that this was not an isolated case but a common occurrence. He added that less than 10% of the armed ELAS-ites in the hills are criminals: but they are discouraged from giving themselves up by fear of the consequences at the hands of the National Guard.

(i) Mr. TSAMBASIS, public prosecutor of all collaborationists for the whole of Greece, informed me that in the PELOPONNESE collaborators are openly protected by the authorities. He cited the public prosecutor of TRIP0LIS and Colonel PAPANIKOLAOU, military commander of PATRAS, as examples. (The former, it seems, has arranged for the removal of his deputy, an admirable Athenian lawyer, for "left wing" sympathies.) He added that right-wing pressure has prevented him from issuing all warrants for arrest of collaborators with very few exceptions, and and has reduced his own position to that or a cipher.

(iii) Lack of control by authorities

(a) Whatever orders are issued on the higher levels, there is no guarantee that they will be carried out. Colonel KONDOLEON, military commander of TRIPOLIS, frankly admitted to Major ORR that he had not a single officer whom he could trust. He was much more reserved with me; but his extreme caution in itself showed how disturbed he was. The Chief of Staff at CORINTH to the Higher Command of the PELOPONNESE admitted to me that he. could never be sure that his orders were carried out unless he supervised them personally. The average local commanders are of poor quality. Captain THEODORAKOPOULOS, in YITHION, is so grossly fat and lazy that he can hardly get into a jeep without being lifted. Lieutenant-Colonel DOURATSOS, in KALAMATATA, is a universally despised and complacent fool. None of them showed adequate personal knowledge of his area.

(b) Examples have already been quoted which illustrate the lack of contact between the levels of command. This is aggravated by confusion over the respective functions of National Guard and Gendarmerie. Colonel KONDOLEON still insists that as commander of TRIPOLIS area, he controls the Gendarmerie as well as the National Guard. Colonel BELINGRATIS, of the TRIPOLIS gendarmerie, insists that he has an independent command. The dispute was unresolved when I left, and the resulting actions were ineffectual.
(c) Most men in authority complacently accept, or even fail to recognise, the irregular situation. They frankly divide all Greeks into Nationalists ("our side") and Communists: these are the actual words of the Major of YITHION. Those who have an objective outlook could be counted on the fingers of one hand. They were the Nomarchs of PYRGOS (Mr. PAPADOPOULOS) and KALAMATA (Mr. KALKANDIS), the Chief of Police in TRIPOLIS (Colonel BELINGRATIS), and the deputy Public Prosecutor in TRIPOLIS (Mr. KHRONAIOS). It was from them that I first heard the suggestion of a general amnesty as a solution.
(d) The Gendarmerie are much more honest than the National Guard about the situation. They admit their limitations. Major KONDOZAMANIS (O.C. YITHION) said that he could not even visit all his posts unless he had a boat at his disposal, since some of them were 20 hours walk apart, through the mountainous peninsulae of the Southern PELOPONNESE. Lieutenant STASINOPOULOS (O.C. R MELIGALA) admitted that he could not guarantee his control more then 5 kilometres outside the town. Two neighbouring villages, both accessible by mo tor-road, were periodically controlled by EAM-ELAS bands from the mountains. (He admitted that no one was suffering the least harm from them). Colonel BELINGRATIS (O.C. TRIPOLIS) violently castigated officials in SPARTA in my presence for forwarding alarmist reports without verification. He emphasised to me that ha could not control his area as lent as local officials were stupid, panic-stricken and incompetent.
(e) The lack of control has lately been aggravated by the temporary withdrawal into the towns of all National Guard units from outlying villages. This is intended to be a preliminary to a re-shuffle. Before leaving the villages, National Guard units used to terrify the villagers by predicting violence from EAM-ELAS in their absence. In a panic, the villagers would exaggerate the slightest molehill into a mountain. This accounts for recent reports of terrorism in the PELOPONNESE, which have without exception been proved baseless. Major KONDOZAMANIS. O.C. Gendarmerie at YITHION admitted to me that he exaggerated his reports in order to induce prompt action.
(f) Post local officials are too attached to ATHENS to concentrate on their jobs. During my visit, the following were absent in ATHENS: the Public Prosecutors of TRIPOLIS and PYRGOS, the Nomarchs of TRIPOLIS and SPARTA, the O.C, Gendarmerie of PATRAS and KALAMATA. In additon the Mayor of KALAMATA and the military commander of TRIPOLIS were about to leave for ATHENS. Of the towns I visited, only YITHION had a full complement of officials in residence.
(g) In the village of EVA, near KALAMATA, the X organisation have established a private government under a man called STAVREAS, which controls several neighbouring villages and runs an armed civilian police force. As EVA lies on the main road from KALAMATA to MELIGALA, the report seemed so astonishing that Captain ANNANT of AGIS sent his NCO to investigate. The story was confirmed.
(h) Captain DIMAS, second in command Gendarmerie at KALAMATA, told me a long story of ELAS terrorism in PYLIA and TAYGETOS. It was soon apparent that he had never been to either. He had not taken the trouble to confirm the stories personally; with his limited resources he was quite unable to act if the stories were true.

(iv) Arming of civilians.

(a) It is reliably reported on all hands that the National Guard arm civilians who sympathise with them, to help them beat up the left. This, of course, is done with weapons recovered from the left. 1 personally saw an armed civilian riding a horse down the public high-way between PYRGOS and OLYMPIA. Colonel KONDOLEON admitted that recently an armed civilian group had appeared one night in TRIPOLIS itself and attacked local EAM-Ites. One method of arming civilians was, until recently, the practice of increasing the AGROPHYLAKI, a uniformed body who were temporarily permitted to carry arms. This has now been forbidden, but the disarming of them does not progress. I have seen armed Agrophylakes in various parts of Greece.

(b) The practice of arming civilians was justified to me by Colonel PAPANIKOLAOU (military commander of PATRAS area). He argued that only by enlisting such help could they be sure of recovering all arms from the communists. It is, in fact, justified, in practice, whatever the legal case against it. It may be significant that Colonel PAPANIKOLAOU's chief of staff, Major VLASIS, was formerly an adherent of ZERVAS, who was held prisoner by ELAS for many months during the first civil war. BLOS report that Colonel PAPANIKOLAOU's rabid anti-communism has abated since a recent visit to his commanding general.

(c) The British unit in PYRGOS reported that they had at last forced the National Guard to arrest an armed civilian who belonged to X. He had walked about PYRGOS unmolested for six weeks, with a revolver on his hip. He claimed to belong to the National Guard, and to have a permit to carry the revolver. The latter claim was correct, though of course totally unjustified. Mr. PAPADOPOULOS, Nomarch of PYRGOS, who expressed himself in violent terms about X, confirmed this case. He quoted a similar instance of a certain Captain KHARALAMBOS STAVROPOULOS, who ran a tavern for the Germans, and now acted as a local leader of X under the protection of the National Guard.

IV CONCLUSION:

My recommendations have already bean stated. I wish to end by emphasising only the existencc of a universal belief that the British are directly responsible for the situation, The right take our approval for granted; the left insist that a remedy is possible in 24 hours. If we do decide. It is not enough to point out that this is false. Concrete proof is needed. The present is probably the best possible moment for decisive action.

Aus: PRO FO 371 R 14973/4/19

THE SECOND PLENUM OF THE CC OF KKE AND THE DECISION FOR CIVIL WAR: A REAPPRAISAL

This essay is concerned with the resolutions of the Second Plenum of the Central Committee of the Communist Party of Greece or - more specifically - the alleged decision of that Plenum to launch the Civil War.[1] Until very recently there has been a general consensus among various schools of opinion that the Second Plenum took such a decision. Anticommunist authors such as Kousoulas, O'Ballance, Pavlopoulos and Averof did not have the slightest doubt about it.[2] Authors close to the KKE such as Foivos Grigoriadis, Eudes, Solaro and Katsoulis came to similar conclusions.[3] The two official accounts of the KKE history of 1952 and 1953 edited by Vasilis Bartziotas upheld the same interpretation.[4] The first to question these established interpretations were Woodhouse and Ole Smith [5] although the first apparently had no access to the important material of the 6th and 7th Plenum of 1956 and 1957 respectively, which was published in *Neos Kosmos* of those years. In view of this unsatisfactory state of research it seems best to go back to the sources.

The direct sources for the Second Plenum are scarce. They consist of the lenghty introductory statements by Nikos Zachariadis published in *Rizospastis* and the resolutions to be found in the March number of *Kommunistiki Epitheorisi* of that year.[6] Neither of these contains any concrete evidence of a decision to move toward civil war - except one rather strange thing: Section 4 of the Resolution has, instead of a text, a row of dots. This "sinister lacuna" naturally gave rise to speculation, even more so because the text of this section was never published. Interpretations and hypotheses all pointed - with hindsight - in one and the same direction: the unpublished Section 4 had contained the Central Committee's decision for Civil War. This theory was apparently corroborated by Zachariadis's own statements at the 6th Plenum of October 1949[7] and the Third Party Conference in the summer of 1950,[8] as well

---

1 This paper is based on my book: British Intervention in Greece: From Varkiza to Civil War, February 1945 - August 1946 *(London: Merlin Press, 1986).*

2 Dimitrios George Kousoulas, *Revolution and Defeat - the Story of the Greek Communist Party* (London: Oxford University Press, 1965) p. 231f.; Edgar O'Ballance, *The Greek Civil War* (London: Faber, 1966) p. 122; Athanasios Pavlopoulos, *Istoria tou Kommounismou en Elladi* (Athens: Geografiki Ipiresia Stratou, 1971) p. 97; Evangelos Averof, *Le feu et la hache* (Paris: Editions de Breteuil, 1973) p. 136.

3 Fivos Grigoriadis, *Istoria tu Emfiliou 1945-1949,* 2 (Athens: Kamarinopulos, n.d.). p. 625; Dominique Eudes, *Les Kapetanios. La Guerre Civile Greque de 1943 a 1949* (Paris: Fayard, 1970) p. 342; Antonio Solaro, *Istoria tu Kommunistiku Kommatos Elladas* (Athens: Plias, 1977) p. 181f.; Giorgios Katsoulis, *Istoria tu Kommunistiku Kommatos Elladas* VI (Athens: Nea Sinora, 1978) p. 99; and more recently: Tasos Vournas, *Istoria tis Sinhronis Elladas. O Emfilios* (Athens: Tolidis, 1981) p. 20f.

4 Chroniko tou Agona, 1878-1951. *Dokumenda ke Ilika apo tin Istoria tou Laikou mas Kinimatos* (n.p.: KE tu KKE, 1952), p. 60 ed. by V. Bartziotas; *Voithima gia tin Istoria tou KKE* (n.p.: KE tou KKE, 1952), p. 233 ed. by V. Bartziotas.

5 C. M. Woodhouse, *The Struggle for Greece 1941-1949* (London: Hart Davis, 1976) p. 169f.; Ole Smith, "On the Beginning of the Greek Civil War", *Scandinavian Studies in Modern Greek* 1 (1977), p. 19.

6 Nikos Zachariadis, "I Simerini Ikonomiki kai Politiki Katastasi stin Ellada kai ta Provlimata tou Dimokratikou Kinimatos kai Agona", *Rizospastis,* February 24, 1946; Apofasi tis 2is Olomelias tis KE tou KKE. I Katastasi stin Ellada. Ta Provlimata tou Dimokratikou Agona kai ta Kathikonda tou KKE", *Kommunistiki Epitheorisi* (March 1946) pp. 105-111.

7 Nikos Zachariadis, "Kenourgia Katastasi, Kenourgia Kathikonda. I Diapistosis, i Grammi kai i apofasis tis 6is olomelias tis KE tou KKE. 9 tu Ohtovri 1949", in: Nikos Zachariadis, *Sillogi Ergon,* (n.p.: KE tu KKE, 1953), pp. 437-476.

8 Nikos Zachariadis, "Deka Hronia Palis. Simperasmata, Didagmata, Kathikonta. Pros ti Sindiaskepsi tou KKE", *Neos Kosmos,* August 1950, pp. 397-453, and September 1950, pp. 509-553.

as by his book *Ta provlimata kathodigisis* of 1952.[1] In 1953 Vasilis Bartziotas gave the *imprimatur* to this interpretation in the already mentioned official accounts of KKE history: that the Second Plenum took the decision to launch the Civil War. Finally, in 1979 KKE Esoterikou's daily, *Avgi*, published a memorandum which Zachariadis sent to Stalin in March 1947, in which it was stated flatly: *"the Plenum reached decisions which resulted in the organisation of the Democratic Army of Greece"*.[2] Thus it would seem that the Second Plenum had indeed taken this fateful decision and all previously mentioned communist and anti-communist interpretations were correct.

There are, however, powerful testimonies contradicting this thesis. The first dissenting voices were heard at the 7th Plenum in 1957. Markos Vafeiadis, for example, stated categorically that the Second Plenum as a body (*san soma*) did not discuss the matter of civil insurrection.[3] Panagiotis Mavromatis took a similar stand.[4] In 1978 Vasos Georgiou, former "ambassador" of the Provisional Democratic Government in Warsaw, stated: *"Contrary to all that has been written, the Second Plenum of February 1946 took no decision for the start of Civil War"*.[5] In his memoirs former Politbureau member Dimitrios Vlandas is even more outspoken: *"Who took the decision for the second armed struggle? Today no one doubts that the Second KKE Central Committee Plenum (February 1946) did not take a decision on armed struggle. Of the still living members of the Politbureau of that time (Partsalidis, Stringos, Bartziotas) not one has said that such a decision was taken, even by the Politbureau alone. In his recent interview Partsalidis said that the Politbureau took no decision for armed struggle. This is the truth."*[6] Similar statements were made by the former editor of *Dimokratikos Stratos* and later news editor of the *Eleftheri Ellada* radio station (afterwards renamed (*Foni tis Alithias*) Lefteris Eleftheriou[7] and by the then Party Secretary for Epirus, Michalis Tsandis,[8] as well as by Dimitrios Partsalidis.[9] Surprisingly enough, during the 7th Plenum in 1957 even Zachariadis admitted that no such decision had been taken by the Second Plenum when, under heavy attack, he stated: *"There was no military plan; we took a political decision. Thus we made no military plan of action; that was worked out later"*.[10] If this important admission has escaped the attention of researchers it is due to the already mentioned fact that the material on the 7th Plenum has been difficult to locate.

But even without the evidence supplied by these sources and testimonies it is hard to believe that, had Section 4 really contained the decision to launch the Civil War, this fact would have been pointed out to the Party's opponents, including the Security Police and the Army General Staff in such an obvious way. Such culpable frivolity - if not downright stupidity - should not be attributed even to Zachariadis, despite his megalomania. The argument that the gap in the text was intended as a kind of threat to the Government side assumes that Zachariadis was capable of highly complicated political manoeuvring, an ability he simply did not possess.

---

1 Nikos Zachariadis, *Ta Provlimata Kathodigisis sto KKE* (n.p. KE tu KKE, 1952).
2 "To Ipomnima tou Zachariadi ston Stalin", *Avgi,* December 14, 1979.
3 Markos Vafiadis, "Omilia pano sto proto Thema", *Neos Kosmos* April-May 1957, p. 50.
4 Panagiotis Mavromatis, "Omilia pano sto proto Thema", *Neos Kosmos* April-May 1957, p. 102.
5 Vasos Georgiu, "Pioi kai pos mas odigisan ston Emfilio", *Eleftherotipia,* December 23, 1978.
6 Dimitrios Vlandas, *Emfilios Polemos 1945-1949,* 2 (Athens 1979) p. 43.
7 Eleftheriu in *Avgi,* February 27, 1980.
8 Tsandis in *Avgi,* February 10, 1980 and March 2, 1980.
9 Partsalidis in *Avgi,* February 24, 1980.
10 Panos Dimitriu, ed., *I Diaspasi tou KKE mesa apo ta Kimena tis Periodou 1950-1975,* 1 (Athens: Politika Provlimata, 1975) p. 92f.

The explanation for the fact that Section 4 of the Resolution of the Second Plenum was not published neither then nor later must be much simpler, much more purely formal. Thus the only reasonable explanation is that the missing text contained a pending matter, a matter on which no decision had yet been reached. According to the internal structure of the Resolution, Section 4 would have dealt with KKE's political tasks. From the statements of Markos,[1] Stringos,[2] Rousos,[3] and Mavromatis[4] at the 7th Plenum and from the so-called "Platform" of Markos of November 1948,[5] the memoirs of Gousias[6] and Partsalidis,[7] we can deduce that the topics considered were the questions of participation in the elections of March 1946 and of limited armed actions by the *aftoamyna* (self-defence) movement.

From the testimony of Markos at the 7th Plenum of 1957 and from a letter by him to *Anti* in 1976[8] we learn the following: When Zachariadis, speaking for the Politbureau, advocated abstention from the elections he met with the opposition of Thanasis Chatzis, Markos, Chrysa Chatzivasiliou and Giorgos Siantos. Chatzis expressed the opinion that abstention did not correspond to the realities of the time; if the KKE participated, 130 to 150 parliamentary seats could be won. Zachariadis, realizing that he could not prevail, closed the discussion on the grounds that one must wait for the views of the Soviet government which would soon be brought back from Moscow by Partsalidis. Therefore it was decided to refer the matter to the Politbureau on the clear understanding that the latter would take into account the Soviets' advice; something which was not done, as is known. Thus the decision whether to participate in or abstain from the elections remained pending and therefore the row of dots in Section 4.

The debate of the Plenum about the armed actions of *aftoamyna* proved similarly inconclusive. From section 3 of the Resolution, which dealt with the duties of EAM, it becomes clear that on this issue, too, the Resolution did not go beyond previous decisions. The right-wing terror was to be met by (unarmed) self-defence (*aftoamyna*) actions by the masses; against physical terrorism the people were allowed to retaliate by the same means. The only new element in this decision was that self-defence could now be directed against the agents of the State as well. But even this was not a completely new feature. At the 7th Plenum in 1957 Mavromatis stated that the Second Plenum took only a very general decision to orient the Party towards armed struggle.[9] Gousias added in his memoirs that the Second Plenum only decided to respond to right-wing terror by the same means,[10] which again must be understood as referring to "reinforced" aftoamyna (self-defence) actions. Further evidence by *Eleftheriou,*[11] Partsalidis[12] and Tsandis[13] confirms this. No fundamental decision was taken on the *aftoamyna* question beyond the previous formula - to meet right-wing terror with the same means, i.e. by limited armed self-defence. All later claims by Zachariadis and his apologists serve only to conceal the fact that the Second Plenum did not take any decision to move

---

1 Vafiadis, "Orailia", pp. 45-72.
2 Leonidas Stringos, "Omilia pano sto proto Thema", *Neos Kosmos* April-May 1957, pp. 82-88.
3 Petros Rusos, "Omilia pano sto proto Thema", *Neos Kosmos* April-May 1957, pp. 89-97.
4 Mavromatis, "Omilia", pp. 98-104.
5 "I Opportunistiki Platforma tu Marku Vafiadi", *Neos Kosmos,* August 1950, pp. 476-480.
6 Giorgios Vonditsos-Gusias, *I aties gia tis ittes, ti Diaspasi tou KKE kai tis Ellinikis Aristeras,* 1 (Athens: Na Ipiretume to Lao, 1977) p. 133.
7 Dimitrios Partsalidis, *Dipli Apokatastasi tis Ethnikis Andistasis* (Athens: Themelio, 1978) p. 196.
8 "O Markos Vafiadis apanta sto Mitso Partsalidi gia ti Synantisi me ton Stalin kai tin Katangelia Zachariadi", *And,* September 4, 1976, p. 33; and Vafeiadis, "Omilia", p. 49; and Stringos, "Omilia" p. 85.
9 Mavromatis, "Omilia", p. 102.
10 Vonditsos-Gousias, *op. cit.*, p..134.
11 Eleftheriou in *Avgi,* January 27, 1980.
12 Partsalidis in *Avgi,* February 24, 1980.
13 Tsandis in *Avgi,* February 10, 1980 and March 2, 1980.

toward civil war. Even the claim by Zachariadis's critics that the Second Plenum generally oriented the Party towards armed conflict should be regarded with caution and be seen only as another reference to limited armed *aftoamyna*. Even for the sternest critics of Zachariadis it has been hard to admit that **no** decision whatsoever was taken. Therefore, Section 4 of the Resolution could at most have contained the demand for limited armed *aftoamyna*, if even that. The ominous Resolution of the Second Plenum is thus reduced to a rather harmless affair.

Now, if the Second Plenum did not take this supposedly fateful decision, could it be that it was taken at the meeting of that mysterious body called the Panhellenic Military Committee which met towards the end of the Plenum?

The Panhellenic Military Committee had been established on 1 October 1945, the first day of the 7th Party Congress.[1] Its task was the study of military problems and it consisted of Zachariadis as chairman of the Committee, Ioannidis representing the Politbureau, Theodoros Makridis (Ektoras), former ELAS staff officer and now military adviser to the Politbureau, and the secretaries and military experts from the Party's provincial organizations.[2] After its constituent session towards the end of the 7th Party Congress it had never been called together again.[3]

From the testimonies of Gousias,[4] Blanas-Kissavos,[5] Markos,[6] Tsandis,[38] and Makridis[39] we can roughly reconstruct the course of the Military. Committee's second meeting and its results. Apparently Zachariadis opened the meeting with a review of the Second Plenum's decisions stressing that it was the Party's first duty to follow the reconciliation policy. However, since under the existing situation armed conflict could not be excluded, the Party must prepare for it. He then put the question, which form the armed conflict might take. It was Makridis who presented the Politbureau's (i.e. Zachariadis's) views: there ought to be an armed rising by the people and the army in the towns, because that was where the movement had its main forces, whereas guerrilla warfare would require long preparation and would give the opponent the opportunity to take better countermeasures. In other words, the Politbureau and Zachariadis advocated a putsch or pronunciamento as Markos later put it.

The Politbureau's concept at once met stern opposition from the majority present and especially from Markos.[40] How could a putsch be carried out and with what forces? How could it be brought off without previous organization of the Party's forces and with the British forces present in the country? Markos then strongly recommended the creation of a guerrilla army based on the groups of the prosecuted which were in the process of formation. When Zachariadis noticed the opposition to his proposal he quickly wound up the conference, which thus lasted only a few minutes. In order to shelve the issue, subordinate party organizations were instructed to examine the means available and the existing possibilities for armed struggle. Thus the Panhellenic Military Committee, too, did not reach any decisions. When a few weeks later the Macedonian and Thracian Provincial Bureaus reported that they would be able to field 25,000 armed men, Zachariadis replied: *"Stop this. The whole business was only a bluff to force the government to give in"*.[41] Thus Kissavos is right when he states that *"Neither the Politbureau of the KKE Central Committee, nor the Panhellenic Military*

1 *To 7o Sinedrio,* I (Athens: KE tou KKE, 1945) p. 10.
2 Giorgis Blanas-Kissavos, *Emfilios Polemos 1946-1949. Opos ta ezisa* (Athens 1976) p. 62.
3 *Ibidem* p. 75.
4 Vonditsos-Gousias, *op. cit.,* p.134f.
5 Blanas-Kissavos, *op. cit*, p..73f.
6 "Platforma" p. 476 and "Omilia" p. 50.

Committee ever undertook to work out or set up a plan to prepare for armed action against enemy forces throughout the whole of Greece".[1]

Thus we may safely reach the following conclusion: Neither the Second Plenum nor the Panhellenic Military Committee took any decision to launch a civil war. At the same time we can distinguish three different opinions about future courses of action in the two leading organs of the KKE i.e. the Central Committee and the Politbureau. The *first* opinion, which was shared by most of the rank and file of the KKE and EAM and a majority of the Central Committee members, advocated a peaceful development and integration into the country's existing system. We may call this line "revisionist". In the Politbureau this line was represented by Siantos, Chrysa Chatzivasiliou and Partsalidis. They, too, were threatening to boycott the elections, but this was only a pre-election political manoeuvre to secure better conditions. Without Zachariadis's influence, the KKE and EAM would very likely in the end have participated in the elections and would have accepted, as did the Communist Parties of France and Italy, integration into the political system as long-term opposition parties in the hope of one day winning over the majority of the electorate and thus bringing about a peaceful transition to socialism. Had there been a democratic vote in the Central Committee on this matter the protagonists of this view would certainly have won. But precisely this was prevented by Zachariadis's manoeuvre to transfer the decision-making to the Politbureau where *he* would prevail.

The *second* opinion we may - with certain reservations - call "Titoist". This line was represented mainly by leading cadres from Northern Greece, many of them former ELAS Kapetanioi, who had not accepted the defeat in December 1944 and had never come to terms psychologically with the Varkiza capitulation. It was their followers who suffered the most from right-wing terror and this strengthened their militancy. Their goal was the revival of the partisan war. Markos Vafeiadis was their main spokesman. But, unlike the "revisionists" they were not represented in the Politbureau.

The *third* opinion was represented in the Politbureau by Zachariadis and his henchmen (regular members Ioannidis, Bartziotas, Anastasiadis and candidates Stringos and Rousos); they had the majority. They rejected both participation in the elections and partisan warfare. The first would have been a right-wing and the second a left-wing deviation from Leninist principles. Zachariadis, who had spent the years 1936 to 1945 in prisons and concentration camps, continued to think in undiluted Leninist-Stalinist categories as he had been taught at the Comintern's cadre school KUTV.[2] Since his return in May 1945 he had tried to bring the KKE back onto the paths of orthodoxy. At the 7th Party Congress he had abandoned the hitherto prevailing line of the 6th Plenum of 1934 when he stated that the process of bourgeois-democratic transformation had been concluded by EAM during the occupation and that the establishing of popular democracy was now the goal.[3] During the following months he had continuously stressed that Greece was going through the deepest crisis of its history. He apparently believed that Greece was rapidly approaching a revolutionary situation. In these circumstances participation in the elections would have been a mistake since it would have stabilised the situation. His plans for a putsch were the orthodox recipe for such a situation. The only obstacle in. his way were the British, but international pressure in the United Nations might soon remove this. His only problem was to bridge the time-gap and to keep the Party away from irreversible deviations such as participation in the elections. This explains

1 Blanas-Kissavos, *op.cit.* p. 59.
2 Kommunisticheskii Universitet Trudyasheshya Vostoka.
3 *To 7o Sinedrio*, 5, 7, 16f.

his manoeuvres during the Second Plenum and at the session of the Panhellenic Military Committee and even more his oscillating policy in the ensuing months which created the impression that he was following a cunning double strategy. In fact, it was merely his attempt to prevent any deviation from the course he had determined. The result was the inconsistent policy which led the Party stumbling into civil war without any clear idea of where it was going.

THE MURDER OF GEORGE POLK IN THESSALONIKI IN MAY 1948

There is almost no field of Greek politics in the year of 1948, the third year of the civil war which was not controlled by AMAG (American Mission for Aid to Greece) headed by the former governor of Nebraska Dwight Griswold..The only exception were the repressive measures against the communists or those persons the Government regarded as such. As long as these reprisals did not trigger bigger protests abroad the Americans did not pay attention. Probably in connection with the banning of KKE, EAM and EA on 8 January 1948 but also in connection with the preparation of the offensive against the Roumeli region a huge operation was set in motion during which 1,400 people were arrested just in Athens and Piraeus. In the following two months 5,000 real or alleged adherents of the Left were arrested all over Greece and many of them were transferred to the island of Gyaros where eventually 10,000 deportees lived. Another 5,000 were exiled to the island of Trikeri. 116 Communists were sentenced to death and a further 688 in 1947. In the first six months of 1948 1,547 death sentences were passed.[1] According to Averoff 2,960 death sentences were passed between January 1945 and January 1948 .[2]

The frequent executions of small groups of those sentenced to death since February was noticed by the US Embassy and reported to Washington but only when Homer Bigart wrote about it in the *New York Herald Tribune* and when the Greek Embassy in Washington protested against the report it became an issue in Washington.[3] The *Washington Post* held that Greece *"under American aid and tutelage, is resorting to some of the terroristic methods that the United States is so sharply condemning in Soviet dominated countries."*[4]

On 1 May, Holy Saturday, of the year 1948 the Minister of Justice Christos Ladas was killed in front of a church in Athens by the KKE-adherent, Efstratios Moutsigiannis who threw a hand-grenade. When he tried to flee he was pursued by policemen and attacked them with other hand grenades. One policeman was killed two others were wounded.[5] The assassination attempt had two results: Vice-premier and Foreign Minister Tsaldaris, the chief of the right-wing Popular Party used it to provoke a governmental crisis, but more important it triggered a wave of executions.

The mass executions which began after Easter, on 4 May 1948 were terrible. During the first two days 184 persons were shot. During the next ten days another 830 persons which had been sentenced to death were to be executed. On 6 May 34 persons were killed. The between January 1945 and January 1948 people executed had been former EAM/ELAS members who had been sentenced to death after the signing of the Varkiza agreement. A lot of them had been convicted based on the flimsiest accusations, many because of alleged crimes during the occupation or during the Dekemvrina. Until the Ladas murder the Greek Government had been cautious in regard to the number of executions. But now they obviously aimed at avenging the murder of Ladas.[6]

---

1 KKE, *I trichroni epopoiia tou dimokratikou stratou Elladas (1946-1949)* (Athen: Synchroni Epochi, 1998), p. 292.

2 Evangelos Averoff-Tossizza, *Le Feu et la Hache. Grèce 46-49* (Paris: Breteuil, 1973), p. 212.

3 *Foreign Relations of the United States 1948,* IV (Washington: Goverment Printing Office, 1974), p. 59.

4 Judith S. Jeffery, *Ambiguous Commitments and Uncertain Policies. The Truman Doctrine in Greece, 1947-1951* (New York: Lexington Books, 2000)., p. 162.

5 *Keesing's Contemporary Archives*, p. 9.342.

6 *Greek News Agency, Survey* (7 May 1948), p. 1f. In *The Nation* (15 May 1948), p. 518 oe read: *"Let us have no illusions about the Greek executions that have horrified Europe these past two weeks; they are plain atrocities*

The London *Times* wrote that these mass executions had nothing in common with justice but with politics. The *Manchester Guardian* spoke of *"profound horror"* and found to be the shootings to be *"an act of revenge"*. The *Daily Mail* opinioned that the were acts of revenge and were reminiscent of the reprisals during the German occupation. A representative of the Foreign Office informed the House of Commons that they had protested in Athens. *"These wholesale executions will come as a grave shock to decent opinion."*[1] Griswold justified the executions. The prisoners had not been shot because they were Leftists but because the were sentenced murderers. This provoked the American correspondent Constantine Poulos to protest in the *New York Herald Tribune*; *"Griswold does not sense any shame in the realisation that the Greek government is now carrying out a deliberate program of liquidation of its political opponents which the British authorities had prevented it from carrying out while they were overseeing Greek affairs."* The protests, however, continued and spread in the West and the East.,[2] and became so loud on 17 May that Foreign Secretary Marshall cautioned against the execution of the 2,000 also sentenced to death. It *"might create grave political difficulties from viewpoint world opinion."*[3]

At the end of May Homer Bigart of the *New York Herald Tribune* complained that the State Department tried to censor American correspondents reporting from Greece.. "It *is the view of certain State Department officials that American correspondents in Greece should give their exclusive attention to the business of saving Greece from Communism which they apparently believe is far worse than fascism. Correspondents are expected to avert their eyes from the suppression of basic liberties, from the mass arrests and mass execution of 'bandits', the closing of the 'bandit' press, the arrests of 'bandit' newsmen, and finally the shipping of whole boatloads of 'bandits' to exile in the islands."* If a correspondent does not comply with this view the US Embassy gave him the cold shoulder. Griswold objects against the expression mass executions and was of the opinion the the inmates of Makronisos were treated well.[4] On Makronisos the Government operated a camp quite similar to a concentration camp.This camp and its facilities should only find accidental mention, just like the two other camps mentioned above.[5]

But the executions went on. In June the US Embassy reported that the Greek military alone had shot in June 147 people who had been sentenced by courts martial. It remains unknown how many executions the Ministry of Justice had ordered. On 6 August Marshall wrote: *"We suggest Gr[ee]k policy regarding court-martial sentences be reexamined with view to reducing executions to minimum and as first step toward eventual halt in cycle of killing in Greece. [...] We would recommend only most heinous be punished by execution, that any executions be postponed for several months, that more lenient policy be adopted by clemency boards with view to commuting vast proportion of sentences..."* On 21 August the new American Ambassador Grady reported: *"Greek Government has executed after legal*

---

without excuse or mitigation. The men killed had been in prison since the 1944 revolt. They were all leftists and members of the resistance; some were Communists but more were not. [...] After four years in prison these men are being marched out and shot in batches. [...] The Greek government says they are not reprisals. If not, what are they? [... It is] wholesale legal murder."

1 *Ibidem*, p. 2f.

2 Greek News Agency, *Survey* (14 May 1948), p. 1f.

3 *FRUS 1948*, IV, p. 86,

4 Greek News Agency, *Survey* (4 June 1948), p. 5. ....In February 1948 UP reported, that the US Military Missioncensored all military operations. American Council, *Facts on Greece*, p. 18

5 Costas G. Sarropoulos,"Makronisos on 29 February and 1 March 1948. The events in the 1st Bataillon of the military detention camp" *Thetis* 3 (1996), pp. 271-280; George Giannaris,"Makronisos and the Greek Intellectuals" *Thetis* 3 (1996), pp. 281-292

process 1824 persons, 234 (2 during last month) as result of crimes arising from and in connection with first Communist attempt (December 1944 revolution) and 1590 (102 during July) arising from current Markos movement."[1]

The American and British Governments were irritated and annoyed the fact that some journalists were not prepared to stay in Athens and rewrite the press announcements of the Greek government as news but went into the province and conducted their own research there.[2] The findings were often shocking. Thus the *Daly Mirror* published a photo of a horseman who triumphantly held up some cut-off heads. Most probably he was a member of those rightist bands who proudly presented his "left" trophies.

For many weeks in the summer of 1947 news about the formation of international brigades and their deployment in the Greek mountains could be read in the American press. But then some war-correspondents managed to get there and they finally reported the truth. After that the Greek army and police did their best to hinder the repetition of these alleged "news". The international brigade were an invention by the propaganda department of the Greek Government. Because the correspondent of the *New York Times*, Dana Adams Schmidt, reported too objectively the editorial staff sent the well known reactionary journalist A. Sedwick to Athens who had presented the events during the Dekemvriana (1944/45) in the "right" light.[3]

Among those which worked independently were Constantine Poulos (*Overseas News Agency, Nation*), Homer Bigart (*New York Herald Tribune*) und George Polk (*Columbia Broadcasting System*). The described the Greek reality and criticised the American policy. In January Bigart wrote that Truman's policy towards Greece: *"stands or falls by the outcome of the Spring offensive [...] If this offensive fails the Americans will be forced to conclude that there is a basic and perhaps incurable rottenness in Greek civil and military administration."*[4] In December 1947 George Polk published a long article in *Harper's Magazine,* which proved that he was well acquainted with the Greek system: *"Thirty-five families dominate the country financially, exerting control or influence through interlocking directorates. The fulcrum for their economic lever is the National Bank of Greece, a private investment institution."*[5]

Polk here described the clientelistic system of Greece in all details though he did not use that term. Polk recognized how much the system had changed: *"What before the war was simply a system designed to make the wealthy wealthier now has become a system designed to squeeze from the country any penny possible as quickly as possible."* Polk then spoke about the "Liberty-ships" which America had given to Greece in order to rebuild the merchant navy. *"After obtaining the ships, the Greek government promptly sold a number of them to private Greek ship owners at extremely low prices. Today most of those ships fly the Panama flag. Some are netting upward of $ 200,000 a year in profits for their owners. Most of the profits are carefully tucked away in private accounts in foreign banks."* 1946 Greece had spent 145 Mio. Dollars for imports. *"Of this sum $ 141,000,000 went into luxury items, deposits of money in foreign banks, purchase of property outside Greece, and other activities that were nonproductive so far as the internal Greek economy was concerned. Only $*

1 FRUS 1948, IV, pp. 114, 119f, 140
2 On 17 January 1948 *The Nation* wrote: *"The reports from Greece [...] are usually based on the handouts issued either by the Foreign Minister Constantine Tsaldaris's royalist information or by the fascist military clique."* "News From Greece" *The Nation* (17 January 1948), p. 50
3 Constantine Poulos, Manuscript in my archives.
4 Greek News Agency, *Survey* (30 January 1948), p. 4.
5 George Polk, "Greece Puts us to the Test" *Harper's Magazine* (December 1947), p. 531.

4,000,000 of the $ 145,000,000 went for machines, parts, and other equipment desperately needed to rebuild Greece's industrial plant." Polk reported how the goods delivered by UNRRA and CARE had been embezzled Griswold had understood the problem but fell foul with the US Embassy. Polk stated: *"The American reconstruction program could not succeed in a country racked by civil war and served by inept, selfish, and corrupt officials. Greece needed a change in officials and policies."*[1]

Polk had called Zervas a gangster but he had also criticised the Communists and criticised the American Government for supporting the repressive right-wing Greek government. During an interview with Tsaldaris on 3 May 1948 Polk allegedly threatened to make public that Tsaldaris had 25,000 Dollars in an account with the Chase Bank inn New York - an enormous sum at that time.[2] Such a disclosure would have been more than embarrassing since the assumption that this money had been diverted from the American aid would have been raised immediately. It was clear that Polk would not find friends neither on the Greek side nor in the US Embassy.

In a letter to his colleague Drew Pearson Polk reported that the reactionaries in the Greek Government did their best to browbeat critical journalists: *"The right wing [...] is trying to get a number of us discredited or removed from Greece ... there are a number of vague hints that 'somebody is likely to get hurt'."*[3]

In February 1948 he complained to the American chargé d'affaires, Karl Rankin about *"the new wave [of] misrepresentation and vilification of Greeks and their Government in [the] US press."* Could the State Department not put pressure on the editors? Marshall replied that they were thinking how the reporting could be improved but *"the most effective corrective action can be taken only in Greece since much material used by American correspondents clearly originates with American sources within Greece."*[4]

For some time Polk had planned to interview Markos Vafeiadis and collect material about children that had been allegedly kidnapped (paidomazoma). On 7 May 1948 Polk wanted to fly to Kavalla but due to bad weather the plane was sent to Thessalonika. Polk stayed at the hotel Astoria. Already on that day but even more so on the following day Polk tried to contact the British and American officials and journalists who could bring him in contact with people who could help him to see Markos. Both sides warned him and made it clear to him that his enterprise was very dangerous and such contacts were prohibited by the Greek authorities. Since the Greek Communists in Thessalonika were either under arrest or under close supervision and because Polk did not speak Greek is it rather improbable that he contacted such persons directly. Nevertheless on 8 May he met people who promised they would organize the desired contact. This becomes clear from two letters he wrote that evening and left his the hotel room. At noon of 9 May he left the hotel and was never seen again.[5]

---

1 *Ibidem*, pp. 532-534.

2 Elias Vlanton, "A Murder and Its Meaning" *The Nation* (28 Januar 1991), p. 93; "The Ghost of CBS Correspondent George Polk" *New Europe* (26 May 2008); http://dlib.nyu.edu/findingaids/html/tamwag/newsmens.html: "Newsmen's Commission to Investigate the Murder of George Polk Records" Tamiment Library/Robert F. Wagner Labor Archives, Elmer Holmes Bobst Library of George Polk Records, New York University Libraries.

3 "The Shape of Things" *The Nation* (29 May 1948), p. 1.

4 Lawrence S. Wittner, *American Intervention In Greece, 1943 - 1949.* (New York: Columbia University Press, 1982, p. 158.

5 Edmund Keeley, *The Salonika May Murder. Cold War Politics and the Polk Affair* (Princeton: Princeton University Press, 1989), pp. 14-27. In the letter to his superior Edward R. Murrow Polk spoke of a "contact through a contact". The description of the Polk-Murder follows this book..

On 16 May a fisherman found the drifting corpse of Polk in the bay of Salonika. There was a bullet hole in the head and his arms and legs were boud together. The autopsy showed that he was thrown into the water while he was still alive. But even before Polk was found strange things happened. On 11 May the 3rd police district anonymously received an envelope with Polk's identity card and other personal items. Obviously it was intended to make the disappearance of Polk publicly known. But the dead body was to remain undiscovered for some time. The murderers apparently knew that a dead body floating in the sea will surface only after two or three weeks. The manner of the killing (a shot to the neck) and the trussing up of the body intended to create the impression that the killers had been Communists. This is confirmed by a report in the *New York Herald Tribune* which said that on 18 May *"a leading Athens Government official, who declined to allow his name to be used, declared: ' We are 1,000 per cent. sure it is the work of Communists'."*[1]

It is quite unlikely that Polk was murdered by adherents of KKE. Which interest would the KKE leadership have to see Polk dead? Markos used every opportunity to be interviewed by western journalists e..g. on 25 June 1948 by Homer Bigart.[2] The first statement by the radio of the PDG (Provisorial Demoratic Government) on 20 May is rather interesting: *"Free Greece Radio stated that the Free Greek Government is in possession of evidence that the same people who were responsible for the murder of the Communist, Zevgos, in March last year, were responsible for the death of Polk. Zevgos' murderers have not been arrested to this day."*[3] The evidence presented on 30 May by the PDG was not really convincing. It was said that the Athens chief of the police Angelos Evert, a former collaborator together with the police officer Tsousis and the CIA had jointly planned the attack. The implementation had been the work of Apostolos Xanthopoulos head of the police in Thessalonika, the chief of the special police (Stefanakis) and Nikolaos Muskoundis chief of the security.[4]

In answer to the question '*cui bono*' there remains only one conclusion: the murder of Polk had been the work of the parakratos of Thessalonika and that it had been diligently planned. The CBS investigative team which was sent to Salonika a little later came to similar conclusions, *"that the likeliest possibility was that Polk walked into a trap which, in view of the short time it took him to find a Salonika 'contact', must have been prepared well in advance by an organization in place and ready, but taking order from 'higher up' outside Salonika, surely from a place where Polk's movements and plans were known: 'almost certainly, from Athens'."*[5] The fact that Polk had lobster and peas before his death does not fits into a Communist surrounding because only rich people could afford lobsters. Probably the alleged Communist contact person invited Polk to dinner and promised to bring him by boat to the coast north of Katerini which was controlled by the DSE (Dimokratikos Stratos Elladas). Where this dinner took place, in which restaurant or on board of a yacht is unknown - but certainly not on board of a kaïki in which the cooking of a lobster would not have been possible. Shortly after the lobster dinner Polk was killed and thrown into the sea. The idea that the murderers

---

1 Greek News Agency, *Survey* (21 May 1948), p. 2.

2 *Ibidem* (25 June 1948), p. 3.

3 *Ibidem* (21 May 1948), p. 2.

4 *Ibidem* (4 June 1948), p. 2.

5 Keeley, *op. cit.*, p. 26. In a CBS Radio transmissionon on 21 June 1948 these three well knowns journalists Howard K. Smith, Don Hellenbeck und Edward R Murrow discussed the murder case of Polk. Murrow said, that the murder *"was a cold, deliberate, political demonstration, planned to be spectacular, planned to intimidate."* Smith expressed the opinion that Polk went into a "carefully prepared trap". *"From the speed with which the trap closed one may conclude that it was organized and directed from a place where Mr. Polk's advance movements were known, in short, from Athens."* Greek News Agency, *Survey* (25 June 1948), p. 3.

killed Polk on land and was then taken on board of a boat is also wrong because whoever knows Salonika knows that the waterfront is full of people even at midnight. It is more likely that Polk entered the boat to be transported to the other beach unnoticed under the cover of the night.

The murder of Polk provoked violent reactions among the American journalists. In New York the Newspaper Guild demanded the sending of an investigating commission consisting of journalists and Governmental officials. In Washington the organization of the *Overseas Writers* set up a commission under the leadership of the well known writer Walter Lippmann which was to investigate the precise conditions of Polk's death. George Sadowski, a member of the House of Representatives intended to demand the creation of an investigative commission of Congress. But the State Department was not interested in the Polk case.[1] Therefore Lippmann organized his own investigating commission and asked the former director of the OSS (Office for Strategic Services, - antecedent organization of CIA) William Donovan, who had a law firm to cooperate. Donovan travelled with the blessing of the State Department.[2] Not one member of the Lippmann commission remained in Athens for a lengthy period of time.

Donovan appeared in Athens and spoke with Greek officials of the Government. When nothing came about he began to exert pressure by hinting that American aid could come to an end. He wanted to see an arrest. The Greek Government did its best to prove that the murder had been committed by the Communists. On 14 August the police of Salonika arrested the journalist of *Makedonia*, Grigoris Staktopoulos, who on 8 May had been introduced to Polk at a happy evening drinking at the hotel bar. The meeting had lasted five minutes at most. Now he was turned into Polk's ominous contact person. After some weeks of humiliations, beating and torture Staktopoulos "confessed" that he had been the contact person.[3]

On 17 October 1948 the Mnister of Justice Melas and the Minister of internal security Rentis announced that the following three persons were responsible for the murder of Polk: Grigoris Staktopoulos, Adam Mouzenidis und Evangelos Vasvanas. During the trial in April 1949 it became known that Mouzenidis who had allegedly shot Polk in the neck had lost his life in the mountains even before Polk's murder and that Vasvanis had been in Western Thrace. Thus only the journalist Staktopoulos and his mother remained who could be indicted. The trial was a farce. The defence lawyers cooperated with the state attorney: *"The defence attorneys from the second day of the trial stressed their solidarity with the prosecution. More than once they made statements such as: 'The defence supports the obvious theory that the Greek Communists decided to execute Polk. We agree with the prosecution; there is no doubt that the Communists committed this crime."* The most grotesque statement in the trial was that by Staktopoulos: *"I was a Communist. I declare my motherland, Greece, innocent of George Polk's murder. I denounce the Greek Communist Party, the Cominform [sic], and Moscow as the perpetrators of this crime."*[4]

Both were convicted but everybody knew that the trial had been a farce. The Lippmann Commission, however, stated in their final report of 1951 that the trial against Staktopoulos and his mother had been fair and was ready to believe that the Communists had murdered Polk.[5] Donovan on the other side was not interested in the truth but only that the whole affair

1 Greek News Agency, *Survey* (28 May 1948), p. 3.

2 Giannis Roubatis & Elias Vlanton, "Who Killed George Polk?" *More Magazine* 5 (1977), p. 15.

3 Elias Vlanton, "Greece's Unfinished Business in the George Polk Affair" *Kathimerini* (19 March 1998), p. 3. In an interview in 1977 Staktopoulos told how he was mistreated for two months. Roubati & Vlaton, *op. cit.*, p. 18.

4 Constantine Poulos, "Who Killed George Polk?" *The Nation* (28 May 1949), p. 605f.

5 Text of the "Polk Report, May 21, 1951" in Keeley, *op.,cit.*, pp. 363-370. A false graphological expertise sstated

was closed with the trial and that the Greek Government could continue to function in the American protectorate.

"It wasn't Walter Lippmann alone who failed George Polk [...] it was American journalism. [...] This was not a gigantic conspiracy, but journalism-as-usual. It was reporters writing about countries whose language, customs and politics they were unfamiliar with and accepting the word of official sources - American and Greek - without doing the necessary legwork to conform information. Worse, there was a failure to apply standards of logic and fairness, whether to a murder confession riddled with inconsistencies or to a trial that mocked the notions of justice and the rule of law." Only a handful of courageous journalists such as Constantine Poulos continued to be of a different opinion and organized a second investigation commission consisting out of Poulos himself, John Donovan of NBC (News Broadcasting Corporation - no relative of William Donovn) and Polk's younger brother William.[1] When Ambassador Grady learned about it he ranted: *"Embassy feels strongly that any new mission to investigate Polk affair, impartial or otherwise, could be undesirable per se. Proposed composition this mission particularly dangerous."* Poulos was a Communist 'fellow traveller'. The best would be to refuse to give Poulos a passport. If this was impossible one should take care that the Greek Government wold refuse a visa for him.[2] When Polk's younger brother appeared in Athens to conduct his own research and asked some inconvenient questions, William Donovan allegedly reprimanded him by asking him whether he intended to ruin his career?[3]

It must be stated clearly that the US Embassy watched the researches of Lippmann-Donovan teams *argus* eyed. When a member of the team, the former Air Force colonel James Kellis came to close to the truth the chargé d'affaires Ranking made it clear to him that the Communists had committed the deed. When Kellis was not ready to accept this version Ranking saw to it that the State Department made the Air Force Command recall Kellis.[4] Kellis report was not shown to the other members of the commission.[5]

Even in 1973 the Greek Right did not have any doubt that the trial of Staktopoulos had been correct. Averoff wrote: *"Finally, after a thorough inquest and an irreproachable trial the court ruled that the unfortunate journalist had been a victim of a secret communist organization which aimed to have his death appear the work of both the Right and to the Centre government which had opposed his visit Markos."*[6]

Staktopoulos was kept in a jail of the Asfaleia for for years in order to keep him "incommunicado". When in 1953 the public was reminded by a series of articles on the Polk affairs Staktopoulos was transferred to a regular prison and his lifelong sentence was reduced to 20 years. After 12 years which he had spent in jail innocently he was released in 1960. After that he again worked as journalist. On 7 July 1976 Staktopoulos revoked the confession of 1948 in the Newspaper *Ta Nea*.[7] In 1977 his lawyer Stelios Papathemelis succeeded in proving that the only 'real' evidence of the 1948 trial had been wrong. He demanded the resumption of the trial which was refused in 1979. In 1977 Vasvanis who had been living in exile in Rumania

---

that Staktopoulos' mother had writte the address on the envelope with Polk's ID card.

1 Vlanton, *Murder and Its Meaning* , p. 94.
2 Roubatis & Vlanton, *op. cit.*, p. 17.
3 Wittner, *op. cit.*, p. 160.
4 *Ibidem,* p. 159.
5 Roubatis & Vlanton, *op. cit.*, p. 17.
6 Evangelos Averoff-Tossizza, *By Fire and Axe. The Greek Communist Party and Teh Civil War in Greece 1944-49* (New York: Caratzas, 1978), p. 265f
7 Roubatis & Vlanton, *op. cit.*, p. 22.

since the end of the war offered to come to Greece and present himself to the court, even though he had been sentenced to death in absentia.. The Greek Government rejected this.[1] In 1998 Staktopoulos died at the age of 88 years. In 2001 his widow tried again to achieve a resumption of the trial. On 16 March 2006, however, the request was finally rejected by the high Greek court (*Areios Pagos*).[2]

Elias Vlanton's commentary of the year 1998 is therefore still valid: *"Gregory Staktopoulos never lived to see the Greek state exonerate him, but even posthumously the Greek judicial system must clear his name. It must do so not for Staktopoulos, but for the integrity of Greece itself. Exonerating Staktopoulos provides Greece with an opportunity to exonerate itself. It will demonstrate to future generations that there is no shame in acknowledging the mistakes of the past, and allow Greece to finally end the drama of the George Polk affair in a way that will help prevent its repetition."*[3]

The murder of George Polk became the topic of books and articles. Many authors adhere to conspiracy theories. There are five groups of alleged conspirators: 1) the Communists; 2) the Greek Right and the Government; 3) the CIA; 4) the British[4] and 5) the contrabandists. It is interesting in this context that in the few studies which suspect the Greek Right to have committed the murder they mention organisation CHI. The parakratos is not mentioned at all.[5] Obviously even those authors who come very close to the truth know the Greek reality ony superficially. The most objective and scholarly book is that of Edmund Keeley of 1980. The earliest book in Greek is that of Kostas Chatziargyris of 1974.[6]The study published by Kati Maron who earlier worked for the CIA, is well researched but only of limited reliability since many assertions are not reliably proven. Many facts cannot be verified.[7] The book by Elias Vlaton and Zak Mettger of the 2006 is well researched but they reach to the wrong conclusions assuming that the murderers were smugglers or drug dealers.[8] Obviously they did not know the Greek world thoroughly enough to understand precisely such people were working for the parakratos. Today it is impossible to detect the real murderers. A scholarly account that includes Greek sources is still missing. To analyse the the contents of these books is not possible in the framework of this article. But one thing seems to be certain that the murderers belonged to the same parakratical circle who killed Lambrakis a few years later.

---

1 Roubatis & Vlanton, *op. cit.*, pp. 13, 22.

2 Reference number of the order to dismiss the case: 1024/2007.

3 Vlanton, *Unfinished Business*, p. 3

4 On the KKE internet pagee http://politikokafeneio.com/dse/dse52.htm an agent of the Intelligence Service is accused but no plausible reason is given.

5 This is especially conspicuous in the article by Vlanton in the Kathimerini. He reports there that in 1953 certain Soula Karanthou had shown up in the US Embassy in Athens and told tht her neighbour, a ertain Zizis Nikzas was mixed up in the Polk-Murdder. *"She reports that Nikzas had a taverna in a remote area along the coast in Nea Krini and that around the time Polk was killed she had observed him taking his rubber raft out from the apartment one day before he was leaving for the taverna. She also said that after returning from work that evening he and his wife had a terrific fight during which she yelled: „Zissis, why did you do it?" And that even later he was visited by men late in the night, but pretended not to be home. What Karanthou did not know but which further research confirmed was that her neighbor was not simply a taverna owner, but that he led one of Salonika's right-wing groups. And a long-time resident of the area knew Nikzas and confirmed that his group [...]and several others in the the area had been engaged in a variety of criminal enterprises."* These groups were part of the parakratos.

6 Kostas Chatziargyris, *I Ypothesi Polk* (Athina: Gutenberg, 1975)

7 .Kati Marton, *The Polk Conspiracy: Murder and Cover-up in the Case of CBS News Correspondent George Polk* (New York: Times Books, 1992).

8 Elias Vlanton /Zak Mettger, *Who killed George Polk? Te Press Covers Up a Death in the Family* (Philadelphia; Templ UP, 1989).

THE OFFENSIVE AGAINST KONITSA

The charming little city of Konitsa is one of those places in Greece which are known to connoisseurs only. Outside Greece not only in America but in Europe as well Konitsa is unknown. There was a time, however, when Konitsa was mentioned almost daily in the New York Times. I am talking of the last week of December in 1947, the week when the battle of Konitsa took place.

I am not going to describe the actual fighting, the dislocation of the troop and the various tactical manoeuvres of the adversaries but I will try and give a picture of the developments which led to the battle and evaluate its results.

The Greek Civil War was the result of the counter-revolution which hit the country after the Varkiza Agreement which ended the *Dekemvriana*. In my *British Intervention in Greece* which was published in 1985[1] I analysed the causes for the Civil War on almost 600 pages. The actual war began in summer 1946 when the first groups of the persecuted Left went into the mountains to escape harassment by the victorious Right and the government. In the course of the following 18 months a wave of escalating violence and counter-violence swept over the country and the isolated tiny groups of persecuted grew into the Democratic Army. In summer 1947 a veritable civil war was fought in Greece. The leader of the Democratic Army was Markos Vafeiadis who was an experienced guerilla leader since his time in ELAS.

Out of ideological reasons, however, the Greek Communist Party (KKE) under the leadership of the Stalinist Nikos Zachariadis did not believe in guerilla warfare despite the fact that during the Second World War the Greek resistance movement had been very successful with partisan tactics. According to his orthodox views the revolution would be carried through by the armed proletariat in the towns. But he knew that such an upheaval was not possible as long as British troops were in the country, because it would end in just another *Dekemvriana*. Thus one had to wait for their withdrawal. In summer 1946, however, the persecutions of the Left assumed such proportions that Zachariadis was obliged to make a little concession: He allowed the persecuted to go to the mountains and fight back. But this was only a compromise to bridge the time until the withdrawal of the British and the takeover in the towns. In other words: until May 1947 Zachariadis was following a double strategy which can be brought to the following simplified formula: guerilla war in the mountains, policy of reconciliation in the towns[2].

Zachariadis' calculation, however, did not work out. Though in 1947 the British were obliged to reduce their military presence in Greece considerably, this was of no advantage for Zachariadis, because the Americans eagerly stepped following the Truman doctrine which was announced in May 1947. At the same time it became clear that not even the United Nations would be of any help. Zachariadis did not know what to do. In April 1947 he demanded from Markos to give up partisan warfare and to go over to regular tactical warfare: First he ought to create a free area in the mountains and then he should liberate Macedonia and Thrace and win Thessaloniki[3]. But this was pure theory. A few days later Zachariadis met Tito and asked whether the Yugoslavs would supply the necessary equipment. Tito reacted very reservedly.

From Belgrad Zachariadis asked Moscow for a meeting with Stalin and Molotov. In mid-May Zachariadis was in Moscow for talks with the Soviet leaders. There is no documentary

---

1 Heinz A. Richter, *British Intervention in Greece From Varkiza to Civil War February 1945 to August 1946*(London: Merlin Press, 1985).

2 Matthias Esche, *Die Kommunistische Partei Griechenlands 1941-1949* (München: Oldenbourg, 1982), p. 229.

3 Christophe Chiclet, *Les Communistes Grecs dans la Gueire* (Paris: L'Harmattan, 1987), p. 201.

evidence on the content of these talks. But we are certainly on the safe side if we assume that Stalin stuck to the percentage agreement of October 1944. But apparently Stalin avoided making his position clear; he did not come out against the Greek civil war as he did a little later towards Yugoslav communists. Instead Stalin told Zachariadis to produce a list with the requirements of the Democratic Army. This list was compiled and towards the end of May Zachariadis was under the impression that the Soviet would supply whatever he needed.

But Zachariadis moved cautiously. He knew that there were forces in the Politbureau and the Central Committee which opposed a course which might lead to another disaster. But fate helped him: In May 1947 Zevgos was assassinated, Siantos died and Bakirtzis committed suicide. Thus in early June the Politbureau i.e. Zachariadis uttered first[1] threats[2] and towards the end of the month the warnings got louder. At the Xlth Party Congress of the French Communist Party in Strassbourg politbureau member Miltiadis Porfyrogenis announced that if the other side continued its irreconcilable course it might be necessary to create a free democratic Greece in the mountains with a government of its own'. But despite these threats Zachariadis still stuck to his double strategy: twice he proposed peace negotiations which might have stopped the escalation. The Liberals in Athens were not unsympathetic to the peace feelers but the Populists and the Americans showed a cold shoulder and intensified the persecution of the Left by arresting large numbers of communists[3] In August a new Government was formed in Athens which offered an amnesty to those who laid down their weapons by the end of October; there was not even a chance for a new Varkiza.

In September the KOMINFORM was founded in Moscow. Three parties were not admitted: the Albanian, the Chinese and the Greek. The first because it was quarrelling with the Yugoslavs, the other two because they were directly or indirectly in conflict with the USA and Stalin did not want to become involved and there was the percentage agreement. Zachariadis, however, misinterpreted the facts completely. He believed that the Soviets would procure weapons *en masse* and that KOMINFORM was a second KOMINTERN.

Zachariadis gave up his double strategy. From 12th to 15th September the Plenum of the Central Committee met at two places: in Athens and somewhere in the mountains[4]. Zachariadis and the hardliners joined the group in the mountains. The CC moved cautiously and did not totally give up the double strategy, but the main weight of the Party's work was from now on on the organisation and the carrying through of the armed struggle. The intention to set up a government in mountains was confirmed. It was decided to split the Politbureau between Athens and the mountains.

After the end of the IIIrd Plenum a special meeting of the CC members and the military leaders of the Democratic Army took place. A far reaching plan which was called "L" or according to another source "S" was conceived. Provided enough weapons' could be found the Democratic Army was to be enlarged to 60,000 fighters by spring 1948. The strategic aim was to liberate Macedonia. During the preliminary phase the Democratic Army was to occupy

---

1 Resolution of the Political Bureau of 8 June 1947 published in *Rizospastis* (12 June 1947)

2 Rizospastis (28. June 1947). The organ of the CPF *Humanité* published a rather toned down version.

3 According to US sources 9,000 Leftists were arrested./7/? *US,* 1947, V, p. 240. Eudes who is not very reliable in number talks about 20,000 arrested. Dominique Eudes, *Les Kapetanios. La guene civile grecque de 1943a 1949* (Paris: Fayard, 1970), p. 391.

4 KKE, *Episima Keimiena 1945 - 1949* Vol. VI (Athens: Synchronii Epochi, 1987), p. 246; The group in the mountains consisted of: Markos Vafeiadis, Giorgis Erythriadis, Giannis loannidis, Miltiadis Porfyrogenis, Petros Rousos, Leonidas Stringos, and some military cadres; the Athens group included: Stergios Anastasiadis, Dimitris Vlandas, Vasilis Markezinis, Achileas Blanas, Panagiotis Mavromatis, Nikos Ploumbidis, Sotiris Soukaras, Chrysa Chatzivasileiou. Istoria tou Kommounistik*ou Kommatos Elladas 1946-1949*. Vol. VI (Athens: Nea Synora, 1977?), p. 184f.

the Metsovon-Pass in order to secure unhindered circulation between Macedonia, Thessaly and Epirus. The Tempi-Valley was to be occupied as well so that contacts with the partisans in mountains of Chasia, Pieria, Olymp and Kissavos could be established. The area comprising Konitsa, Metsovo, Grevena, Tsotyli and Nestorio should be liberated. After that they would conquer Thessaloniki and hold it. They would defend it with heavy anti-aircraft batteries. They even dreamed of creating an air force and a navy[1]. Markos much later characterised the atmosphere as fictitious (mia atmosfaira panigyrismou).[2]

On 8 October *Rizospastis* published parts of the resolutions of the Illrd Plenum and appealed to the members to assist the military efforts. The Government retaliated by having ten Communists sentenced to death and shot. Thus another escalating process was triggered off: the process of terror and counterterror which was to last until the end of the Civil War. On 18 October *Rizospastis* and *Eleftheri Ellada* were prohibited. In order not to arouse world public opinion too much KKE and EAM were not yet banned. On the same day a big partisan unit of 3,000 men attacked the Metsovon-area to get this important pass under the control of the Democratic Army. The heavy fighting lasted twelve days and at the end the Democratic Army gave up."[3] A similar attack against Grevena failed as well. Guerilla attacks in Northern Macedonia especially in the nomarchies of Serres and Kavalla were rather successful. Thus already in October and November 1947 it was evident that partisan warfare was far superior to conventional warfare. However, the amateur strategists of the CC did not understand this lesson.

On 2 December 1947 the five-member Politbureau of the mountains met and heard the report on the progress of the military preparations of the three-member committee which had been set up after the Illrd Plenum. This committee consisted of Markos Vafeiadis, Giannis Ioannidis and Leonidas Stringos. Zachariadis criticised their work. The realisation of the resolutions of the Illrd Plenum was late. There were still opportunistic deviations from the Party's line. The military leadership of West-, Central- and East-Macedonia had not managed to recruit enough fighters. Thus the building up of reserves had been delayed. Each Party member should consider himself as drafted by the Democratic Army. Any delay was considered as treason. The Party organisations in the towns should organise the safe transfer of their members to the mountains. By February Plan "L" should be completed.

Towards the end of the conference Zachariadis announced his intention to set up a provisonal government in the mountains. The seat of this government would be Konitsa. Markos asked whether there was any chance of recognition and suggested that Politbureau-member Ioannidis should become president. The latter suggestion was a clever move to force the eminence gris of the Politbureau to the fore so that he was obliged to shoulder responsibility. Turning to the idea to conquer Konitsa Markos opposed: It was impossible to take Konitsa by frontal assault. The Democratic Army neither had the necessary material nor enough men. But Zachariadis and his henchmen insisted on the attack.[4] From the wording of the resolution passed at the end of the meeting it becomes clear that the dogmatic theoretician Zachariadis had prevailed over the military pragmatist Vafeiadis. The only astonishing thing is why did Markos not resign from his post as Commander-in-Chief of the Democratic Army although he knew that this attack was going to lead to disaster. The answer is simple: party discipline and believe in the leader.

---

1 Christophe Chiclet, *Les Communistes Grecs dans la Gueire* (Paris: L'Harmattan, 1987), p. 21 If.

2 Memorandum of Markos Vafeiadis dated 15 November 1948 printed in: Panos Dimitriou, *I diaspasi ton KKE*, Vol 1 (Athens: Politika Provlimata, 1975), p. 23.

3 Evangelos Averoff-Tozizza, *Le Feu et la Hache. Grece 1946-49 (Paris: Breteuil, 1973), pp. 192-5*

4 Markos Vafeiadis, Memorandum, p. 23; *Episima Keimna*, pp. 249ff.

During the following three weeks the Democratic Army prepared the attack on Konitsa. On 14 December the New York Times reported that the formation of a government by the guerillas was seen as imminent. This government would be recognised by Yugoslavia, Albania and Bulgaria. The Soviet stand was reserved. American military sources did not believe that the guerillas would risk the setting up of a stationary headquarters.

But precisely this happened: On 24 December the radio station of the Democratic Army transmitting from Albania announced the formation of a Provisional Democratic Government of Free Greece. Vafeiadis was Prime Minister and minister of war, Ioannidis became vice-premier and Minister of the Interior, Porfyrogenis was in charge of Justice, Rousos of Foreign Affairs, Bartziotas of Finances, Stringos of Economics, Vlandas of Agriculture, Kokkalis of Health, Education and Social Security. The new government announced a program of ten points which were a combination of serious ideas and communist theory. Point 9 was important as it stipulated the creation of an army which could repulse even external aggression i.e. a tactical army[1]. Zachariadis kept clear. If the enterprise went wrong he would not be damaged. All members of the Provisional Government except Kokkalis were Communists and all except Vafeiadis were staunch supporters of Zachariadis. Vafeiadis became a kind of romantic fig leave of Stalinism in action.

The attack on Konitsa began on Christmas Day 1947 and ended on 4 January 1948 when the partisans withdrew. Both sides had suffered heavy losses[2], which were painful for both sides but disastrous for the Communist side: The government losses amounted to 0,3% of the available force. The Democratic Army lost 1 % and had already difficulties in recruiting new fighters. I do not want to go into the tactical details of the battle, these can be found elsewhere [3] but I want to comment on certain other important implications.

The decision to select Konitsa as the first target of a tactical attack was taken for a variety of reasons. Markos lists four main ones: In 1947 Konitsa was linked with Ioannina only by one narrow road. The area is extremely mountainous with few passes which are almost impassible in winter. The distance to the Albanian border is short. This was of double advantage: Supply and reinforcement routes were short. Thus the counter offensives of the enemy could only be directed at certain passages: flank attacks were rather difficult[4].But alarmed by the rumours of an imminent proclamation of the Provisional Government the analysts of the VIth Division had come to precisely the same conclusions and had increased the garrison of Konitsa before the attack started. After the failure Markos admitted that the first trial to fight as a tactical army had failed. The attacks on Grevena and Metsovo had been guerilla attacks. The attackers against Konitsa were equipped in a much better way. But - so Markos - the whole offensive was very badly organised and it was carried out even worse *(Ολη όμως η επιχείρηση οργανώθηκε πολύ άσχημα και εκτελεστηκε ακόμα χειρότερα)*. The military leaders could not adapt to tactical warfare and lead their units as such. The opponent had a much better moral and better American equipment.

---

1 According to Kanellakis they mentioned even the creation of a fleet and an air force. FES , *op. cit.*, p. 318.

2 C. M. Woodhouse, *The Struggle for Greece 1941-1949* (London: Hart-Davis, MacGibbon, 1976), p. 221 gives the following numbers: Losses of the National Army 500, among them 104 dead and 356 wounded; Democratic Army 250 dead. The official history of the Greek General Staff gives these numbers: Democratic Army dead 458, wounded 217, National Army dead 149, wounded 548, missing 69. The latter numbers include the losses in the Mourgana area.

3 *Genikon Epiteleion Stratou, O EWu|vixoc Zxquxo? xaxct τον AvxiauttpoQiaxov Aycova (1946-1949) To Seuxepov sxogxou avxiaupiroQiaxou ayo'tvoc 1947 (Athens: ΑΙΕΥΟΥΝΟΕΟΚ loioQi'ag Ixpaxoti, 1980), pp. 311-40; Maxkos Vafeiadis, «H ejttx^e i6n^o l xr|5 Kovixoac» Thetis 1 (1994), pp. 155-162. This text is reproduced as an annex to this paper.*

4 Markos, *Konitsa,* p. 155.

It was clear that the Democratic Army could fight successfully as a partisan army but never as a tactical one. In pitch battles against a well trained tactical army with plenty of equipment and thus high firepower it had no chance. The only logical conclusion of the battle of Konitsa would have been to abandon tactical warfare and return to guerilla tactics. The final result would have been a compromise with the government side, a second Varkiza. Though, normally, a partisan army cannot win a war, it is, however, impossible that it can be defeated provided its commanders know their profession well - and Markos Vafeiadis knew his job. Thus the only way out of this dilemma would have been a compromise.

However, this simple logic was not understood by the orthodox leadership around Zachariadis. He was not ready to accept the simple logic that a rigid defence of a mountainous area with lightly armed guerilla units against a well equipped tactical army well trained in mountain warfare leads with deadly consequence into a catastrophe. It is well known that when Markos later in 1948 criti-cised Zachariadis suicidal tactics he was removed from the scene for reasons of health and a little later he was exiled to a little town in the Ural where he lived until the end of 1970s. Zachariadis on the other side had the "chance" to carry through his blinded experiment to the bitter end in summer 1949.

As we mentioned earlier, Zachariadis trusted that the communist who ruled countries in the north of Greece would recognise the Provisional Government. But as early as the 25th December the American Charge d'Affaires in Athens advised the State Department, to make it clear to the Soviet side, that the United States would not be prepared to accept a recognition of the Markos government by Soviet satellites. On 30 December the State Department published a statement in this sense. Especially the Yugoslavs got a stearn warning since they were believed to be ready for recognition. Early in January the American and British Ambassadors in Belgrade and Sofia warned the two governments that recognition would have serious consequences. Under American influence the United Nations reacted in the same sense. The United Nations Special Subcommittee on the Balkans appealed to all nations concerned to refrain from recognition, since recognition would violate international law. The Roumanians apparently played with the idea of recognition but Moscow ordered them back. In February 1948 Stalin told the Yugoslav Communist Kardelj that the Greek rebellion should be stopped as quickly as possible. It had no perspective[1]. It was pretty clear that Stalin was not ready to risk a direct confrontation with the Americans and by doing so possibly lose his sphere of interest.

After the end of the battle Queen Frideriki appeared in person in Konitsa to congratulate the courageous defenders. In Athens a wave of arrests swept over the town. Though a few communist cadres, among them Partsalidis managed to escape from their exile, tens of thousands were placed in the concentration camp on Makronissos. On 27 December KKE and EAM were outlawed. The Americans considered the attack on Konitsa as a kind of provocation and decided to strengthen the National Army even more. The final round of escalation towards full scale civil war began.

Thus the battle of Konitsa assumes the character of a watershed in the course of the Greek civil war. Until the failure of the Konitsa battle the Democratic Army had fought rather successfully. From then on it was doomed. Until the battle of Konitsa there had always been a chance for compromise and reconciliation. For the National Army the battle of Konitsa was the first true success against the partisans. The prize however was first paid by this little town - and then naturally by the whole of Greece, a prize which was much too high according to my book.

1 Vladimir Dedijer, *Tito Speaks* (London, 1953), p. 164.

THE GREEK COMMUNIST PARTY (KKE) 1944 - 1947: FROM THE MASS-PARTY TO CADRE-PARTY

During this period mentioned above the development in Greece is the antithesis of the developments in all other European countries. At the beginning of this period KKE[1] was a mass party with about 200,000 members and within the framework of the National Liberation Front (EAM) they achieved a unification of all leftist forces of which most other CPs could only dream. A the end of this period KKE is entangled in a civil war and is fighting without any hope against the Greek Right which was supported by the USA.

In the following study I will try and describe this development leading back to a cadre party and compare it with the developments on the international level.

The Development in 1941

In October 1918 after the first pan-Hellenic trade union congress the Socialist Workers Party Greece, SEKE was founded.[2] In 1919 it broke its ties with the Second International and it joined the Communist International in 1920. A little later it changed its name to KKE (Kommounistiko Komma Elladas). A few members of SEKE refused this step and joined the SEKE, the Socialist Party of Greece. But the SEKE degenerated soon into a sectarian tiny group which remained far under one percent in the elections. A socialist party of some importance came into being only much later when Andreas Papandreou founded the PASOK in 1974.

Though KKE was the only leftist party after the Socialists left it, it remained almost invisible. The bourgeois parties still controlled the political field. Central events of Greek history such as the expansion attempt in Anatolia which ended in the Asia Minor Catastrophe and the ensuing struggle for the form of the government saw KKE in a passive role.

Even after the foundation of the republic KKE remained a political quantité négligeable which gained scarcely more than one percent of the votes. The reason for this miserable result of the CP were manifold. 1) Though Greece was still an agrarian country KKE did not take the revolutionary potential of the peasants into account and confined themselves to the almost not existing industrial proletariat of the towns. 2) The acceptance of the anti-Greek Macedonian policy of Komintern[3] made it easy for bourgeois side easy to denounce KKE as anti-

1 A history of the Greek CP (KKE - Kommounistiko Komma Elladas) meeting scholarly claims does not yet exist. A short survey.is contained in: Heinz Richter: "Kommunistische Partei Griechenlands", in: *Lexikon des Sozialismus*, hg. von Thomas Meyer u.a. (Köln, 1986), pp. 361-363. The 1965 published history of the KKE - D.G. Kousoulas: *Revolution and Defeat, the Story of the Greek Communist Party*, (London, New York) - is of limited use only. The militant anticommunism of the author misleads to a nonscientific view. In a reduced manner this is true also for Basil P. Mathiopoulos: *Die Geschichte der sozialen Fracge und des Sozialismus in Griechenland, 1821-1961* (Hannover, 1961). The book by Antonio Solaro: *Storia del Partito Communista Greco,* (Milano, 1974) reflects the position of the Italian CP. The seven volumes work of Giorgis Katsoulis: *Istoria tou KKE*, (Athina, 1976-8) is a compilation of known texts with some connecting text without any analysis.
Whoever is interested in the history of KKE has only one chance i.e. working through a great number of memoirs and detailed studies. A guide is the bibliography published in 1984: Heinz Richter: *Greek Communism, Socialism and Trade Unionism, in:* Idem., *Greece and Cyprus since 1920. Bibliography of Contemporary History*, (Heidelberg, 1984), pp. 263-325. A comprehensive history of the Greek Left can be found in: Heinz A. Richter, *Geschichte der griechischen Linken* (Wiesbaden: Harrassowitz, 2017)

2 On the development of KKE from its foundation to the dictatorship of Metaxas: Angelos Elefantis: *I epangelia tis adynatis epanastasis, KKE kai astismos ston mesopolemo,* (Athens, 1977). The best description of the general political development of Greece in the inter-war period is still: Grigorios Dafnis: *I Ellas metaxy dyo polemon 1923-1940*, 2 vols, (Athens, 1955).

3 At the Vth. World Congress of KOMINTERN the leadership of KKE was forced to accept the policy of indepen-

national. 3) Additionally there were fights between the various factions within KKE that absorbed a great part of its strength. Decisive, however, was that the party itself was a foreign element in the Greek political system. The bourgeois parties did not know party programs, organizations or congresses not to mention decision-making process within the party as their Western European counterparts. They were clientelistic networks which ruled the country by a highly refined system of favouritism, nepotism and favours (rousfetia). Those in power distributed rousfetia; the Greek voter did not vote for the policy of a party but against the party which had not granted him the expected rousfeti.[1]

In view of this system it is not astonishing that KKE did not even manage to attract the about 1,5 million refugees from Asia Minor who made their living under miserable conditions in the outskirts of the Greek towns. The KKE did not have a chance to come to power, could therefore not distribute rousfetia and thus was not elected.

Consequently KKE could expect noteworthy influx only when the system failed, i.e. if parts of the voters of the traditional clientelistic parties left their parties because of desperation and frustration and voted KKE out of protest and KKE became the carriers of hope for improvement of their living situation (of course on the basis of rousfetia). If KKE achieved this breakthrough the old basic clientelistic networks of the old parties would quit their old parties and shift their loyalty to KKE, after all nothing is more attractive than the success.

Consequently KKE achieved its first successes when the effects of the world economic crisis were felt in Greece: in the elections in 1932 and 1933 KKE achieved almost five percent of the votes. At the same time the fights of the fractions within the party were ended by Komintern and KKE was transformed into a Leninist-Stalinist cadre party. Until 1936 the number of the membership increased to 14,000 of which 2,000 can be regarded as real Communists. Ideologically KKE followed the Komintern-line and since 1934 it propagated the popular front. At the end of 1934 it succeeded in concluding an alliance with some tiny leftist clientelistic parties and a few trade union groups which presented itself as popular front at the elections of September 1935 and gained almost 10 percent of the votes because the Liberals boycotted the elections. But already in the next elections in January 1936 the popular front dropped back to six percent. A permanent incursion into the clientele of the bourgeois parties was not achieved.

The popular front in Greece was totally different from the corresponding groups in Western Europe. There the popular fronts were real party alliances against Fascism but in Greece this was a theoretical concept only. Though KKE steered a course consistenr with Komintern and took over its ideological position and analyses and projected them on the Greek situation - despite they had nothing in common with Greek reality. A independent analysis of the specific Greek conditions was not made, KKE slavishly followed the orthodox recipes provided by Komintern. If these were not congruent with reality the latter was adjusted to it by dialectic acrobatics to orthodoxy and the postulate demanded by ideology was "discovered", a proceeding which would never have succeeded in normal times.

Times, however, were not normal in Greece, too. The elections in January 1936 produced an impasse between the two big bourgeois parties. Since one alone could not form a Government both tried to find an agreement with the CP in order to form a government. Therefore

---

dence of Macedonia and Thrace propagated by the Bulgarian CP which meant the integration of these provinces into Bulgaria in the long run.

1 On the Greek clientelistic system: Heinz Richter: "Zwischen Tradition und Moderne. Die politische Kultur Griechenlands", in: Peter Reichel (Hrsg.): *Politische Kultur in Westeuropa, Bürger und Staaten in der Europäischen Gemeinschaft*, (Bonn, 1984), pp. 145-66. Also the article in this study: Heinz A. Richter, *Another Type of European Democracy: The Political Culture of Greece"*

KKE won a more than proportional importance as the party which might help to form a Government. This in turn caused the Greek Right analog to the German example to conjure up a Communist menace. The result was the coup d'état by general Metaxas on 4 August 1936 who together with the king erected a dictatorship which was the exact copy of the Italian or German model.[1]

During the dictatorship KKE was persecuted massively. The imprisoned Communists were not killed as in Hitler Germany but Metaxas was the first who made physical torture an instrument of the power apparatus of the State and together with the system of the so-called repentance statements (*diloseis*) which were exacted by torture as well, they had found a highly efficient method to decimate the Communists. Until 1941 only 2.000 party members resisted this psychological and physical terror and of these 800 managed to escape when the Germans invaded Greece.

1941-1944 The Breakthrough as Mass Party

Paradoxically[2] it was the war with Italy and Germany and the ensuing occupation which led to the comeback of KKE. During the dictatorship the bourgeois parties had been prohibited and their clientelistic networks had been broken up and dissolved. The successful defence against the Italians at the Albanian front had changed the psychological climate. Events no longer had to be accepted passively. One was able to fight even against a stronger power. The people discovered their strength and saw how weak their leadership had been hitherto.

This will to resist was not broken by the occupation of the country by the Wehrmacht either. Already in summer 1941 the first resistance groups formed themselves spontaneously. The bourgeois politicians did not have part in this process. Some of them went abroad as government in exile, others collaborated, the biggest part, however, indulged in a honourable wait and see position and intended to outlive the war relatively comfortably in a kafeneion. The people discovered their power and saw how weak the old leadership really was..

The horrible famine during the first winter of occupation showed to the masses that their former leaders abandoned them. Help came from a new organization he EA, the National Solidarity which saved ten thousands from dying of hunger. In the course of the following years EA turned into a mass organization. The biggest organization became the EAM (National Liberation Front) which together with its half-dozen sub-organizations counted 1,5 million members of a population of 7,5 millions. until the end of the occupation . Its members stemmed from all classes and strata of society. The army was represented by 16 generals, 34 colonels and further 1,500 professional officers, the church by 6 bishops and a great number of priests. The president of the polytechneion, two members of the academy of science and 30 professors of the University of Athens were members of EAM as well.

Especially the youth reacted enthusiastically because in the youth organization EPON they had the chance to transfer their energies in deeds, something which had been impossible in the patriarchally structured prewar society with its gerontocracy.

The women became especially loyal adherents of EAM since it accepted them as equal members.The EAM became the vehicle of their emancipation. The old trade unions which had been split in over 1,000 tiny groups were united in one unitary organization of the wor-

---

1 On the dictatorship of Metaxas: Heinz Richter: *Griechenland zwischen Revolution und Konterrevolution 1936-1946,* (Frankfurt, 1973), pp. 54-81; Jon V. Kofas: *Authoritarianism in Greece, the Metaxas Regime*; (New York, 1983).

2 The narrative follows Richter (footnote. 5). On the British policy: Prokopis Papastratis: *British Policy towards Greece during the Second World War 1941-1944,* (Cambridge, 1984).

kers-EAM (EEAM) which succeeded in impeding German plans to gather forced labourers for the German industry.

At the same time EAM began to rebuild the state from the grassroots. The introduction of a local self-administration system on a democratic basis offered an opportunity to the rural areas and communities, which had been ruled from Athens, to determine their own fate. The creation of a people's jurisdiction which had been tied up by traditions of Ottoman times and the codification of the developing laws which replaced the rights imported in the 19th century from Western Europe enabled the peasants for the first time to understand what was going on in court because the new law was written in the people's language, *dimotiki*.

In March 1944 EAM created the Political Committee of National Liberation (PEEA) which soon took over the function of a Government in the areas controlled by the Resistance. In order to gain the necessary legitimation in early May about 1 million voters (women could also vote) elected in secret and equal ballots 250 delegates for a parliament, into the National Council. This council formed a representative cross section of the Greek society. During its constituent session in May the Council enacted a kind of constitution which contained the following typical features: people's sovereignty, local self-administration, people's courts, equal rights for men and women, responsibility of the Government and the introduction of dimotiki as common language.

Though all this was controlled by PEEA and EAM respectively but this radical renaissance of the Greek State ultimately rested on the devoted cooperation of its members and their readiness to make sacrifices as well we the broad masses of the people, i.e. on the grass-roots democracy.

Critics and enemies of this development denounced EAM and its suborganization as Communist front organizations; KKE allegedly built up EAM to erect - with its support - the dictatorship of the proletariat after the war .

Though it is right that KKE participated in the creation and leadership of EAM and its sub-organizations but EAM never became a creature of KKE. But with growing success and growing number of members the influence of KKE diminished. It is true that KKE had placed its cadres at the decisive points but these were not enough to keep the mass-organization in the path of orthodoxy. Additionally new ways of forming the political will came into being, the central elements of which were open discussion and free vote.

Simultaneously KKE experienced a massive influx of new members. Until the end of the occupation their membership rose to (a realistic) 200,000. The number 400,0000 found in KKE documents is certainly much exaggerated. The increase of members changed the character of the party: The monolithic cadre party of Stalinist character became a mass party in which pluralism of opinion and disputes between the different wings were normal.

The new members were not disciplined cadres or ideologically uniform Communists but human beings who wanted social change and a democratic post-war Greece but not a return to the clientelistic prewar system. In other words: KKE was developing towards a heterogenous, democratic mass party which attracted all progressive forces. The union of the Left, which was often the aim in the other European countries and could often achieved only by force had become a reality in Greece at the end of the war. A Greek road to Socialism appeared on the horizon.

From the programmatic declarations of EAM and EEK of those years the post-war aims can be derived: national independence and creation of a democratic social postwar republic.

December 1944: The British Intervention

These aims were accomplished to a vasr degree as far as they regarded for the internal policy of Greece. They could have been easily be achieved after the withdrawal of the occupying forces because at the eve of the German withdrawal the resistance controlled 90 percent of the Greek state territory.

But the demand for national independence required a reorganization of the relations with the traditional protective power Great Britain, whose protectorate Greece had been since the 1860ies with short interruptions.

The main guarantor of this relation was the Greek monarchy. The demand of EAM to abolish the monarchy and to establish a republic would remove the traditional control mechanism but it did not imply any means that Greece would take an anti-British course. The traditional dependency would be replaced by a relation based on partnership and equal rights. This was made clear during negotiations between EAM and the British authorities and in programmatic declarations. But for the British PM of the war years this was unacceptable and unimaginable.

For him was a pro-British Greece was an essential chain-link of the life line of the British Empire through the Mediterranean to India and to the oil of Mossul. He could imagine this if Greece was a protectorate under a British controlled monarch. Thus the Greek monarchy had to be restored at all cost.[1]

When in summer 1943 in the context of a conference with Greek resistance leaders it became clear that the majority of the Greeks were against the return of the monarchy he gave the order to prepare for a military intervention in Greece. The excuse was that after the German withdrawal a Communist take over loomed.

If the Greek CP had really planned to take over the power it could have done this without any trouble in October 1944 during the German withdrawal by occupying those 10 percent which were not already controlled by the resistance, by rejecting the return of the Greek Government in Exile and by not allowing the landing of British troops to go ashore in Greece. Instead they jubilantly welcomed the Bitish troops as liberators.

Only when it became apparent that the British wanted to disarm the Left unilaterally and disempower it in order to help the Right and the old politicians to regain their their former power positions, the Left adopted a tough attitude. Proposals for compromises failed because of Churchill's hard course. He believed he could steer a tough course since he had concluded the notorious percentage agreement with Stalin in early October which defined the spheres of interest in the Balkans. Mistakes of the EAM and KKE leadership facilitated Churchill's course of action. On 3 December the pent-up tensions exploded when Athens policemen fired at an unarmed demonstration of EAM - a police force which had served under the dictator Metaxas and afterwards the Italians and Germans. The EAM reacted by attacking the police. The civil war for Athens began.

British troops intervened in this inner-Greek conflict. The civil war turned into a fight between the British and the Athens reserve ELAS which lasted over 30 day and took place at the same time as Hitler's battle of the Bulge.

Despite heavy protests in England and the US Churchill annihilated the Athens resistance. From Moscow not one word of critique was heard. Staling stuck to the percentage agreement. Greece was the first case of a liberated country after WWII where the victorious power enforced a regime which was suitable for the victor. It provided a model case for Western and Eastern Europe.

In mid-January the British troops had defeated the Athens reserve ELAS but EAM still controlled the rest of Greece. If EAM had really fought for power it could have continued the fighting outside Athens by turning to the form of a partisan war. But instead they looked for

---

1 On the events in December: Richter (footnote. 6); John 0. Iatrides: *Revolt in Athens. The Greek Communist Second Round 1944-1945*, (Princeton, 1972).

a compromise which would enable the integration into postwar system and therefore it concluded the Peace Treaty of Varkiza on I February 1945 .

This peace treaty was a fair compromise. If its conditions had been fulfilled according to the text and its spirit a peaceful and democratic postwar development would still have been possible.

1945-1946: From the Mass Party to the Cadre Party

The beaten Left fulfilled its obligations punctually, disarmed itself and demobilized its fighting units. The Greek Right and the Government violated their obligations systematically and rode roughshod over the freedom rights guaranteed by the treaty.[1] Between February 1945 and March 1946 Greece underwent a counterrevolution of unimaginable degree. The balance of power which had existed at the time of the liberation was reversed. Greece became the only country in Europe where the Right and the collaborators were in power and ten thousands the former members of the resistance were in prison by or were on the run. Even the moderate bourgeois politicians gave way to the Right because of a pathological fear of the Communists and did not stop the White terror.

The Right itself had drawn specific conclusions during the occupation. In their eyes only the reconstruction of the old clientelistic networks and the reconstruction of the state apparatus was not enough to get the masses of the Left under their absolute control. Therefore they began to infiltrate the armed forces and the security apparatus. Parallel it built a power apparatus, the so-called parakratos, which existed in parallel to the state, competed with it but was also closely linked to it. While the power apparatus of the state acted in relative legality the parakratos outside of any legality. The parakratos became an underground terror and murder apparatus the aiming of which was to destroy the clientele of the Left by terror.

In the course of the year 1945 this parakratos permeated the whole country and became the main carriers of the White Terror. This counterrevolution took place under the eyes of the British occupation power which had penetrated the whole state with its various advisory missions. It would have been easy for them to stop this development and as participants of the peace negotiations of Varkiza they would have morally been obliged to do so. The necessary instruments and the competences were there. Ambassador Leeper was de facto High Commissioner, who administered the British protectorate in a sovereign manner - both terms stem from documents of the Foreign Office of the time.[2] Even when in summer 1945 Labour won the elections British policy towards Greece did not change. Labour Foreign Secretary Bevin followed a Tory foreign policy.

The defeat in December 1944 and the Peace Treaty of Varkiza had thrown EAM and KKE into a deep crisis.[3] Moderate and radicals criticized the leadership. Some leading Socialists left EAM and with them their clientele went away. On the radical side there was talk of treason and an attack on the the party leadership was contemplated. Obviously disintegration of the mass-movement of EAM threatened.

The reaction of the KKE leadership to these disruptive tendencies was characteristic: it tried to discipline its members by prohibiting to discuss the situation within the party about the situation. This once more showed that the KKE leadership itself had never understood the

1 The description of the counterrevolution and the development of KKE between February 1945 and summer 1946 is based on Heinz Richter: *British Intervention in Greece, from Varkiza to Civil War, February 1945 to August 1946* (London, 1986).

2 Churchill to Sir Orme Sargent 22. April 1945. Prime Minister's Personal Minute Serial No. M 382/5 in: PRO, FO 371 R 7423/4/19.

3 Richter (footnote. 8), pp. 235-87, 457-95.

real character of the mass movement as a spontaneous democratic grass roots movement. Instead of making the forthcoming difficulties clear to the basis by elucidation and discussion and prepare the members psychologically for the forthcoming problems the KKE leadership acted bureaucratically and threatened to purge the "unreliable" elements. When criticism did not end the 11th plenum made a halfhearted self-criticism and promised a general debate on the forthcoming 7th Party Congress. But before this Congress could be convened the former secretary general of KKE, Nikos Zachariadis, returned from the Dachau concentration camp to Athens.

Zachariadis belonged to the few cadres who had been trained in the Soviet Union. In 1931 during the Komintern intervention he had been made party leader. During the years until the prohibition of the KKE he had become the 'Stalin' of the party. In view of the early personality cult it is not astonishing that he was welcomed now as a messias. Willingly the party transferred the lead of the party to him in the hope he would overcome the crisis and correct the mistakes of the past.

Instead of informing himself about the development during the last years Zachariadis went to work and tried to promote the so-called democratic centralism. The first victim became the prominent partisan leader Aris Velouchiotis. During the 12th Plenum in June 1945 Zachariadis stated that the reasons of the wrong development was the socially wrong composition of the party. Only 18 percent of the party members were workers. In order to correct this the party organizations in the villages had to be dissolved and the peasant party members transferred to the Agrarian Party AKE.

This was done during the following months. Until April 1946 KKE lost over 100,000 members. Though a part of this loss of members was caused by the effect of the Right terror but it was decisive that AKE - a Communist Front Organization - was organisationally not capable to integrate these new members. The peasants who had formed more than 60 percent of the members of EAM and KKE were left to their fate - and - the persecutions by the parakratos. KKE became a cadre party. The 7th Party Congress appreciated this measure and in order to discipline the party members created the Party Control Commission. KKE had successfully been re-Stalinized.

During the following months Zachariadis left the party line which had been followed until then. He stated that the process, prescribed by the ideology, of transforming society into a bourgeois-democratic one had been achieved during the occupation and now the task was to introduce popular democracy. He "discovered" that Greece was approaching the revolution which of course would take place in the towns and cities..

This tremendous misjudgement of the real situation explains his ambivalent policy during the following months. On the one side he allowed that the hard pressed rural cadres to defend themselves against the repression of the Right and the Parakratos but on the other side he prohibited the formation of a new partisan movement. The revolution would take place in the towns. Though the Soviets recommended participation in the elections in March 1946 he boycotted the elections arguing that the climate of terror did not allow free elections.

Though the bourgeois parties boycotted them with exactly the same arguments but there was one decisive difference. Even after an election victory of the Right the bourgeois parties would continue to exist but KKE and the whole Left would be annihilated. If KKE and the Left had participated in the elections they would - according to British estimates - have gained 25-35 percent of the votes and 100-120 mandates of the 300. They would have become a opposition party for many years but by its presence in parliament its members would survived the postwar years. By the election boycott KKE exposed itself to a annihilation campaign of the legitimate victorious right Government. The decision to boycott the elections was the greatest and most momentous mistake which the KKE leadership ever made.

Immediately after the elections an escalation of terror began which led to the civil war. Contrary to the expectations of Zachariadis, this war was fought as a partisan war in the mountains of Greece. The Right used this opportunity to decimate all left forces including the left liberals. At the end of the civil war the Right totally controlled the Greek state. KKE's mistakes had blocked for many years all reform for many years as well as any modernisation of the Greek state and thus even tiny moves in direction of a democratic left policy were compromised. Whoever questioned the existing system was denounced a Communist.

The Greek state needed the shock of the military dictatorship in 1967 and its fall in 1974 that a new socialist movement - the PASOK - could come into being.

ANOTHER TYPE OF EUROPEAN DEMOCRACY: THE POLITICAL CULTURE OF GREECE[1]

In 1943 the head of the British Military Mission to the Greek partisans, Brigadier C. E. Myers, groaned in exasperation about Greek politics: *"The Greeks are Asiatic. One cannot judge them by European standards."*[2] Despite the fact that this statement is factually wrong, it shows clearly that the English Brigadier recognized that there was a difference between the political cultures of Greece and those of Western Europe. Having no background knowledge he helplessly characterized it as Asiatic. Recently a similar helplessness was noticeable among EU-leaders when the Greek financial crisis broke out late in spring 2010. The recommendations and suggestions voiced in Berlin and Paris demonstrated clearly that none of them had the slightest idea how the Greek political system functions. This brings us to the question of the real difference between the Greek and "European" political culture.

What is a European?

In 1930 the famous Spanish cultural philosopher Ortega y Gasset stated that at a first glance the western Europeans differ widely but that taking a closer look at their theories, value system, and political aims one easily discovered that most of these stemmed from the common European heritage and that only a few are specific of an individual nation. The basis of Europeaness is the unique blend of Greek-Roman philosophy, Jewish-Christian religions, and - as is currently being rediscovered - Arab/Islamic influence. These elements have shaped the ethical, religious, legal and cultural ideas of the Europeans. During the Renaissance these elements became more and more influential and brought about the Reformation. The confessionalization of politics triggered a counter-movement focussing on the individualisation of human life. New ethical values brought about by Calvinism led to the emergence of a new elite, the bourgeoisie. The mediaeval feudal order with its decentralised power structures could not adapt itself to the need for larger economic units. Thus a revolution from above took place and creating the monarchical absolutism. Politics became more rational and the governmental administration more efficient. The Enlightenment and French Revolution proclaimed the universal human rights. Rousseau's concept of the a national state based upon the sovereignty of the people, the idea of the freedom of the individual and the right of the individual to participate in the exercise of power became an integral part of European political thinking. At about the same time political ideas such as liberalism, democracy, socialism, conservatism and nationalism came into being which ideologized politics. The concept of left-right antagonism became an accepted pattern of European politics, and political pluralism became a central feature of European political culture.[3] The idea of multiculturalism will be another feature despite the fact that it was recently declared dead by the German Chancellor.

The process which led to this result began at the end of the 15th century and 300 years were needed to develop the main components. But this process was confined to western and central Europe alone. Emigrants took it with them to America but in Eastern Europe outside

---

1 This article was written for the University of Crete on the occasion of my being awarded a honorary doctoral degree.. It was uploaded to this internet address: http://www.soc.uoc.gr/political/wp-content/uploads/2012/01/-2014-Political-Culture-of-Greece.pdf. After the honorary title was conferred to me inappropriate and insulting accusations were made and I was brought to a Cretan court. With the help of my two brilliant Athenian lawyers I won the trial. Nevertheless the University of Crete blocked the article. Therefore it is republished here.

2 Myers in a "Report on Experience" in 1943. Copy in my archives.

3 Peter Reichel (ed.), *Politische Kultur in Westeuropa. Bürger und Staaten in der Europäischen Gemeinschaft*, (Frankfurt: Campus, 1984), p. 12f.

the Hapsburg Empire it did not take deep roots as can still be seen today. Southeastern Europe remaining outside the Austrian-Hungarian monarchy was excluded from these developments.

Different developments in Greece

In the Balkans outside the Hapsburg monarchy the European Roman Catholic Middle Ages had not taken place. Huge parts of the Balkans had belonged to the Byzantine empire and thus had never encountered the vitriolic quarrel between Pope and Emperor known as the Investiture Conflict. But just as the West was beginning its comeback the Ottomans conquered the Byzantine Empire; in 1453 Constantinople fell. The Ottoman occupation lasted 400 years in large areas of Greece and other parts of the Balkans until the end of the Balkan Wars in the early 20th century. As Ottoman provinces Greece and the other Balkan countries did not experience the subsequent periods of European history: Renaissance, Reformation, Counter-Reformation, Absolutism, Rationalism, Enlightenment and Bourgeois Revolution. Time almost stood still for almost 400 years .

The 300 to 400 years of Ottoman occupation led to deep changes. One of the first measures of the conqueror was the eradication of the respective ruling oligarchy i. e. the aristocracy in order to deprive the subjected peoples of their leadership thus precluding potential insurrections. The surviving local notables slowly obtained a double function. They became the leaders and guardians of the local population and at the same time the objects of Ottoman repression if something went wrong in the sphere of their responsibility. They protected the locals from the Ottoman overlords thus gaining prestige and power in their eyes. As a quid pro quo for their intercession they expected loyalty from their local wards. In the course of time these notables became rich because their position and wealth acquired through their positions enabled them to obtain ever more powerful positions: they became usurers. Although this was less honest than interceding selflessly on behalf of their weaker co-villagers but money-lending was a more solid basis for the growing dependency of the peasant on the patron. This patron-client structure, called the muchtar system, existed all over the Ottoman Empire and is the basis of today's clientelism.[1]

Additionally the influence of the Christian Orthodox church increased during this period of Greek history, because it contributed to the preservation of the Greek identity. On the other hand the church collaborated with the Ottomans collecting taxes for the Porte. The European principle of separation of Church and State has never been fully realised in Greece. The Greek church has remained attached to state power.

Beginning of clientelism

When in 1821 the Greek struggle for independence began these clientelistic structures were the only existing nuclei of crystallization for the political organisation of the struggle, during which these structures grew horizontally and vertically. Refined clientelistic networks came into being. When the struggle was over clientelism became a system of government: When King Otto came to Greece there was no other governmental structure. He could not run the country with the help of a handful of Bavarian civil servants, but had to use the existing clientelistic networks for ruling the country. By taking over civil administrative responsibilities the patrons gained access to the money of the state.

Now two developments took place: first, clientelism assumed a new character. Until then the relationship between client and patron had been more or less on a voluntary basis with a mutual advantage. Now it became a means of coercion to integrate the individual into society.

---

1 Keith Legg, *Politics in Modern Greece* (Stanford: UP, 1969), p. 34.

Secondly, the patrons began to meddle in politics and quickly learned that the clientelistic system could be used for political purposes. The patrons used their political position and power to accord favours (*rousfetia*) to their clients by stealing money which belonged to the state. In return they expected their clients to vote for them in the elections.

At first the new Greek state was a European protectorate and the Greek King was a kind of viceroy by grace of the big European powers of the time. Greece was a European client state. The European powers exerted their influence by controlling their adherents organized into "parties" which were in reality clientelistic networks. There were three "parties", the Russian, English and French. In 1862, however, Britain installed a new dynasty and from then on the Greek kings were British viceroys and Greece a British client state or protectorate. From now on Greek Kings and politicians acted on the maxim of *"τι θέλει ο ξένος παράγοντας"* (what does the foreign factor wish). If a king tried to get rid of this clientelistic relationship as King Constantine I did during WWI, Britain intervened and undermined his power. During the difficult years right after WWII, Britain still considered Greece a "protectorate" und the British ambassador acted as a "High Commissioner".[1] Until 1946 Britain was the protector state of Greece. In 1947 a kind of *translatio imperii* from Great Britain to the US took place within the framework of the Truman doctrine.[2] Greece remained an American client state until 1974. The Turkish invasion of Cyprus triggered by a putsch by the Greek military junta caused the end of this clientelistic relationship. For the first time in modern times Greece became a really independent state. Cyprus paid the price by being divided ever since.

When Britain became the sole protector the "parties" changed their character. They became political parties and there now existed now a conservative and a more liberal clientelistic network in structured like pyramids. Despite being labelled as liberal and conservative they did not differ much. Both ruled on the basis of a highly refined system of favouritism, nepotism and *rousfetia*. The state became the object of exploitation by the chiefs of the respective clientelistic pyramid. Trading of posts, patronage, a spoils system and a total corruption of the state administration, the judicial system and the military were the rule. The buying of votes and the falsifying of election results were a normal feature of political life. Towards the end of the 19th century a Greek deputy had called this system political procuration.[3]

Clientelistic parties

The political parties which emerged had nothing in common with their European counterparts except the names. Party programmes, party organization, or party congresses were unknown let alone the forming of a political will by discussion inside a party. The party was the clientele of the party leader and he alone decided about the party's course. Conflicts within a party led to the breaking off of sub-networks. Party loyalty become functional to the success of the party leader, i. e. loyalty depended on the *rousfetia* which the party leader was able to convey to his clients. Change of power came about, when sub-networks shifted their loyalty to another party leader. In parliamentary elections the Greek voter did not vote *for* a party but *against* that party which had not done him the expected favour of *rousfeti* during the previous legislative period.

---

1 The term "protectorate" stems from PRO F.O. 371/48.256/R 4385/4/19 and the High commissioner from PRO F.O. 371/48.257/R 3559/4/19.

2 Dan Diner, *Das Jahrhundert verstehen. Eine universalhistorische Deutung* (München: Luchterhand, 1999), p. 278.

3 Hariton Korisis, *Die politischen Parteien Griechenlands. Ein neuer Staat auf dem Weg zur Demokratie 1821-1910* (Hersbruck: Pfeifer, 1966), p. 105.

Clientelism survived even the great crises of the 20th century. It proved to be so deeply rooted that it was able to force the two central ideologies of the century to adapt itself to it. In the Balkans Fascism became clientelistic fascism, i.e. the ideological features were taken over but modified. Instead of creating fascist mass parties which would have been alien to the system the people as a whole were declared the clientele of the fascist leader.[1] Only if one recognizes this modification of the fascist mass movements one can understands that most of the dictatorial regimes of the 1930s in the Balkans were indeed fascist regimes, indeed. After the end of WWII Greece's northern neighbours of Greece encountered a similar modifying process in relation to Communism. Ceaucescus system, for example, can be described as clientelistic communism.

In the 20th century Greece had three chances to overcome its clientelistic system. The first chance came after the Asia Minor catastrophe when the defeat and the influx of 1,5 million Greek refugees rocked the system to its foundations. But the traditional clientelistic network of Venizelos was strong enough to absorb the shock and survive and become even stronger. The second chance came at the end of the occupation in WWII. During the war years a new political system emerged which was based on forces which had never been part of the ruling clientelistic networks of the Venizelists and Anti-Venizelists. It was the leftist EAM-resistance movement created by the communist party (KKE), several socialist parties (SKE/ELD) and independent leftists and liberals. This movement rebuilt the Greek state from the grassroots and a democratic postwar republic with Europeanized structures was emerging on the horizon.

This new state would have terminated the clientelistic relationship with Britain: the King would not have been allowed to return and Greece would have become an equal partner of Britain. But for Churchill who wanted to restore the monarchy at all costs, this was unconceivable and unacceptable. He denounced the resistance movement as communist struggling for the imposition of a dictatorship of the proletariat. The armed British intervention in December 1944 ruined this chance of a renaissance of the Greek state. The state which emerged after the 1946-49 civil war had the old clientelistic structures. There was a ruling network called ERE, under Karamanlis and an opposition network based on George Papandreou's Centre Union. The short period of rule of Papandreou did not change anything and the dictatorship from 1967 to 1974 was a repetition of clientelistic fascism.

A spoiled chance in 1974

During the dictatorship discussion began among Greeks in European exile about the overcoming of the old system by the creation of parties of the European type (ευρωπαϊκόυ τύπου), i.e. parties with a programme, congress, internal democracy, and leadership elections. There was consensus that the Greek system had to overcome clientelism. A new left-programme party was to be created after the downfall of the junta. However, when the junta fell in 1974. Karamanlis returned and - hesitatingly - revived the old clientelistic party of the right, calling it *Nea Dimokratia*. When Andreas Papandreou returned he deliberately left aside all the plans for the creation of a programme party despite the fact that he had participated in the discussion about the renaissance of the Greek political system. He founded a new left party, PASOK. This party was from the beginning the clientelistic network, with A. Papandreou as its patron. Opposing groups such as the resistance group *Δημοκρατική άμυνα* (democratic defence) which in the beginning tried to stop the development towards a clientele party where purged.

1 Heinz A. Richter, *Griechenland im 20. Jahrhundert*, I, (Köln: Romiosini, 1990), p. 204.

During the rule of Konstantinos Karamanlis that lasted until 1981, clientelism worked in the traditional way. The conservatives did not exaggerate the clientelistic *rousfeti* system. Karamanlis greatest achievement was Greece's entry into the EU. But when PASOK came to power in 1981 A. Papandreou considered the EU funds as an unlimited source for the distribution of *rousfetia*. EU money was fed into the clientelistic system in an unprecedented way. When Mitsotakis and his Nea Dimokratia took over in 1990, not much changed, and on Papandreou's return to power in 1993, the distribution of *rousfetia* on the basis of EU money reached a climax. When in 1996 A. Papandreou had to resign over financial scandals Kostas Simitis, a German trained lawyer, took over.

Until 2004, Simitis made great efforts to reduce clientelism, but discovered that the clientelistic system was too strong for him. Despite the fact that he was prime minister and head of PASOK he could not control the clientelistic network. His misfortune showed clearly that the clientelistic system had again changed its character. It was no longer a monolithic pyramid under the control of the patron on top but a network with influential sub-patrons who could distribute *rousfetia* on their own because they themselves had direct access to necessary funds of the Greek state or of the EU. When the conservatives returned to power in 2004 this tendency became even stronger. The new generation of their leaders considered it legitimate to enrich themselves and their followers in an even more unprecedented way. The end of the road is known - the Greek bankruptcy.

The present crisis

The Greek state is in such a fundamental crisis that there is again a chance to overcome its basic evil - clientelism. In order to achieve this uncontrolled access to financial resources must be denied to all those who are not legally entitled. At the same time the procurement and spending of money must be closely controlled by suitable persons. If no further money for *rousfetia* is available clientelism will be weakened. A purge of the inflated civil service of all those superfluous civil servants who were employed on the basis of *rousfetia* will be a further blow to clientelism. Ending of the sport of tax evasion is another means. The rich must be taxed adequately. The measures to destroy clientelism and install a democratic system in accordance with western European standards are rather clear. The political system of Cyprus might provide a model.

But in order to achieve this Greece will need external help. The financial help is only one aspect of the necessary measures. If the clientelistic system is not eradicated European financial help will be in vain, because the moment the state is stabilized the old system will reemerge and continue its old games. European help must not confine itself to financial support. Europe must help to reform Greece's political system. But in this context a thorough understanding of Greek clientelism is necessary.

Most Europeans do not understand the phenomenon of clientelism and react in a bewildered way. Apart from the Austrians who show some understanding due to their past as a Balkan power the Europeans react in a negative way. They project European political ideas and ethical principles on Greece and the other Balkan countries, without understanding that these ideas and principles are alien to the society and the political culture of Greece. Clientelism is an Ottoman heritage. In the eyes of the Europeans, the outward signs of clientelism such as favouritism or *rousfetia* are registered through moral glasses and identified as corruption. Thus one can confine oneself to bristling at this, and swinging the moral hammer demanding that the Greeks overcome their corruption and clean their house. This simplistic approach is absolutely counter-productive. Greece does not need moral sermons but efficient help from competent experts, in her effort to reform her political system.

Hoping that such competent experts will be found it should be understood that the Greek problem is only the first of its kind which has surfaced so far. All Balkan states suffer from this Ottoman heritage albeit at various degrees. Berlin, Paris and Brussels should make an effort to understand the real problem - clientelism. - Unfortunately this has not happened. Clientelism survived even this severe crisis. The only state which got rid of this Ottoman heritage is Cyprus but it needed 70 years of British reeducation.

GREECE IN CRISIS 1965-1967

The Athanasiadis-Novas Government

The most decisive political event in Greece in 1965 was the overthrow of Prime Minister Georgios Papandreou by the royal coup d'etat when King Constantine II pushed Papandreou out of office on 15 July 1965; an event which became known as *Ta Iouliana*. After this the country plunged into an almost permanent governmental crisis which paved the way towards the coup on 21 April 1967.[1]

A few minutes after the King had overthrown Prime Minister Papandreou he appointed Georgios Athanasiadis-Novas Prime Minister, the hitherto president of the parliament, who belonged to the same party (EK). The new PM was 72 years old and came from Nafpaktos, a small seaport town in the gulf of Corinth. He was a typical career politician. In 1926 he ran for a seat in the parliament of Venizelos' Liberals for the first time and was elected as deputy of his home constituency (*Aitokarkania*). Later he joined the progressive party of G. Kafandaris and represented it in parliament until 1936. In 1945 he became Minister of the Interior in the Plastiras government. Since the Liberals boycotted the election of 1946 he returned to parliament as late as 1950. Between 1950 and 1952 he held various ministerial posts in the cabinets of the Liberals. In 1961 he joined the Centre Union (*Enosis Kentrou* - EK) of G. Papandreou. In 1964 he was elected president of the parliament. At the same time he made a literary career under the pseudonym of Georgios Athanas. He published ten volumes with poetry and prose and in 1955 he became a member of the Academy of Athens.[2]

Shortly after the appointment of the new Prime Minister, at 8 p.m. on 15 July the King called the former admiral and de facto deputy of the EK Georgios Toumbas to the Palace. He appointed him the soldier "loyal to the Crown" Minister of the Interior and Security. Thus the King himself exercised control of the security forces because Toumbas would obey him completely. After Toumbas Foreign Minister Stavros Kostopoulos appeared and raised some objections but obeyed the King and additionally took over the Ministry of Defence. At 8.25 p.m. the Archbishop of Athens, Chrysanthos, inaugurated the three politicians. This act completed the change of power.[3] In order to assess this act correctly it is necessary to take a close look at the Greek party system at that time.

Greek parties were and still are clientelistic networks which are kept together by *rousfetia* (favours). Democratic structures inside these parties are almost unknown and played no role because the forming of the political will runs from top to bottom. Party programs as they exist in eastern European parties are unknown. A party, which was in power could distribute *rousfetia* through its hierarchical structure, and thus was kept together. The change of power in 1963 had taken place because all small opposing clientelistic networks from the moderate leftists and the conservative liberals had united under the lead of G. Papandreou who, however, did not succeed in binding the chiefs of these sub-networks to himself so that they could no longer be influenced from outside. The usual method to obtain the loyalty of a sub-leader was to offer him a ministerial position which enabled him to offer *rousfetia* to his followers and become rich himself. The loss of a position meant that the loyalty of this chief and his clientelistic network towards the highest chief became dubious and a change was threatening. Exactly this situation had come about in 1965.The only exception of this system was the Greek Communist Party (KKE) and its successor party EDA (*Eniea Dimokratiki Aristera* - United Democratic Left) because they could not distribute *rousfetia*.

---

1 Heinz A. Richter, "Der Weg zum Putsch des 21. April 1967" *Thetis* 13/14 (2007), pp. 254-259.

2 *Keesing's Contemporary Archives*, p. 20.867; *Ellinikon Who's Who 1962*, p. 18.

3 Spyros Linardatos, *Apo ton emfylio sti chounta,* V (Athen: Papazisis, 1986), p. 234.

When Toumbas had resigned as Minister of the Interior allegedly for "national reasons" in reality it had been the acceptance of the Leftist Ilias Tsirimokos into the cabinet. Papandreou appointed Tsirimokos Minister of the Interior and made Ioannis Glavanos Minister of Trade. However, he refrained from integrating Savvas Papapolitis, who was the leader of a group of 16 deputies, into the hierarchy, whereupon the latter distanced himself a bit b forming an independent group within the EK. In other words: When the EK government was formed the centrifugal forces began to become stronger and by the integration of Tsirimokos into the cabinet the Right could conjure up a Communist danger because Tsirimokos had been a member of the left resistance organization EAM during the occupation.

A little later the newspaper *Eleftheria,* which belonged to Panos Kokkas and was close to right wing of the EK around Konstantinos Mitsotakis, began to attack Archbishop Makarios of Cyprus and Andreas Papandreou the son of the PM. The reasons for these attacks were relatively clear. On the one hand Papandreou's son was to be weakened because since his visit of Cyprus in autumn 1964 he had won the sovereignty of interpretation of the Cyprus question within the EK and had influenced his father accordingly. On the other hand this manoeuvre to position himself as successor of the 77 years old G. Papandreou. Here the forthcoming fights between the wings in the EK, between the "Leftists" around Andreas Papandreou and the "rightists" around Mitsotakis, became visible. Since Foreign Minister Kostopoulos had good relations with Kokkas it may be assumed that he took part in the game. Whether other "Rightists" grandees of the EK such as the Minister of Defence Garoufalias were in the game is unknown but cannot be excluded as his later behaviour proved.[1] But let us return to the events of 15 July 1965.

Shortly before 9 p.m. the new PM announced his appointment and proceeded to his political bureau were he was expected by Minister of Economics Konstantinos Mitsotakis, the deputy Minister of Coordination Georgios Balkatselos, the Minister of Transport Stylianos Alamanis and the Minister of State in the office of the PM Dimitrios Papaspyrou. Next morning on 16 July it was announced that Mitsotakis would take over the Ministry of Coordination, Bakatselos the Ministry of Labour and Industry, and Alamanis the Ministry of Economics. Nine other ministries would be given to apostates (renegades) of whom none had ever served as minister. On 20 July the ex-diplomat and former Minister of Trade Georgios Melas was appointed Foreign Minister and four other backbenchers also. Obviously all renegades were rewarded by ministerial posts.

Already during the night of 16 July on order of the King officers under the command of the royalist general Kyriakos Papageorgopoulos took over control of KYP (*Kentriki Ypiresia Pliroforion* - Central Information Agency). Their first action was to make material disappear which incriminated the King. During the following days KYP was purged rom all supporters of Papandreou.[2]

In the evening of 15 July the leading cadres of the EK assembled in Papandreou's house in the Athenian suburb Kastri. Papandreou formulated a press declaration which was signed by all present including Stefanos Stefanopoulos.[3] In the morning of 16 July Papandreou spoke to the press and referred to the appointment of the new Government of Athanastiadis-Novas as a coup d'état by the King and all those who had formed it as traitors of the EK. Then he appealed to the Greek people to demonstrate for democracy: *"I promise you that we will return to power. Only we represent the will of the sovereign people. Today an new incessant*

1 *Ibidem*, V, p. 129f.

2 *Ibidem*, p. 248f; C. M. Woodhouse, *The Rise and the Fall of the Greek Colonels* (New York: Franklin Watts, 1985), p. 11.

3 Andreas Papandreou, *Democracy at Gunpoint: the Greek Front* (New York: Doubleday, 1970), p. 176.

fight (anendotos agonas) for democracy begins."[1] Already the first (unauthorized) demonstrations began in Athens. On Syntagma Square and the streets leading to it clashes with the police occurred. The demonstrators shouted "democracy", "Papandreou", "down with the apostates" and the number of the constitutional article (114 - *ena ena tessera*) which explicitly transferred the protection of the constitutional order to the people.[2] Deputies of the EK and of the EDA participated. The coupists were not impressed and announced that Mitsotakis and his group were inaugurated as ministers. Opposition leader Panagiotis Kanellopoulos declared himself ready to support the new government together with the 99 members of the ERE (Ethniki Rizospastiki Enosis - National Radical Union) fraction.[3]

On 17 July there were protest demonstrations all over Greece. As Papandreou was afraid that the government would prohibit a mass rally the party members were informed that on 19 July Papandreou would drive from his home in Kastri to the headquarter of EK. When Papandreou drove down town on that date allegedly 180,000 people lined the streets waving at him enthusiastically. On 21 July thousands of students and pupils demonstrated in Athens and Thessalonika. When the security forces used force against them more than 100 were injured and 25 years old student Sotiris Petroulas was killed. His funeral on 23 July turned into yet another demonstration against the government. At a press conference shortly thereafter Papandreou demanded the immediate resignation of the government, the existence of which was a pure provocation. There were only two ways out of this crisis. After the fall of the government the King was obliged to ask him, Papandreou, as the leader of the biggest fraction in parliament to form a new government or call for elections. *"There is no unbridgeable personal feud between the King and myself. [...] Our difference lies in the proper functioning of our constitutional regime. The King refused to let me take over the Defence Ministry. He had the right to advise but not to decide. [...] In a crowned democracy the King reigns and the people govern through the Government. [...] We continue to believe that the lawful regime in this country is crowned democracy. We are not asking for a change. What we are questioning is the democratic functioning of the regime."*[4]The leftist trade union federation GSEE (*Geniko Synospondia Ergaton Elladas*) called for a general strike on 27 July in Athens and Piraeus but not many people participated. On 29 July the fraction of the EK met. 143 of the 171 deputies signed a protocol which condemned the government Athanasiadis-Novas and in which they declared their readiness to vote against the government if it asked for a vote of confidence.[5]

On 28 July the newspaper *Eleftheria* which was close to Mitsotakis began an indirect attack on Andreas Papandreou by publishing a letter by Margaret Papandreou, the American wife of Andreas, which she had written on 8 and 15 July to some good friends and acquaintances in the US. In this letter which was addressed, among others to Mrs. Lady Bird Johnson, Foreign Secretary Dean Rusk and Vice-President Hubert Humphrey, Margaret vented her anger about the political intrigues of the enemies of her father-in-law and at the same time she informed the addressees about the political situation in Greece. One of the recipients passed the content on to the well known American columnist, Drew Pearson, who took over a paragraph in his column which appeared regularly in well over 100 American newspapers. Obviously one of the letters had been opened and copied by KYP agents because now the whole text was published in *Eleftheria*:

---

1 Linardatos, *op. cit.*, V, p. 238; *Archiv der Gegenwart* (25 September 1965), p. 12.085.
2 Peter Cornelius Mayer-Tasch, *Die Verfassungen Europas* (Stuttgart: Kröner, 1966), p. 160: *"Die Einhaltung dieser Verfassung wird dem Patriotismus der Griechen anvertraut."*
3 Linardatos, *op. cit.*, V, p. 242.
4 *Keesing's Contemporary Archives*, p. 20.868.
5 *Ibidem*, p. 21.006.

"The essence of my letter was this: that the King and the rightist forces in the country were working together to oust unconstitutionally my father-in law, the Prime Minister, and to attack and discredit my husband, Andreas, by linking him to a supposed conspiratorial group called ASPIDA. I pointed out the strong anticommunist stance of my father-in-law, and that he was, by the will of the Greek people, leading them toward real democracy, and that if the scare tactics of 'communist infiltration' used by the Right succeed, the country would be plunged into turmoil, perhaps even civil war, which could result in a military take-over of the government."[1]

Foreign Minister Melas used the opportunity to attack Margaret Papandreou in parliament massively. This provoked deputies who were true followers of Papandreou and there were nefarious scenes when they threw paper balls and newspapers at the minister. At the subsequent press conference Melas showed himself totally disappointed because Margaret Papandreou had told Mrs. Johnson that there were two camps in the American embassy: *"In one were the CIA and the military attaches, who favoured the king and his armed forces. In the other were Henry Labouisse, ambassador [...] and the minister counsellor, Norbert Anschuetz, who favoured her father-in-law's majority. [...] If America has no involvement, and I hope she hasn't then she must indicate she stands on the side of democracy."*[2] In order to carry the case to the extreme the government made sure that Margaret Papandreou was examined by the state attorney. During the hearing officers were present. Margaret Papandreou understood that this was the beginning of the power take over by the military.[3]

On 30 July 1965 the new PM intended to deliver a declaration of the government in parliament and ask for a vote of confidence. The building of the parliament was surrounded by armoured police vehicles and all entrances were guarded by a huge police force. But in the plenum only the presidency of the parliament, the members of the government and a few deputies were present. The EK boycotted the session so did the EDA. When the opposition leader of the Panagiotis Kanellopoulos heard of this he told the deputies of the ERE to stay away from the session. The president of the House, Immanouil Baklatzis, conceded that the necessary quorum for a vote of confidence was not present and the government was in a crisis. In the streets leading to Parliament thousands of demonstrators were demanding the resignation of the Government. The PM refused to accept this as defeat in the vote and therefore parliament adjourned the session to Monday the 2 August.[4]

The session on that day was a travesty of a parliamentary session. When Athanasiadis-Novas and his ministers entered plenary hall and took their seats hell broke lose. The deputies of the EK hissed and booed. G. Papandreou had not appeared. When the PM began to read the governmental declaration he was constantly interrupted by hecklings such as "traitor", "Judas", "shame", "liar". Other deputies chanted an ambiguous line from a poem by Athanasiadis-Novas.[5] Nobody listened to the declaration of the PM. Andreas Papandreou described the scene as follows: *"All in all, it was chaos. Parliament had lost its decorum. But that was only*

1 Margaret Papandreou, *Nightmare in Athens* (London: Prentice Hall, 1970), p. 87.
2 *Ibidem*, p. 86.
3 *Ibidem*, p. 89.
4 Linardatos, *op. cit.*, V, p. 256.
5 An Athenian newspaper had re-published a failed poem of the PM which contained a line of unintentional humour. These lines of the poem had distinctly dubious sexual connotations. The line sounded: *"ήταν τα στήθεια της άσπρα σαν τα γάλατα"* [her breasts were white like milk] / "*και μούλεγε γαργάλα τα"* [and she said to me tickle them (in the sense of "stir them")]. The slogan heard in Parliament "*Γαργάλα τα*" ridiculed the manliness of the PM, which was extremely provoking in the Greek macho society. *Ibidem*, p. 257.

secondary to the fact that it had lost its purpose, its role, its raison d'être, for the King had dealt it a deadly blow."[1]

During the continuation of the debate on 3 August the head of the right-wing progressive party, Spyros Markezinis, said that Greece was in a national crisis and a government of national cooperation had to be formed. On 4 August Kanellopoulos declared that ERE would vote for the government. During the debate there constantly were ugly scenes which culminated in a brawl between two deputies. During the days of the debates thousands demonstrated on the Syntagma Square outside the parliament, astonishingly there were many young people among them. The building of the parliament was protected by a large police force. At the voting on 5 August 131 deputies voted for the Government i.e. the 98 deputies of the ERE, the 25 apostates and the 8 progressives of Markezinis, i.e. together 65 deputies. Thus the government Athanasiadis-Novas fell. The PM declared his resignation and the King told him to remain in office until a new government was formed. Thus the first attempt of the King to install a government convenient for him, ended in a fiasco.

Background Manoeuvres

The King had already begun consultations with the party leaders in the afternoon of 3 August. But in this case he changed the usual procedure by talking not only with the leaders but also with the sub-leaders of the parties. G. Papandreou was the first who presented his ideas: He should be the first to be entrusted with the forming of a new government or the acting government should hold new elections. Papandreou was followed by Kanellopoulos who suggested the formation of a new government from of the existing parliament; should this not succeed new elections should be held. On 6 August the King received the leader of EDA, Ioannis Passalidis. It was the first time since the end of the war that a leader of the Left entered the royal palace. Passalidis demanded the restoration of democratic conditions by asking Papandreou to form a government. In order to gain the necessary majority EDA was ready to vote for such a government. If this proposal was not accepted new election should be held. The leader of the Progressives, Markezinis, repeated his demand for the formation of a government of national unity.

After the leaders of the parties Constantine received the grandees of the EK: Stefanos Stefanopoulos, Georgios Athanasiadis-Novas, Savvas Papapolitis, Ilias Tsirimokos, Alexandros Baltazis, Konstantinos Mitsotakis, Stavros Kostopoulos and Stylianos Alamanis. It was obvious that the King was looking for other shaky candidates in the EK which he could pull on his side, and, indeed, these existed. In order to tarnish his interference into the internal affairs of the EK Constantine talked with two grandees of the ERE, with the former Prime Minister Panagiotis Pipinelis and the former president of the parliament Konstantinos Rodopoulos.[2]

It was clear that the King opposed yet another government by Papandreou and this the more so since it would be supported by EDA. But new elections were equally unacceptable for him because he knew that Papandreou would emerge from them as victor. He was looking for a third solution which would keep the status quo, deepen the tensions within the EK and would lead to a schism.

In the meantime speculations began in the newspapers about a possible solution. An important role played the editors of the Athenian papers *Vima* and *Nea* (Christos Lambrakis), *Athinaiki* (Ioannis Papageorgiou) and of Macedonia appearing in Thessalonika (Ioannis Vellidis). They had observed that the circulation figures of *Eleftheria* had dropped considerably

1 A. Papandreou, *op. cit.*, p. 179.
2 Linardatos, *op. cit.*, V, p. 263f.

when its editor Kokkas supported Mitsotakis wheras the circulation of the other paper rose. They wanted to avoid a similar fate and therefore proceeded cautiously by not openly opposing Papandreou. In private they favoured the following solution: Papandreou should restrict his activities on the party and leave the office of the PM to Stefanopoulos. Thus the unity of the EK could be preserved, the King would be satisfied and the country be lead out of the crisis. This proposal they submitted to Papandreou on 6 August in the presence of Tsirimokos, Papapolitis, Stefanopoulos and other grandees of the EK. Papandreou rejected the proposal.[1]

The reason of G. Papandreou's negative reaction was clear: The proposal would have been feasible in any party system elsewhere in Europe but in the clientelistic system of Greece it would have meant the de facto disempowerment of Papandreou because only he could distribute rousfetia as he had access to the resources of the State. Allegedly on 7 August the three editors and Stefanopoulos, Tsirimokos and Papapolitis met and signed a protocol on the future course of action. Accordingly Papandreou was to remain uncontested leader of the party. A split of the EK was to be avoided so that the party could remain in power for the whole legislative period. If the King rejected Papandreou's proposals (fresh formation of a government or new elections) a government under Stefanopoulos should be formed. The formation of an unpolitical government shad to be avoided at all cost; this was a hint at an extra-parliamentary solution, i.e. a military coup. New elections were not in the interest of the party.[2]

Apparently Stefanopoulos informed the King via about the conversation and his intention to find a solution. The King hoped that this meant that Stefanopoulos was ready to form the new government. Via go-betweens the King informed the American embassy and expressed the hope that the Embassy would render their good offices in this case.[3]

In the evening on 8 August the King and G. Papandreou met again. Constantine told Papandreou that he rejected his proposals and asked him whether he had a third alternative proposal. Papandreou denied this and added that solution could only be found by respecting the sovereignty of the people. Each effort to create a government by on of the leaders of the EK would be considered as an attempt to split the EK. Later the King called Stefanopoulos to the Palace and asked him to find out if there was majority in the EK that would accept the formation of a government led by him. If this was confirmed he would ask him to form a government.[4] Linardatos characterized this manoeuvre as salami technique.[5]

On 9 August the deputies of the EK met. G. Papandreou criticised the effort of the King to mingle into the internal affairs of the EK by trying to find a PM acceptable to him. This would split the party. He had submitted two proposals for a solution: *"It has never happened in the past for a King to survey the parties and pick among their members whom he likes in order to construct governments. This method [...] violates [the party's] constitution, which provides that the party is headed up by a leader, who represents it. ... If the King attempts a dictatorial solution, he will never be justified. There is open to him only the solution of elections."*[6]

After him Stefanopoulos spoke; he stressed that the King had given the task to form a government to the party but he would submit to the vote of the deputies. The former General and present deputy Pavsanias Katsotas spoke out for immediate new elections. Tsirimokos pre-

1 Giorgios Leontaritis, *Ilias Tsirimokos kai i krisi tou 1965. Apostatis i martyras?* (Athen: Olkos, 1977), p. 50.
2 *Ibidem*, p. 50f; A. Papandreou, *op. cit.*, p. 180, gives a wrong date, writing that the meeting took place on 26 July.
3 United States Department of State, *Foreign Relations of the United States, 1964-1968, XVI, Cyprus; Greece; Turkey* (Washington: US Govt. Printing Office, 2000), p. 426. From here quoted as *FRUS 1964-1968,* XVI.
4 *Archiv der Gegenwart*, p. 12.085; *Keesing's Contemporary Archives,* p. 21.006; A. Papandreou, *op. cit.*, p. 180.
5 ThatLinardatos, *op. cit.*, V, p. 266.
6 *Ibidem*, p. 268f; A. Papandreou, *op. cit.*, p. 180.

ferred a compromise solution. He stressed that he, too, was against the interference of the King. He could not elect the Prime Minister and the Ministers at will but these were theoretical considerations. Fact was that since George I all Kings had done exactly this. Tsirimokos mentioned the case of Karamanlis who had been overturned because of differences with the Palace and had been replaced by another grandee of the ERE. He considered the reduction of the political confrontation to the alternative "with or without Papandreou" and "Papandreou against the King" as dangerously simplifying because it was not known whereto this split might lead. In his eyes this was harping on about principles. If elections were held now they would assume the character of a plebiscite over the form of the state triggered by the confrontation of the King and Papandreou, and the King would loose. The subsequent triumphal celebrations of the people might force the King to leave the county as this had happened in the past. In view of this situation it was the duty of the democratic camp, Tsirimokos continued, to avoid the direct confrontation and to search for a compromise. A tactical compromise was no defeat but a victory. He would vote for a Stefanopoulos solution.[1]

Alexandros Baltazis demanded new elections. Savvas Papapolitis was of the opinion that Stefanopoulos' proposal should be accepted and that both proposals of Papandreou could not be implemented. Primarily a split of the part had to be avoided. Papapolitis was ready to accept the opinion of the majority. Among the deputies there were many who agreed with Tsirimokos argumentation but did not dare to state this publicly because they would have taken position against the old one (*o Geros* - Papandreou).

Tsirimokos' view of the situation was much closer to reality than that of Papandreou. As a leftist he knew the possibilities of the *parakratos* and royalist army which were close to the King. Astonishing, however, is the assumption that the King might leave the country; this was a total underestimation of the possibilities and the real reactions of the King because the latter would if he felt pressured use the army to establish a dictatorship. But perhaps Tsirimokos did not want to be too clear. He knew the consequences of a policy based on confrontation from the time of the civil war and wanted to avoid a repetition of that situation. Tsirimokos course was not heroic, populist but pragmatic, and realistic. As his policy went against Papandreou's course he was quickly suspected to be a renegade, an apostate because the right to interpret - the events rested with Papandreou.

Papandreou on the other side had always loved the great gesture. He was a gifted populist with a touch of demagogy. The adoration of the people (*o geros tis dimonkratias*) alienate him from reality. He was somewhat detached and a little bit beset by old age stubbornness opinionated and not ready to renounce power. He was the greatest opposition politician in Greece in the twentieth century; But when he was in power he both times proved to be rather incapable making a compromise and both times, 1944 and 1965 a catastrophe for Greece resulted: 1944 the Dekemvriana with the ensuing civil war and 1965 the destabilisation of the political system with the ensuing military dictatorship 1967. If the dictatorship could have been avoided had Papandreou accepted the proposal of Stefanopoulos must remain speculation of course.

At the ensuing voting of the EK fraction Papandreou's proposals received 113 votes and 26 deputies voted for those of Stefanopoulos. Quite rightly Linardatos speaks of a Pyrrhic victory of Papandreou. His inability for a compromise coerced a large part of the EK in an oppositional direction and out of the party. Even though a few who had voted for Stefanopoulos e.g. Papapolitis and some adherents of Baklatzis remained in the Papandreou fraction but the

1 Linardatos, *op. cit.*, V, p. 269f; Leontaritis, *op. cit.*, p. 52.

political spirt of discord had infested the party.[1] The editor of *Vima* and *Nea*, Lambrakis, who feared a reduction of the circulation figures of his papers and made a 180 degree turn and the headline of *Nea* announced the next day that all Greeks were on the side of Papandreou.[2]

But the adherents of the change of course did not give up. At a meeting of Stefanopoulos with Papapolitis, Mitsotakis, Tsirimokos and Ioannis Tsouderos they tried to convince Stefanopoulos to continue his efforts. Afterwards Tsouderos visited the deputy chief of the American embassy, Norbert Anschuetz: *"A word of encouragement from the Embassy at this point could be extremely important. [...] There is increasing amount of disgust and unhappiness among the 116 [sic] deputies who had supported Papandreou [...] Although it is not at all certain that all the 26 who had supported Stefanopulos [...] would necessarily support him if he proceeded without formal support of CU [Center Union], there is undoubtedly significant number of deputies [...] who would switch their allegiance if Stephanopoulos' determination to accept mandate and seek vote of confidence became clear."* Stefanopoulos was in an awkward position especially because Lambrakis did not support him. He hoped that Stefanopoulos would change his opinion.[3]

Before Stefanopoulos went to the King on 10 August he rang up Anschuetz and informed him that he intended to give back the royal mandate. He had other ideas for a solution.[4] Later in the morning he saw the King and gave back the mandate to form a government. It is unknown whether on this occasion they already talked about the formation of the government by Tsirimokos. It cannot be excluded but it is not likely. However, the further development hinted in this direction. Anyway on the same day Stefanopoulos and Tsirimokos broke off their relations to Papandreou and the EK-party. At the same time followers of the King and the acting Novas government planted the rumour that Tsirimokos was asked to form a new government. The newspaper *Eleftheria* which was close to Mitsotakis published this rumour as a fact. It was obvious thatthey tried to promote the split of the EK. The King did not know what he should do because he had bet on Stefanopoulos.[5]

On 11 August Papandreou asked fo an audience with the King which then took place in the later afternoon on 12 August and lasted minutes. Papandreou informed the King about voting results of the fraction on 9 August and mulishly repeated his two demands. However, the King did not move. He rejected new elections and regretted that he could not ask Papandreou to form the new government because he had lost the majority in parliament as he added shrewdly.[6] Papandreou replied that if the crisis continued the question concerning the form of the government would arise, i.e. the abolition of the monarchy and he asked himself whether it would be possible to avoid a coalition with the EDA among the rank and file. He told this to the King as a last warning which he felt obliged to do as a leader of the people.[7]

Shortly after Papandreou Kanellopoulos visited the King and told him that the ERE was ready to support a government of the EK provided it was not led by Papandreou.[8] Following a conversation between Constantine and Athanasiadis-Novas it was heard that the EK was steering course of confrontation and wanted to provoke a constitutional crisis. Kanellopoulos purpoted that Papandreou actually was aiming at the formation of a popular front government

1 Linardatos, *op. cit.*, V, p. 270.
2 Leontaritis, *op. cit.*, p. 54.
3 *FRUS 1964-1968,* XVI, p. 426.
4 *Ibidem.*
5 *Ibidem*, p. 427.
6 Linardatos, *op. cit.*, V, p. 273f.
7 *Keesing's Contemporary Archives*, p. 21.006; *Archiv der Gegenwart*, p. 12.085.
8 *Keesing's Contemporary Archives*, p. 21.006.

together with the EDA. On 13 August Stefanopoulos and Tsirimokos, who were among the eight founding members of EK, issued a declaration announcing that from now on they would be independent deputies in parliament. The latter had enough support to form a government of their own. This was understood that more deputies of the EK would quit the party.[1]

On 14 August the newspapers released several critical remarks by G. Papandreou about the policy of the King. Constantine tried to find out from his followers in politics and as well as civilian life whether a solution Tsirimokos would be acceptable. He intended to authorize Tsirimokos to form a government. During a meeting of the EK parliamentary group the option Tsirimokos was discussed: A little bit earlier the former socialist leader had been classified as a danger for the nation and he had been insulted as EAMoVoulgaris Now some spoke for him, others stills distrusted and rejected him. But in the end they bowed to the will of the King and besides they were convinced that Tsirimokos could tame the Left more easily. Kanellopoulos had a long conversation with Constantine and at the press conference after this he lauded Tsirimokos' mediating role.[2]

On 16 August Stefanopoulos and Tsirimokos announced in parliament that they would leave the EK and form their own parliamentary group - "independent EK". They did not mention names but the press wrote that the new group allegedly counted 30 deputies. Obviously it should be avoided that these deputies would be put under pressure by the leadership of the EK around G. Papandreou. In a declaration to the press this group accused Papandreou of inadequate behaviour and complete disconnect from reality. He led the country into a deep crisis by his unrelenting demeanour.[3] On the same day a conversation took place between Stefanopoulos and Tsirimokos and the head of the political office of the King, Konstantinos Choïdas. The content of this conversation remained unknown.[4]

The fact that this conversation had taken place was sufficient for Papandreou to give the statement to the press on 17 August in which he denounce Stefanopoulos and Tsirimokos as traitors. Their treason was even worse than that of Athanasiadis-Novas. After all Stefanopoulos had promised to respect the unity of the party. The King behaved like Kirke, the sorceress; he used the human greed to power to seduce them. He, himself, had never put the form of the state into question and had never toyed with the idea of forming a popular front government together with the communists. The traitors should be subjected to the righteous anger of the people. Infuriated Stefanopoulos counterattacked and revealed that Papandreou himself had played hanky-panky with the King and the ERE leadership and Tsirimokos added insult to injury by stating that when they founded EK they had known exactly what was going on but neglected it because Papandreou purported himself as lawyer of democracy.[5] In short: Both sides attacked each other below the belt and burned their bridges.

All this was accompanied by vast demonstrations of the adherents of the EK and the EDA which assumed a more and more anti-royalist character. In the evening of 17 August a huge rally took place in the biggest football stadium in Athens (Panathinaiki).The main speakers were the leaders of the GSEE and the union of democratic lawyers, After the end of the meeting a crowd of 39,000 people, marched to the Omonia Square while chanting "Down with the junta", "Shame on the traitors", "Democracy" , "Down with Fascism" and "There is only one

1 *Ibidem*.
2 Linardatos, *op. cit.*, V, p. 275f.
3 Leontaritis, *op. cit.*, p. 55.
4 Linardatos, *op. cit.*, V, p. 276.
5 *Keesing's Contemporary Archives*, p. 21.006; Linardatos, *op. cit.*, p. 276f.

leader, the people". More than 4,000 policemen had been gathered there but nothing happened.[1]

The Tsirimokos Government

On 18 August Stefanopoulos and Tsirimokos were again called to the Palace whee they conferred with the King more than two hours. When they left the Palace Tsirimokos declared to the waiting journalists that he had accepted the mandate of the King to form a new government with full agreement with Stefanopoulos. The question arises why the King did not entrust Stefanopoulos with this task but Tsirimokos ostracised until that time and why he accepted the mandate. The answer regarding Stefanopoulos is easy. Stefanopoulos knew that he would never find a majority. Only the 98 ERE deputies, the eight Progressives of Markezinis and the 25 Apostates of Athanasiadis would vote for him. Added to them might be the 26 deputies who had voted for him the day before. Numerically he would thus have a comfortable majority of 14 votes . However, it was not sure that all these deputies would be on his side. Time was badly needed and therefore Tsirimokos took over this task and accepted the mandate. It must have been clear to him that he could never win the vote of confidence but that he would remain in power only as long as Stefanopoulos needed to swear enough deputies on to himself. The temporal restriction of the Tsirimokos option explains why the King and the parties of the Right accepted it. The frequent accusations that Tsirimokos had been an opportunist are not true because the disadvantages of the take over of the government outnumbered the advantages. Tsirimokos knew that he engaged himself in an unpopular enterprise: *"A true leader does not allow the masses to control him instead he leads them there where he wants to have the. I will take the way which I believe to be the only one to save democracy, if we succeed in saving the situation before the army takes action."*[2] But Tsirimokos knew that he was facing heavy going.

Papandreou expressed astonishment that the King himself had opted for Tsirimokos. When he, Papandreou, had wanted to make Tsirimokos Minister of the Interior the King had objected, And when Tsirimokos tried to become speaker of the House ERE had again opposed him.[3]

While on 19 August Tsirimokos made an effort to form his cabinet big demonstrations began in Athens. About 15,000 youths marched through the town centre of Athens despite demonstrations being prohibited and shouted slogans against the royal family and Tsirimokos and demanded the reinstallment of Papandreou as PM. During the night of 20 August violence escalated when the police advanced against the youths. Dozens were injured on both sides. The security forces arrested 226 people, of which on 23 August 116 were brought to court. In the city shops and offices were devastated.[4]

The Tsirimokos Government which was inaugurated on 20 August consisted exclusively of the dissidents. Four ministers had belonged to the previous government (Alamanis, Kostopoulos, Toumbas and Papaspyrou). Stefanopoulos made an efforts to draw these 26 deputies, who on 9 August had voted for his proposal, on to his side, but when Markezinis declared that he would not vote for the government in parliament it became clear that the Government would not reach the magic number of 151 votes for the majority in parliament.

1 Linardatos, *op. cit.*, V, p. 277.
2 Leontaritis, *op. cit.*, p. 62.
3 Linardatos, *op. cit.*, V, p. 278.
4 *Keesing's Contemporary Archives*, p. 21.007.

In the evening of 20 August there once again serious clashes between the demonstrators and the security forces occured. 31 persons were hurt among them 10 policemen.[1] The banners carried by the demonstrators showed a growing antiroyalist tendency; especially ex-Queen Frideriki was targeted. The meddling of the King with daily politics made the question of about the form of state pressing again. Chants demanded that Frideriki leave the country, some even widened this demand and included mother and son. In the demonstrations the supporters of Papandreou and those of the EDA commingled thus enabling the Left to leave their ghetto. *Vima* and *Nea* did their best to heat the atmosphere towards the King.[2]

Papandreou betook himself into the province in order to mobilize his adherents. On 22 August a great rally took place in Larisa to which people had been brought from afar. It became clear that Papandreou was already in campaign-mode. This in turn strengthened the obstuction of the Right and the Palace because they feared to be decimated in the elections and the King saw his throne shaking. All conservative forces, even those in the EK were afraid of a shift to the left which would strengthen Andreas Papandreou: *"For these reasons, King, supported by ERE, Progressives and sizeable element of CU [Center Union], strongly oppose elections, and would consider instability for indefinite period preferable to return of Papandreou."*[3] In order to avoid elections the Right was even ready to support the "leftist" Tsirimokos.

In the evening of 24 August the discussion of following the government declaration began. The parliamentary building was guarded by a huge police force. The apostates formed a closed group. When the PM began his declaration he was constantly interrupted by critical shouts. If Athanasiadis-Novas declaration had been tragic-comic in character now pure hatred surfaced and the scene became ugly in character. The abuses were directed at a proven democrat and exponent of democracy in Greece who had always fought for human rights. He was the first social democrat who became PM although by King's grace and in confrontation with the progressive forces in the EK and the EDA. Though Tsirimokos knew that in the end he would be voted down he did his best to present his governmental program.[4]

The continuation of the debate on 25 August was accompanied by mass demonstrations against the new government outside the parliament building. 4,000 policemen had been concentrated in the centre of Athens and they closed off the streets leading to the parliament building. Water cannons had been put into positions. In parliament P. Kanellopoulos was the first speaker. He announced that his party group would vote for Tsirimokos though it was known that many ERE deputies rejected the "communist" Tsirimokos. Deputies of the EK interrupted his speech constantly by shouting "elections, elections". There were even some brawls between deputies of the ERE and the EK so that the session had to be interrupted. Kanellopoulos reacted to the demand of elections by saying that he also preferred election but not in the presence of the street terror. Ilias Iliou spoke for the EDA. He was afraid that the army would intervene if the new government did not find a majority. After this remark chaos broke out in parliament and the session had to interrupted again.[5]

While on 25 August the feelings ran high in parliament attemps in the background tried to create the necessary majority be it by political pressure or bribery. Because Markezinis had declared that he and his adherents would not vote for Tsirimokos he was urged by Choïdas and Athanasiadis-Novas to vote for him nevertheless, even the King called him by telephone.

1 *Archiv der Gegenwart*, p. 12.085.
2 *FRUS 1864-1968*, XVI, p. 429.
3 *Ibidem*, p. 430.
4 Linardatos, *op. cit.*, V, p. 284.
5 *Ibidem*, p. 285; *Keesing's Contemporary Archives*, p. 21.007.

Markezinis, however, remained stubborn but five deputies from his fraction yielded to the pressure and promised to cast their vote for Tsirimokos. But even this did not bring a majority. Now legal as well as illegal means were applied. Five EK-deputies later told parliament that they had been promised financial means and ministerial posts, if they joined the "apostates". One of them mentioned the name of a great importer of Mercedes cars and industrial plants (Michail Fostiropoulos) who had made these offers.[1] Allegedly the governor of the National Bank (Ethniki Trapeza), the former EK politician Georgios Mavros was approached by Tsirimokos for support. When he rejected this he received a telephone call from the chief of the general staff General, Ioannis Genimatas, who demanded from him that for national reasons he should support Tsirimokos. Even the Greek-American representative of Esso Greece, Tom Pappas who had close relations to the CIA contacted Mavros and advised him to support Tsirimokos who was an honest fellow. Mavros rejected this again.[2] Obviously attempts were made to buy the necessary parliamentary majority.

When on 26 August the debate continued Markezinis again refused to vote for Tsirimokos and demanded instead the creation of an all party government. On this day, too, there were tumults in parliament when the deputies insulted each other and lashed out against their colleagues. G. Papandreou presented a compromise to the public: A managing government should be created which would organize elections in December1963. This proposal was rejected by the advisors of the King. In the session on 27 August Mitsotakis, Stefanopoulos and Tsirimokos appealed to the deputies to support the government. Else the government Tsirimokos would be the last EK government. On Monday 29 August the end of the Tsirimokos government came: 159 deputies voted against (EK 134, EDA 22, Progressives 3) and 135 deputies voted for it (ERE 98 and Apostates 17) and 5 deputies of the progressive abstained. Tsirimokos declared his resignation but continued to carry on the work of the government temporarily.[3]

The Meeting of the Crown Council

On 30 August the King announced that he would convene the Crown Council *(Symvoulio tou Stemmatos)* the next days. The Crown Council was an consulting assembly not provided for in the Constitution consisting of former prime ministers who should advise the King during critical times. Tsirimokos suggested that the leaders of the parties represented in parliament should also participate. King Constantine agreed but did not invite the leader of EDA Passalidis. Thus on 1 September I. Tsirimokos, G. Papandreou, P. Kanellopoulos, Sp. Markezinis as well as the former prime ministers Stylianos Gonatas (1922), Konstantinos Tsaldaris (1946), D. Kiousopolos (1952), G. Athanasiadis-Novas, K. Dovas (1961), I. Paraskevopoulos (1963) and P. Pipinelis (1963). Karamanlis had been invited but had refused to participate. St. Mavromichalis (1963) was abroad and K. Georgakopoulos (1958) and P. Politsas (1946) were sick.[4]

The Crown Council met on 1 September for three hours and 7 hours on the following day. With the exception of Papandreou and the 85 years old Gonatas they all rejected new elections. Kanellopoulos was against elections at this time because the country was in uproar and a interim government would not be able to restore peace and quiet which were the prerequisite for free elections. Markezinis as of the same opinion; according to him the atmosphere in the

1 *Efimeris ton Syzition tis Voulis - Synedriasi 3i tis 21is Noemvriou 1965*, p. 104.
2 *Linardatos, op. cit*, V, p. 286.
3 *Ibidem*, V, p. 286.
4 Linardatos, *op. cit.*, V, p. 288. Alkiviadis Provatas, *Politiki istoria tis Ellados 1821-1980. Nomothetika kai ektelestika somata* (Athen, 1980).

country forbade new elections, and asked again for the formation of a government of national unity. For Tsaldaris elections equalled national suicide. Kiousopoulos, Novas and Dovas expressed themselves similarly. Pipinelis conjured up the communist danger, the popular front was threatening.

Kanellopoulos proposed that the King should ask him to form a government and then dissolve parliament. He would organize new elections. Papandreou agreed to this proposal yet with some reservations. Markezinis, too, was ready to support this proposal. Pipinelis and Dovas rejected it, probably with the connivance of the King. Thus the Crown Council meeting ended without any result.[1]

On 4 September Papandreou talked with the deputies of his party and then announced that in principle he was ready to accept a government of Kanellopoulos provided it organized new elections with the period of 45 days as the constitution prescribed and that these would be free. The EDA leadership distrusted the proposal because it was afraid of the use of force and falsifications. The royalist forces in the ERE were alarmed and the press close to them accused Kanellopoulos of delivering the country to the popular front and thus to the Communists. The eminent ERE-grandees e.g. Pipinelis, Sp. Theotokis, E. Averof and K. Maniadakis were opposed to new elections. Only Grigoris Kasimatis and G. Rallis and P. Papaligouras supported Kanellopoulos. King Constantine called Kanellopoulos and spoke out against new elections. He stressed that his foreign advisors were against new elections as well. The behaviour of the right wing of the ERE was influenced by two factors: On the one side the King was against new elections and on the other these forces were rightly afraid that their party would loose the elections. Their tactical manoeuvring and feinting in the context of supporting of the support to the governments of Athanasiadis-Novas and Tsirimokos had alienated their traditional clientele. New elections would have meant a catastrophe for ERE.[2]

The Americans on the other side were afraid that Papandreou might win the elections: *"Embassy has concluded George Papandreou's return to power should be avoided if this can be done without a direct and open confrontation with him: George Papandreou at this moment commands wide popular support among Greek people. This popularity has temporarily been raised to artificial levels in current crisis by Papandreou's clever exploitation of latent hostility towards the Monarchy. I am keenly aware that inasmuch as we may have to deal with Papandreou again in future, utmost discretion and avoidance of open hostility toward him are essential."* Though these sentences show a certain respect for Giorgios Papandreou the opinion on Andreas Papandreou was completely negative: *"Andreas is neutralist, ambitious, amoral, and emotionally unstable."* Anschuetz suspected him to be one of the leaders of the ASPIDA, who he tried to gain control over the army. Since he was steering a neutralistic course the extreme Leftists and the Communists would be his natural allies. His policy concerning the Cyprus question which was against *enosis* was an attempt to make himself acceptable to the Soviet Union.[3]

In view of this situation on 5 September Kanellopoulos visited Papandreou in his residence in the suburb Kastri. He had to admit to Papandreou that he could not stand to his proposal due to the opposition in the rows of the ERE. Papandreou regretted this deeply. Kanellopoulos had to recognize that he only controlled ERE conditionally.[4] On 8 September the talks between the two politicians on this topic ended for good. The liberal Kanellopoulos could not

1 Linardatos, *op. cit.*, V, p. 294.
2 *Ibidem*; A. Papandreou, *op. cit.*, p. 183.
3 *FRUS 1964-1968*, XVI, p. 431.
4 Panagiotis Kanellopoulos, *Istorika dokimia, I, Pos efthasame stin 21i Apriliou 1967* (Athen, 1979), p. 88.

prevail against the united forces of the Palace, the Right and the so-called foreign factor.[1] Thus these forces returned to the original idea to create a new government under a prime minister from the rows of the EK. The new candidate as Stefanopoulos.

The Stefanopoulos Government

Stefanos Stefanopoulos, born in 1898 in Pyrgos, was the right man in the eyes of these circles. After studying law, economics and political science in Athens and Paris he entered the field of politics. In the elections of 1930 and 1936 as well as 1946 and 1950 he was elected deputy of the conservative party (*laïko komma*) in the Iliaia constituency in the Northwest Peloponnese. Before the Metaxas dictatorship he had served - being an specialist of economics - as secretary of state and minister in the ministry of economics. At the time of the liberation of Greece in October 1944 he belonged to the all-party government of Papandreou as expert for economics. After the war he became a member in the leadership of the *laïko komma* and was minister of coordination in almost all government. In 1951 he joined the party of Papagos and became Foreign Minister and vice-prime minister. When Papagos resigned in 1955 he hoped to advance to the leader of the party but the Palace decided that Karamanlis should take this post. Rather hurt he left the party and founded his own party (Laïkon Koinonikos Komma - Social Peoples Party) with which he entered the EK in 1961. In the second government of Papandreou (19 February to 15 July 1963 he was vice-premier and minister of coordination.[2] In other words: Stefanopoulos was a much more acceptable candidate for the opposition and the Palace than the Leftist Tsirimokos.

After negotiations with the leadership of the ERE and the Progressives of Markezinis it was decided that each of the parties should send a representative into the cabinet Stefanopoulos who were to advance the interests of the parties. The leaderships of both parties agreed and thus the votes of these two conservative parties were assured at for the vote of confidence. However, as these votes were not enough for the absolute majority of 151 votes some deputies of the EK had to be won over. The methods applied were all but clean: Though there were a few deputies who changed their sides because they were convinced that a compromise was necessary to lead the country out of the crisis. But their motives were hardly honourable. Some wanted to settle old scores, others saw the chance to enrich themselves or satisfy their ambitions. The latter knew that hey had to seize this chance because a switchover to the apostates would bring their political career to an end. The potential defectors were allured by posts as ministers or secretaries of state, though some of them were absolutely not qualified for these jobs. The number of the ministers was raised significantly that all defectors would get a post, others would receivet money.[3] Under Tsirimokos such manoeuvres took place in the background but now the leader of the apostates were directly involved and were morally responsible for these machinations.

As the King was not sure that Stefanopoulos and the other apostates would succeed in finding the necessary majority, on 16 September he turned to the American chargé d'affaires Anschuetz and asked for support. The embassy should bring its influence to bear. Elections

---

1 Linardatos, *op. cit.*, V, p. 295.

2 *Poios einai poios eis tin Ellada. Viografiko lexiko* (Athen: Eklogis, 1958), p. 497f.

3 Linardatos, *op. cit.*, V, p. 296. Andreas Papandreou reports these incidents: *"All the forces of the Establishment were mobilized. The Americans, the foreign investors, Greek businessmen - all went to work. It was not an easy task, for a would-be defector demanded all kinds of things. He knew that once he took the jump, the chances of his re-election to Parliament would be nil, so he wanted to achieve honors, powers, and riches all at once. A ministerial post was the minimum requirement. Beyond that there were other demands. And it is not surprising that one of the slogans that emerged at the time was 'How much?'"* A. Papandreou, *op. cit.*, p. 183.

would be held but only if the situation allowed it. The election system would have to be changed to a proportional representation. Though this would strengthen the election results of the Left but Papandreou would be decisively weakened. The King remained rather vague in the case that Stefanopoulos would fail: *"King did not specify what remedy he might seek in event current effort to form government fails nor did he specifically exclude extra-Parliamentary solution."* In other words: The King did not exclude the introduction of a royal military dictatorship.

In the afternoon of 17 September the necessary quorum had been achieved. Stefanopoulos, Mitsotakis, Garoufalias, Kostopoulos and Bakatselos met in the house of the shipowner Anastasios Potamianos in the Stisichorou street a few steps from the royal Palais on the Irodou-Attikou street. The *Neue Zürcher Zeitung* reported on the further development the : *"The method how on Friday afternoon the 6 or rather 8 followers of Papandreou in the EK were won over for the new government tells its own story. The negotiations had been directed by the mediation of the big Greek shipowner Potamianos. At about 7 p.m. 8 deputies were made to go to the private house of the shipowner which is directly near the royal palais where leading members of the EK were present. When the whole group was present it was proposed to go directly to the royal palais to be inaugurated as ministers. 6 deputies agreed, one asked for time to think and one rejected it. The 6 were diligently accompanied by the leaders of the new government over the street and a few minutes later they were sworn in as ministers as if it was feared that they might change their mind at the very last moment. It could not be assured whether the principle of material interest played a role."*[1]

In the meantime the Archbishop had arrived and when all future minister had assembled in the Palais he inaugurated them, first Stefanopoulos as Prime Minister and then the Ministers among them a representative of ERE (Dimitrios Vourdoumbas) and the Progressives (Alexandros Karathodoros). The whole affair took place in hit-and-run style as is shown by the fact that the new minister were inaugurated wearing lounge suits. Athanasiadis-Novas and Tsirimokos were inaugurated as executive vice-premiers and the latter additionally Foreign Minister. The other grandees obtained the following posts: Mitsotakis coordination, Kostopoulos defence, Melas finances, Toumbas industry, Bakatselos work, Alamanis education and Papaspyrou law. On the next day Stefanopoulos declared in parliament that elections would be suspended for the moment, until the country became quiet again. Papandreou characterized the behaviour of the apostates as shameful.[2]

---

1 *"Die Art und Weise, wie am Freitag nachmittag die 6 bzw. 8 bisherigen Anhänger Papandreous in der Zentrumsfraktion für die neue Regierung gewonnen werden mußten, spricht für sich. Die Verhandlungen waren vor allem durch Vermittlung eines der großen griechischen Reeder, Potamianos, geführt worden. Gegen 7 Uhr abends brachte man 8 Abgeordnete dazu, sich in der Privatwohnung des Reeders, die unmittelbar unterhalb des königlichen Stadtpalais liegt, einzufinden, wo auch die führenden Zentrumspolitiker anwesend waren. Als die ganze Gruppe vollzählig war, machte man den Deputierten den Vorschlag, unverzüglich ins Königspalais hinüber zu gehen, um sich auf der Stelle als Minister vereidigen zu lassen. 6 nahmen an, 1 erbat sich Bedenkzeit, und 1 lehnte vorläufig ab. Die 6 wurden dann sorgfältig von den Führern der neuen Regierung eskortiert über die Straße geführt und bereits einige Minuten später als Minister eingeschworen, als ob man befürchtet hätte, sie würden sich im letzten Moment wieder anders besinnen. Inwieweit man auch das Prinzip der materiellen Interessiertheit gegenüber ihnen walten ließ, ist nicht festzustellen."* Quoted from *Archiv der Gegenwart*, p. 12.086; Linardatos, *op. cit.*, V, p. 297.

2 Linardatos, *op. cit.*, V, p. 297. A CIA-report of October 1966 characterized the new government: *"Many members of the government are obscure politicians with no recognized administrative ability, their qualification based solely on their former leader and make themselves available for high office. Some have engaged in corrupt practices in dealing with the financial and patronage connected with their office. Stefanopoulos himself has described many of them as being 'sick or psychopaths'."* CIA, *Special Report "The Greek Political Scene on Eve of Parliamentary Session"* (Washington: CIA, 28 October 1966), p. 4.

On 22 September Stefanopoulos entered parliament and delivered his Government's policy statement. Again he was insulted as a traitor by deputies who were followers of Papandreou. As he was certain of his majority of votes he retorted in a menacing manner. His government represented freedom of speech and the freedom of the citizens but illegal mob actions would be persecuted. Exaggerated political agitation would postpone the elections. The army must be kept from interfering into politics and the economy of the country had to be rehabilitated. In foreign policy Greece would continue to remain loyal in the Western Alliance. The Greeks would never give up their desire to be united with Cyprus but its implementation had to be achieved in close contact with Turkey. At the same time the obligations towards the UN would be met by supporting the demands of Cyprus to gain "unfettered independence in the name of the principle of self-determination of the people."[1]

When on 25 September the vote of confidence took place the new government received 152 votes, 148 deputies voted against it. Since the ERE had 99 and the Progressives eight seats the apostates counted 46. The absolute majority of the EK was gone. King Constantine had prevailed. The methods used provoked Kanellopoulos some months later to utter critical remarks against the King: The manner how to achieve this majority was no an example for the younger generation. The worst, however, was that the majority had been bought with money, ministerial posts and other unacceptable means. If he had foreseen this he would have absented himself from the voting in parliament. By such means the country would not be led out of the crisis.[2] Indeed by this manoeuvre the ruling class had discredited itself. Greece developed features which were normally associated with a banana republic.

Another important personal change took place when the Minister of Defence Kostopoulos adviced the highest general staff chief, General Ioannis Pipilis and the chief of the army general staff General Ioannis Genimatas to resign. This resignation was put into effect during a session of the Hight Defence Council under the presidency of Stefanopoulos. They were replaced by Lieutenant General Konstantinos Tsolakas who had commanded the 3rd Army Corps in Northern Greece and Lieutenant General Grigorios Spandidakis. The King had dropped Genimatas and replaced him by Spandidakis who was loyal to the Crown but had contacts to the clique around colonel Georgios Papadopoulos who staged the coup on 21 April 1967. But at this time almost nobody knew anything about his plans. Fact, however, is that by establishing the Stefanopoulos Government the acute crisis was warded off and a period of relative stability began. Since the parliamentary holidays lasted until November 1965 the Government succeeded in stabilizing its position. The new cabinet ruled Greece until 23 December 1966.

The Downfall of the Stefanopoulos Government

Georgios Papandreou had begun his new never ending fight (news *anendotos agon*) against the royal coup d'état which, in summer 1966 reached a critical phase. The success of Papandreou's EK in the elections of 1961 and the victories of 1963 and 1964 had been achieved at the expense of the leftist EDA. Additionally the "left" wing of the conservative ERE had ro suffer losses.[3] During the new "untiring fighting" the danger threatened that many former

---

1 *Keesing's Contemporary Archives*, p. 21.007.

2 Linardatos, *op. cit.*, V, p. 296.

3 In 1958 EDA (24,43 percent of the votes) had been the second strong Party. The Liberals of Venizelos and Papandreou had reached 20,68 percent. After the foundation of the EK, in which all liberal, left-liberal and progressive forces had concentrated, this new party reached in the elections of 1961 366 (EDA: 14,63 percent) and in the elections of 1963 42,04 percent (EDA: 14,34 percent) and in the election in 1964 even 52,72 percent (EDA: 11,80 percent). Meynaud, *Les Forces Politiques en Grèce* (Paris: Études de science politique, 1965), pp.

protest voters might return to the Left and the Right if they were not kept by the means of an appropriate rhetoric and promises. Out of his anti-Communist position G. Papandreou had constantly announced that for him a coalition with the EDA was excluded. His son Andreas agreed with this course but wanted to embed the left-leanig floating voters to the EK by producing leftist slogans and by attacking the monarchy all through the country.[1] G. Papandreou was afraid that such rhetoric would move the country towards a dictatorship, recommended to the King by Queen Frideriki, the former ERE Prime Minister Panagiotis Pipinelis and the former Minister of Defence Petros Garoufalias. In a speech on 23 July 1966 he criticized the behaviour of the King in the past but spoke in a more conciliatory manner about the future. The King could overcome the present hopeless situation by announcing free and fair elections by proclaiming his support for a democratic government in Greece, and showing respect for the constitution. He, Papandreou, would support him in this.[2]

In a conversation with US-Ambassador Talbot on 11 August 1966 Papandreou went one step further. The real contentious issue was who controlled the army. The army should serve the state and not a party. *"Papandreou could assure King that, if there were elections and he came to power, he would appoint as Def[ence] Min[ister] someone in which both had confidence. Neither he nor Constantine wants to see organizations in army of IDEA and Aspida type. However, King wants an army loyal to him personally."* He needed the help of the Americans who should use their influence to make the King understand that he should give up his course which led to a dictatorship. Talbot himself had no contact with the Palace. *"Someone needs to convey his views to the King, someone outside invidious Psychiko circle (meaning Queen Mother and her confidantes). If he (Papandreou) attempts to convey this kind of feeling, it would be interpreted as compromising his position, and both sides would suffer. Gesture to be effective must be spontaneous initiative on part of King. It must not appear that there are secret agreements. Papandreou added he had not heretofore intimated these thoughts to anyone, not even to his friends."* He admitted that in the EK there were younger politicians *"eager for applause who have found that anti-monarchist statements bring this applause. Today they say these things for demagogic reasons; if allowed to continue, they only become persuaded. [The] longer present course continues [the] bitterer are public emotions."*[3]

Though Talbot recognized that G. Papandreou wanted the Americans to recommend early new elections to the King but he informed the chief of the royal protocol, Ambassador Dimitrios Bitsios on 18 August, about the ideas of Papandreou.[4] He had the impression that G. Papandreou had recognized that the time was working against him and his son was gaining more and more influence on the EK. Therefore he wanted to get in contact with the King as long as he was in control of the party.

On 29 September Talbot had another conversation, this time with father and son Papandreou. Both rejected the formation of a government in coalition with the EDA. Under Papandreou Greece would remain a reliable NATO-partner the voice of which - added Andreas - would be heard more than in the past. Both suggested that the King should install a managing government whose members should be politically independent personalities who would be accepted by EK and ERE. This government should remain in power for certain period of time

502-505.

1 A. Papandreou, *Democracy at Gunpoint*, p. 186.

2 *FRUS 1964-1968*, XVI, p. 500.

3 *Ibidem*, 501f.

4 *Ibidem*, p. 502 Fußnote 4.

and work out an election law based of the proportional representation system. After this task was completed elections should take place.[1]

In October, however, the developments began which lead to a rupture between father and son. After three years the trial against the probable murderer of the deputy Lambrakis. Iolved the police and linked with them the parakratos. There were speculations that the entourage of Frideriki had been behind the attack. Because it could be assumed that there would be demonstrations and unrest during this process the ASPIDA trial was begun as well. The beginning of that trial had been postponed in the hope that its beginning would divert attention from the trial in Thessalonika during which the ties of the then ERE government would come to the light. Its final stage would take place early in election campaign of the elections of 1968 scheduled by the constitution.[2]

Even before the trial began it became clear that the military court would try to put Andreas on trial. However, they allowed him to leave the country for a lecture tour through Scandinavia. He used this chance to speak very critically about the situation in Greece which was enthusiastically noted by his adherents in Greece but was furiously registered by the establishment and the press connected tied in to it. When he returned he was welcomed by a huge crowd at the Ellinikon airport. The roads towards the town centre were lined with adherents and allegedly Andreas needed four hours to reach his home. A little later Andreas toured accompanied by a number of EK deputies through Crete where he attracted the masses by his aggressive rhetoric. His talent as populist speaker influenced the listeners and their exaltation provoked him to ever more aggressive rhetorical heighlights.[3] He and the deputies allowed themselves to be swept away by their own rhetorics and the chanting of the masses. They had the feeling that any attempt by the establishment to take over power by means of the military would be impeded by the masses.[4]

Father Papandreou and other grandees of the EK, among them the editor of To Vima and *Ta Nea*, Christos Lambrakis watched the provocative behaviour of Andreas with regret. At the beginning of November Papandreou secretly got in contact with the King helped by the deputy and former minister, Stylianos Choutas.[5] Allegedly he forwarded the following five proposals: Each of them was to keep his opinion about the events in the past to himself but they should not become topics for political disputes. The Stefanopoulos Government should be replaced by an interim-government with a lengthy tenure and this government should prepare the country for the elections. The new government should pass an election law on the basis of proportional representation voting. If the EK won the elections but did not get the absolute majority it would not enter a coalition government with EDA. If the King undertook a change of the government on the basis of these ideas the EK would praise this initiative and refrain from any critic against the King.[6]

On 30 November the King informed Kanellopoulos about the initiative of Papandreou. Papandreou had submitted to him five proposals to which he would agree if Kanellopoulos also approved. Papandreou would do likewise. Kanellopoulos agreed to these proposals and informed the King. The latter asked Kanellopoulos to keep this totally secret and not even talk to his closest friends about it. In the first half of December there were two secret meetings in

---

1 *Ibidem*, p. 511f.
2 Stephen Rousseas, *Militärputsch in Griechenland oder im Hintergrund der CIA* (Reinbek: Rowohlt, 1968), p. 42.
3 Papandreou, *Democracy at gunpoint*, p. 193.
4 Rousseas, *op. cit.*, p. 44.
5 Kanellopoulos, *op. cit.*, p. 98.
6 Linardatos, *op. cit.*, V, p. 376f; Kanellopoulos, *op. cit.*, p. 98.

the royal summer residence in Tatoi. At the first meeting Papandreou and Kanellopoulos met and at the second the King joined them. Top secret measures were taken and only the chief of the royal protocol, Ambassador Dimitrios Bitsios and the aide de camp of the King Colonel Michail Arnaoutis participated in the Tatoi meeting.

Papandreou and Kanellopoulos discussed the five proposals. Kanellopoulos agreed to the change of government and the formation of an interim-government with a lengthy tenure with the agreement of both parties. He also accepted the change of the election law. The election were to take place in May 1967 at the latest. Both party leaders agreed that the political passions should be bottled up. And they quickly agreed on the head of the interim-government; Ioannis Paraskevopoulos who had led the country to the elections of 1964.[1] Bitsios kept the minutes at the meeting on 18 December with the King. The King accepted all five proposals, which Papandreou and Kanellopoulos had submitted to him. Additionally Papandreou proposed that regarding the Greco-Turkish negotiations re Cyprus the Crown Council should come together, and rhat the party leaders should be invited. A memorandum prepared by Bitsios was signed by Papandreou and Kanellopoulos on 19 December.[2] Since the King and Papandreou insisted on the secrecy of their talks it was Kanellopoulos who on 20 December 1966 told PM Stefanopoulos that the ERE withdrew their support for him. The next morning Stefanopoulos declared his resignation and the King received all party leaders, among them also G. Papandreou, who recommended the formation of an interim-Government and new elections. The King asked Paraskevopoulos to form a new government.[3] The whole matter was typical manoeuvre of Greek politics. The party leaders made their lonesome decisions and expected that their followers to join in. A discussion within the parties about the lonely decisions of the leaders was not provided for in the clientelistic system.

On the same day the CIA reported from Athens that on 13 December 1966 the revolutionary council of the military plot under the leadership of Georgios Papadopoulos had met. The report mentioned the names of the seven committee members and stated that the group had discussed the actual situation but had not yet taken the decision to establish a military dictatorship, as G. Papadopoulos had demanded on 22 November. The report added that the group had been plotting since the end of 1963.[4] Obviously the colonels were waiting for a suitable moment to launch their attack.

In view of this situation it would have been necessary for all democratic forces of Greece cooperated, including Andreas Papandreou. But he followed his own instincts for power. His father had not informed him about his rapprochement with the King because he rightly fear violent reactions. On 17 December 1966 Andreas had a conversation with the vice chief of the US Mission in Athens, Norbert Anschuetz. The latter had suggested that Andreas should meet the King. He himself was ready to organize such a meeting. Andreas could erase the impression that he was a diehard revolutionary. Andreas rejected this proposal because, if it became known, he would be finished as the leader of the "anendotos agon". Anschuetz proposed that Andreas should appoint a representative who could talk with Bitsios. Andreas rejected this proposal, as well. However, the King would be free to talk to all important party leaders including him. Anschuetz, who obviously was informed of G. Papandreou's plans spoke about the possibility of a interim-Government, which would be supported by EK and ERE and would govern the country for a lengthy period. *"Passions would calm down, the attacks*

---

1 Kanellopoulos, *op. cit.*, pp. 99-101.
2 Text des Memorandums in Linardatos, *op. cit.*, V, pp. 378-380.
3 Einzelheiten Kanellopoulos, *op. cit.*, pp. 104-110; *Archiv der Gegenwart*, p. 12.891.
4 *FRUS 1964-1968*, XVI, p. 520. Die Namen waren G. Papadopoulos, I. Ladas, D. Stamatelopoulos, D. Ioannidis, A. Lekkas, M. Roufogalias und I. Mexis.

against the King would die out, the situation would be 'normalized', and then, then and only then, we could have elections. I answered that Norbert should not be wasting his time over such pipe dreams. But I was wrong. They turned out not to be pipe dreams at all."[1] Andreas did not understand the range of the proposals and remained stubbornly on his own course. When on 20 December 1966 he heard about the resignation of Stefanopoulos and his father's approval of the Paraskevopoulos government of he broke with his father.[2]

On 22 December 1966 the cabinet Paraskevopoulos was inaugurated. In a radio message to the Greek people the King announced that after consultations with the leader of the political parties he intended to install an interim-Government which would prepare the country for election which would take place et the end of May 1968. It was necessary to lead the country back to quietness and order. Foreign Minister Oikonomou-Gouras added that they would take care of the existing serious national problems re the dialogue with Turkey.[3]

From December 1963 to the elections in February 1964 Ioannis Paraskevopoulos had led the country to the complete satisfaction of everybody. He was governor of the National Bank of Greece and now on 22 December 1966 he became PM and minister of coordination and defence. The general director of the Foreign Ministry, Pavlos Oikonomou-Gouras became Foreign Minister. Christoforos Stratos became Minister of the Interior and Sofoklis Tzanetis Minister for public security. Most of them had a professional qualification, an academic career and and were politically neutral. Since most of them had become minister under a ERE government they sympathized of course with the conservatives but they were no party politicians and did not follow traditional party politics.[4]

Thus the country could have come restbut now the ASPIDA affair boiled up and poisoned the political climate completely and led to the retreat of Paraskevopoulos on31 March 1967. The Iouliana which had been triggered by the royal coup on 15 July 1965formed a break in Greek history. It lead to a renewed polarization of the political forces. From now on the left centre and the moderate left fought against the right centre and the right. The radical Communist Left (EDA) did scarcely play any role any more despite the fact that the Right and their sympathizers in the US Embassy were still conjuring the Communist danger. The weakening, even paralysis of the democratic camp by the King opened the door to the establishment of the military dictatorship on 21 April 1967.

1 Papandreou, *Democracy at Gunpoint,* p. 195.
2 *Ibidem*, p. 196.
3 Nikos Kranidiotis, *Anoxyroti politeia. Kypros 1960 - 1974. I* (Athina: Estia, 1985), I, p. 393f.
4 Provatas, *op. cit.*, p. 730; *Archiv der Gegenwart*, p. 12.891.

THE ROAD TO THE PUTSCH OF APRIL, 21 1967

In the autumn of 1966 the ASPIDA-trial had begun before the military court in Athens. On 29 September 1966 the fact finding commission submitted a report of 457 pages which intended to prove that over 700 officers had participated in an effort in July 1965 to overthrow the King. But only 28 officers were indicted. Te evidence presented was very doubtful and only based on hearsay. The accusations were grotesque or wild claims without any evidence. Andreas Papandreou had been the leader of the conspiracy; he had planned a coup à la Nasser that was to bring him to power. He had intended to announce a republic and lead Greece out of NATO. [1] Papandreou's reply to this attack was characteristic: *"After fifteen months, the edict on the Aspida affair has finally seen the light of day. [...] Everyone knows the reason. Since there was no evidence, evidence had to be manufactured. Since it could not be discovered, it had to be forged. Finally, today came the disclosure. Never has there been a judicial report as empty as this one in positive evidence. Despite the illegitimate means that were employed, convincing evidence could not be forged. [...] Both the names and the depositions of the witnesses for the prosecution created a general feeling of hilariousness. This is today the general impression. Among the circles of the opponents of the Center Union there is deep disappointment, as a result of the empty edict, which is not a judicial document, but a miserable editorial of the worst type of yellow press. Among democratic citizens, the feeling has gone beyond contempt and has reached the tone of comedy ... The number of officers in the Greek Army is greater than ten thousand. Following fifteen months of investigations, twenty-eight officers are referred to trial. When this happens, we shall find out how many among them are guilty, and to what degree. Today we restrict ourselves to noting the number. For was it possible that these twenty-eight officers could have overthrown the regime?"*[2]

Even at this stage there were efforts to bring the ASPIDA affair to an end by an amnesty because the ASPIDA report mentioned Mitsotakis who had been the strongest person in the Stefanopoulos cabinet. But G. Papandreou knew that an amnesty would weaken EK and hurt the position of his son in the party and in politics. Therefore he turned to the public: *"There is circulating a rumour that amnesty will be given to those charged, in order to terminate this adventure. Before the people we answer: No! We decline. The affair should be taken to the courtroom in order to have the truth emerge from the confrontation with the witness for the defence, in order to prove that we are not guilty of this conspiracy. Rather are guilty those obscure forces that have pushed the nation to anomaly, and that are now preparing even greater adventures for it. This is what we demand, that the truth may shine."*[3]

On 1 October 1966 the ASPIDA trial began. The prosecutor accused the 28 officers of high treason and claimed that Andreas Papandreou had been their leader and Georgios Papandreou had been informed about the events as well. In the right wing press the wildest rumours were spread and most absurd assertions were printed.[4] The real trial began in the middle of November. Quickly it became clear that was a travesty of justice and that the verdicts had

---

1 Jean Meynaud, *Bericht über die Abschaffung der Demokratie in Griechenland* (Berlin: Wagenbach, 1969), p. 45; C. M. Woodhouse, *The Rise and the Fall of the Greek Colonels* (New York: Franklin Watts, 1985).

2 Andreas Papandreou, *Democracy at Gunpoint*, p. 190; Linardatos, *op. cit.*, V, p. 363f.

3 *Ibidem*, p. 190f.

4 Dimitrios N. Chondrokoukis, *Oi anentimoi kai o ASPIDA* (Athen: Kedros, 1976), p. 217; Aris Bouloukos, *Ypothesi ASPIDA. ..I alitheia pou kaiei* (Athen: O Typos, 1989), p. 340. The are the names of the accused officers.

been determined. On 21 November the court listened to the witnesses of the prosecution. Andreas Papandreou participated in this session and gave a statement to the press: *"I wish to point out, through my presence here, the flagrant violation of the constitution and of the Greek citizen's basic rights upon which the Aspida frame-up rests. ... It is clear that the whole procedure is null and that the verdict will be unfounded. It is also clear that, despite all the violations of the constitution, despite all the desperate efforts to justify the July 15 [1965] royal coup d'état through a prepared Aspida verdict III a military court, the plot against the nation, the national Army, and democracy will be uncovered. And the real plotters will also be uncovered, to be forever sentenced by public opinion, the nation, and history."* [1] It was obvious that Andreas wanted to provoke the King, the parakratos and the military.

In the course of the trial the prosecutor did his best to accuse leading members of the EK of cognizance of the ASPIDA plot but he did not succeed. On the contrary at the Lambrakis trial in Thessalonika more and more leading officers of the gendarmerie were called to account. The plan of the Palace, the Greek right and of the parakratos to weaken the EK did not succeed. This contributed to the willingness of the King to reconcile with G. Papandreou. The inauguration of Paraskevopoulos as Prime Minster on 20 December provoked the break up between father and son Papandreou.

Andreas Papandreou did not grasp that Greek politics had gone through a decisive change and clung to the old course: If they supported the Paraskevopoulos government they would legitimize the overthrow of the King and ridicule the past struggles. If they cooperated with ERE on this question it would be impossible to gain an absolute majority in the elections. Then followed the analysis of the situation which was correct in certain points but rather wrong in general: *"It is therefore clear that we would be playing right into the hands of the Establishment, of hands of the Establishment, of the Palace, and of the Americans. Even if we managed to obtain a relative majority [...] we would have to collaborate with the National Radical Union to form a government. And this would mean that we would be unable to carry through our basic program. For there exists no minimum program today that could be accepted by both the National Radical Union and the Center Union. Such a collaboration, post-electorally, would require a total capitulation on our part. The Greek people are politically mature; they would sense the meaning of our vote of confidence to Paraskevopoulos. They would feel that our 'unyielding' fight against the King's arbitrariness, against his flagrant violation of our constitution, was a sham. But beyond this, it should be clear that Paraskevopoulos will not move directly to elections. He will not act as a caretaker government. For a caretaker government dissolves Parliament immediately and proceeds to elections within forty-five days. Why does he need a vote of confidence? Because he intends to stay in power for some longer period of time. Why? In order to lay the foundations for a military take-over, in case popular sentiment has not switched away from us. No! It is our clear duty to vote down the Paraskevopoulos government. But, of course, there exists the danger of a split of the Center Union. If George Papandreou insists in his support of Paraskevopoulos, if I insist on voting against it, the Center Union has come to an end. And this too meets the requirement of the Establishment, of the Palace, of the Americans. So our first task is immediately to develop maximum pressure on George Papandreou to revise his stand before he takes a public position. Later it will be too late. We move tonight."*[2]

During the following hours Andreas put pressure on many deputies of the EK in this sense. Since his father could not play with open cards and admit the existence of the agree-

1 Papandreou, *Democracy at Gunpoint*, p. 194.
2 *Ibidem*, p. 196f.

ment between the King and Kanellopoulos these counterarguments failed their outcome but doubts remained. Attempts of friends to reconcile father and son failed because Andreas was stubborn and when he heard that his father would support the government Paraskevopoulos he openly attacked the policy of his father in the press: He appealed to the leaders of the EK to reconsider the matter once more and vote against the government of Paraskevopoulos. A vote in its support would mean treason to the principle of the party and submission to the King. The army would remain a party army and under the control of the King. Greece would remain a satellite state of the Americans. The future prime minister would be representatives of the oligarchy. A new government would solve important national issues e.g. the Cyprus problem by suppressing the rights of the Cypriot people. The government promised new elections in cooperation with the King as soon the country was quiet again. This could only mean that the government was pursuing a merciless policy of intimidation. At the end of his speech followed the formalistic appeal that according to the situation the EK should close its rows and fight against the government jointly.[1]

The situation became even more confused when on 1 January 1967 the newspaper *Eleftheria* which was close to Mitsotakis published a protocol of the talks between Kanellopoulos, the publishers Eleni Vlachou and Christos Lambrakis and the political advisor of the King, Dimitrios Bitsios, in which the overthrow of the Stefanopoulos Government and the establishment of a Paraskevopoulos Government was discussed. The question from whom the protocol originated and whether it was true remained unclear. There were rumours that the "protocl" was the result of a wire-tapping action. Decisive, however, was its political effect because its content coincided with the historical facts. It was obvious that G. Papandreou and P. Kanellopoulos had discussed the overthrow of the Stefanopoulos Government and to establish a new Government and to hold new elections. Though Kanellopoulos and Vlachou denied the whole event and the leadership of the EK (Enosis Kentrou) denounced all statements regarding G. Papandreou as falsifications, the effects on the public and the deputies of the EK were immense, because in parliament the vote on a motion of confidence of the Paraskevopoulos Government was imminent.[2]

The deputies of the EK did not know anything about the manoeuvres in the background and only knew that G. Papandreou had decided to support the Paraskevopoulos Government. In the eyes of many EK-deputies this meant that the *"annnendotos agon"* had come to an end and they had fought 18 months in vain. The majority of the deputies accepted this this change of course by the leadership with discipline but a greater number of deputies of the left wing of the EK was not ready to follow the leadership unconditionally. They gathered around Andreas Papandreou. He understood that the final breakup with his father was threatening, if he should be fighting against his father. He might create a new party together with the left "apostates"(renegades) of his own party but this party would scarcely succeed between the EDA and the EK. The remaining EK would find itself in a middle-right position of the political spectrum which would reduce their chances in election massively. This would have forced them into a coalition with the liberal part of the ERE around Kanellopoulos. If Andreas knuckled down to the will of his father he would loose face towards his followers. Andreas was confronted with a classical dilemma he could overcome only by a most complicated manoeuvre.

He agreed with his adherents that they would absent themselves from the session of the parliamentary group on 4 January 1967. This came about and 45 of the 122 deputies and Andreas himself did not show up. Allegedly more deputies were ready to boycott the meeting.

1 *Ibidem*, p. 199f.
2 Linardatos, *op. cit.*, V, p. 390f. Papandreou was not mentioned.

But G. Papandreou was not impressed and declared that whoever voted against the party line in the decisive vote of parliament or abstained from voting would be excluded from the party. Now hectic indirect negotiations between father and son via intermediaries began. Even Margaret Papandreou, the wife of Andreas, was involved. Finally a compromise was found: The left deputies of the EK would voted for the Paraskevopoulos Government in the vote of confidence. In return G. Papandreou would nominate only those 122 deputies who had remained true as candidates. The other 178 candidates would be nominated by Andreas which was a theoretical number because the Greek parliament counted 300 deputies only. In reality the number was 80 candidates who had a real chance to be elected. The were Andreas' personal followers and the apostates and their clique. Andreas and his followers mad it known in the press that they would vote for the Government but their reservations still existed. The vote of confidence on 9 January 1967 showed 216 votes for the Government, 61 against it and 15 deputies - mainly apostates of 1965 - who had abstained.[1]

For the time being the conflict between father and son, the right and left wings within the EK was reconciled but a new conflict was brewing. Reactionary forces continued to involve Andreas in the ASPIDA-trial. G. Papandreou had assumed that because of his support the Paraskevopoulos Government would drop the indictment against Andreas or at least not continue the trial. Allegedly there existed an agreement between G. Papandreou and Kanellopoulos about this. This, however, was a typical Greek method to get rid of the problem. But precisely this did not happen because the control of the ASPIDA trial regarding the indicted officers was in the hands of the military court and could only be influenced by the King. On the other hand the part of the trial in which civilians were involved - especially Andreas - was under the control of the General State Attorney, Konstantinos Kollias, who had close connections to Queen Frideriki. As long as parliament was not dissolved Andreas was protected by his immunity as deputy and could not be indicted, But as soon as new elections were announced and parliament would be dissolved his immunity protection would end.[2]

How precarious the situation really was is shown by the development of the court martial. There it became increasingly clear that it was a rigged game. Witnesses of the indictment told fairy tales. When on 26 January the public openly criticized the obvious scandal the military tribunal decided to meet in camera to protect the public order. G. Papandreou and Mitsotakis criticised this procedure strongly. G. Papandreou saw the constitution violated and Kanellopoulos condemned the the exclusion of the public severely.[3]

Though the King had concluded a preliminary truce this was not effetive for everybody in the whole royalist camp. In a conversation with Talbot G. Papandreou expressed the opinion that Queen Frideriki was against the truce, as she. but had fortunately been in India when the negotiations about the Paraskevopoulos Government took place. But on the other side the truce did not hinder Andreas to badmouth the monarchy though in agreed that the attacks on the monarchy from the side of the EK would be stopped. *Eleftheria* at once published Andreas' remarks probably as a small revenge of the editor for the overturn of the Stefanopoulos Government. G..Papandreou additionally assured Talbot that he would support the interim-Government if it kept its promise and to hold free elections.[4]

---

1 Linardatos, *op. cit.*, V, pp. 390-392, 395f; Papandreou, *Democracyat Gunpoint*, p. 201f; M. Papandreou, *op. cit.*, p. 124; Rousseas, *op.cit.*, p. 48f. He speaks of a party congress but it was a caucus.

2 M. Papandreou, *op. cit.*, p. 124.

3 Linardatos, *op. cit.*, V, p. 397f; Papandreou, *Democracy at Gunpoint*, p. 203f.

4 Alexis Papachelas, *O viasmos tis ellinikis dimokratias. O amerikanikos paragon, 1947-1967* (Athen: Estia, 1997), p. 276.

Andreas' constant attacks on the monarchy on 28 January 1967 prompted the political advisor of the King, Bitsios, to rat on Andreas at the CIA station chief, John Maury, worked under cover as first secretary of the Embassy. Andreas allegedly tried to instrumentalize the ASPIDA trial for his purposes: *"Bitsios went on to say that it now seemed perfectly clear that Andreas was serving the purposes of the Communists and the Soviets."* When Ambassador Maury wanted to have evidence for these claims Bitsios admitted *"that there was no 'direct' evidence, but he felt the 'circumstantial' evidence was conclusive. He said that he had no doubt that Andreas was receiving generous financial support from Moscow and from KKE."*[1] When Maury wanted to learn details Bitsios became vague but he stressed, that *"everything that Andreas has said and done demonstrated his sympathy with Communist and Soviet aims and his hostility to constitutional government in Greece and to Western unity."* When Bitsios asked how the Americans would react at "extreme measure", i.e. a coup d'état Maury replies clearly that the reactions would be very negative. *"It is our general observation around the world that unconstitutional measures rarely solve knotty political problems, and once such a course is embarked upon it is dificult to turn back. Whatever we may suspect of Andreas' motives and affiliations, there is still no proof of active Communist or Soviet connections. However Andreas may look to us from the perspective of Athens, the fact remains that in the US and perhaps in several other countries, he has influential admirers in intellectual, political and academic circles."*

Maury asked Bitsios under which circumstances he would consider a putsch necessary. Bitsios gave to understand that if an absolute majority of the Centre Union in the elections was imminent a putsch might be necessary to avoid that. However, he left it open whether he meant the next elections or future elections from which Andreas emerge victorious. Maury replied: *"I reiterated that whatever justiication might be found here for an unconstitutional solution, I saw no way in which it could be justified [...] If Andreas was the threat that many believed him to be, it was difficult to see why influential and responsible Greeks did not work more vigorously against him."* Bitsios agreed and declared that in ERE there was no strong leader. The purpose of the conversation was to find out the American attitude i.e. of the CIA in regard to a putsch.[2]

In early February Maury tried to convince Ambassador Talbot that a covert operation should be begun aiming to influence the election result, Talbot rejected this idea.[3] But the CIA resident did not give up and thus this topic continued to be discussed during the following days. It became obvious that Norbert Anschuetz, too, favoured covertly influencing of the elections.[4] On 11 February 1967 Talbot gave in and demanded from Washington the permission of a *"limited covert political action in connection with the forthcoming Greek elections."* He reminded the State Department that in former times such actions had been made against EDA. But this time the task is, *"to restrict dimensions of power base being built by Andreas Papandreou, by encouraging support for certain competitive elements."* In the text published by the State Department any explanatory statement is missing because this information was

---

1 In the Greek right wing press, especially in *Kathimerini similar* contentions were raised. On 2 March this paper alleged that the Communists were controlling the Centre Union. On 14 March they wrote that the Communists used the Papandreous to conquer Greece. Taki Theodoracopoulos, *The Greek Upheaval. Kings, Demagogues and Bayonets* (London: Stacey, 1976), p. 161.

2 *FRUS 1964-1968*, XVI, pp. 528-530.

3 Laurence Stern, *The Wrong Horse. The Politics of Intervention and the Failure of American Diplomacy* (New York: Times Book, 1977), p. 37. Maury wrote: *"The initial reaction of the American Ambassador, Phillips Talbot to this proposal was ambivalent. For a deep believer in both the evils of military dictatorship and the sinfulness of CIA covert operations, it was not any easy choice."*

4 Papachelas, *op. cit.*, p. 279.

not "declassified". Obviously the CIA had censored the text of the telegram but in the footnote of the document there is reference to the study of Papachelas where details be found about deputies, which were inimical to Andreas. Among them members of the Centre Union, the FIDIK (the recently founded party of the Apostates), of ERE and the Independents. Details of the action would be conveyed to the State Department and the CIA. The latter telegram was of course not "declassified".[1]

Talbot explained that he had agreed only after long hesitations but a success in the elections might prompt Andreas to change course of his foreign policy. Though Andreas was not controlled by the Communist Party he had embraced many foreign policy aims of EDA and propagated them intensively *"significance is that he gives respectable centrist cover to advancements of Communist policies. Moreover, his public commitment to these policies has become so complete that EDA and his personal supporters from the left will have effective grip on him should he attain high office after elections. American interests in Greece would be vulnerable to substantial erosion in such an atmosphere."* In these elections Andreas might succeed in taking over the leadership of the Centre Union, other forces might take over the lead. If they succeeded in weakening Andreas. *"Upsurge of Andreas' strength is deepening dichotomy in Greek public life to degree his incipient success might set off rightist counterrevolutionary attempts with prospectively adverse consequences for Greece and for the Alliance. What we don't need in NATO now is a Greek military dictatorship."* On the other side, the forces which rejected Andreas had the majority but were totally disorganized.[2] They were not capable of stopping Andreas..The necessary financial means for this operation were estimated to amount to 100,000 $.[3]

On 8 March the 303 committee responsible for covert operations among other things discussed the proposal of the Athens Embassy. The US Deputy Secretary for defence, Cyrus Vance, had already expressed doubts. Secretary of State Foy D. Kohler and Presidential advisor Walt W. Rostow voiced greatest reservations: *"Was the threat that great? [...] Was it not possible that we were attributing more potential to Andreas than he deserved?"* Since Vance had to go to another meeting the group adjourned to 13 March.[4] On that day Vance let it be understood that he was against a realization of the proposal except if there were overwhelming reasons that asked for it. Kohler reported that the State Department was of different opinions and would ask Secretary of State Rusk for his view. At the same time it was stated that *"if it looked likely that Andreas was moving closer to victory, the monarchy and the military could well suspend the constitution and take over. The military was estimated as being loyal to the king."* On 14 March Kohler spoke with Rusk about the project and the latter flatly rejected it. The political gain would be nothing in comparison to the damage that would be caused if it became known in the public.[5]

The decision of the military tribunal to negotiate behind closed doors in the ASPIDA trial triggered waves of protest. All 45 defence lawyers resigned from their office. On 23 February the Chief of the General Staff, General Tsolakos, gave testimony to the tribunal and showed that some of the officers indicted were totally innocent. The courts martial was a shame for

---

1 *FRUS 1964-1968*, XVI, p. 541; Papachelas, *op. cit.*, p. 280.
2 *Ibidem*, 541f.
3 Papachelas, *op. cit.*, p. 280.
4 *FRUS 1964-1968*, XVI, p. 551f.
5 *Ibidem*, p. 554f; Peter Murtagh, *The Rape of Greece. The King, the Colonels and the Resistance* (London: Simon & Schuster, 1994), p. 106f. The reason for this restrained position of the US-Government was double. Firstly the Vietnam war was on its climax and secondly in the US press articles had appeared about covered operations in the form of financing student organisations, trade unions etc.which had caused great indignation.. Stern, *Wrong Horse*, p. 37.

the Greek Army.[1] On 24 February the office of the Athens district attorney requested that the immunity of the deputies Pavlos Vardinogiannis und Andreas Papandreou, should be repealed so that they might be charged with treason. Both agreed that their immunity could be suspended by the appropriate committee but Andreas added that in this case the ASPIDA affair and the breaches of the constitution by the King had to be discussed in parliament. Andreas was informed that Frideriki was the driving force behind the manoeuvres of the State Attorney. The political climate deteriorated day by day. The right wing press agitated against Andreas and on 6 March even attacked Kanellopoulos who was too moderate in their eyes. As the newspapers of the Centre Union counterattacked the old lines of confrontations became visible again and the relations between G. Papandreou and P. Kanellopoulos became tense because deputies of both parties turned against each other. 11 member (10 of the EK and one deputy of EDA) voted against the suspension of the immunity during the meeting of the committee of immunity questions and 6 deputies of ERE and one FIDIK who wanted to take revenge and one deputy of the Progressives voted for the suspension of the immunity. Three other FIDIK deputies did not show up at the session. In short it was a question of time when the cooperation between G. Papandreou and P. Kanellopoulos would break apart. After the dissolution of parliament the conflict would become visible. Then Andeas Papanderou's immunity would ended and he could even be arrested.[2]

On 6 March the CIA rsident in Athens reported that the chief of the army general staff, Lieutenant Grigorios Spandidakis had told him that during the previous ten days a greater number of low-ranking officers in key positions had been transferred for the implementation of the operation "Ierax". *"Ierax Number Two is a plan for the military take-over of Greece contingent upon the occurrence of another political crisis. In the event such a crisis occurs, the plan outlines the role of the key military units which would be involved in the take-over."* Spandidakis added that these preparations had been made by order of the Palace. There followed a list of the commanders, mainly generals, but among them was the name of Lieutenant Colonel Papadopoulos. Additionally 35 higher officers had been transferred to command pots in the vicinity of the capital. Similar measures had been taken in the Air Force. These had been ordered by the aid de camps of the King, major Michail Arnaoutis.[3]

Later Spandidakis told that he himself had ordered Papadopoulos and Makarezos to plan the operation Ierax II. The 35 officers mentioned by Spandidakis probably belonged to the small junta, that of the colonels. Operation Ierax II is mentioned in the literature and it often means the Big Junta , the junta of the generals. Woodhouse who is rather well informed of Greek developments wrote about it: *"The so-called Generals' plot was lso an almost total fiction. [...] There was no evidence that they had conspired with each other; nor that they had even discussed the possibility of a military intervention with each other until the day before the Colonels' coup."*[4] The big junta was formed by the clique from the Palace (Frideriki, Arnaoutis) and right-wing politicians (Pipinelis, Garoufalias). The members of this clique, Generals and rightwing politicians regularly met in the house of Konstantinos Maniadakis the former police minister during the Metaxas dictatorship. IDEA, a right-wing secret organization provided most of the members of the big junta, while the colonels belonged to the EENA.[5] The aim of the big junta was he introduction of martial law and the establishment of an interim-government headed by Panagiotis Pipinelis. They worked rather carefully and

1 Papandreou, *Democracy at Gunpoint*, p. 204.
2 *Ibidem*, p. 208; Linardatos, *op. cit.*, V, p. 404f; Rousseas, *op. cit.*, p. 56f.
3 *FRUS 1964-1968*, XVI, p. 552f. On the tight atmosphere M. Papandreou, *Nightmare in Athens*, p. 126.
4 Woodhouse, *Rise and Fall*, p. 16.
5 On the pre-history of IDEA and EENA see vol. 3, pag 590ff.

wanted to act only a short time before the elections and even then only in agreement with the King. The activities of the big junta di not remain secret. Andreas Papandreou reports in his memoirs that he was constantly informed and passed this information on to his father.[1] The colonels', however, whose plans, remained secret, pressed for action. In early March Papadopoulos informed his co-conspirators that they would act on 25 March, the National Greek Holiday, but the date was postponed.

On 10 and 11 March the military state attorney presented a 10 hours summary attacking father and son Papandreou but also Mitsotakis and Tsirimokos. On 16 March the courts martial pronounced a verdict: Of the 28 officers indicted 15 were sentenced to prison and 13 discharged. Four officers were sentenced to 18 years, three others to 13 years and 3 others to 8 years prison and were discharged from the army. Five other officers received three to eight years of jail. Among them were three offiers who were acquitted of the origunal charge but were condemned because they had not passed on their knowledge of the conspiracy. 14 of those sentenced asserted their innocence to the end. Among those condemned most severely was the former vice-chairman the KYP during the Papandreou Government, Colonel Paterpos and lieutenant colonel A. Damvoulis, the former chief of the Greek military secret service in Cyprus. In the course of their interrogation the attorny had tried to drag A. Papandrou into the case which he failed to do even in the closed sessions.[2] The ASPIDA trial was a farce like the Lambrakis trial in Thessaloniki some months earlier when the assassins were sentenced to 11 and 8½ years of jail on grounds of bodily harm with fatal consequences by a heavy traffic accident. Snf not for first-degree murder. The officers of the gendarmerie who had been involved in the murder were acquitted.[3] Both trials served as means to intimidate the political opponents of the Right.

In early March Andreas Papandrou delivered a speech in the Athenian representation of the foreign press. In the introduction he compared the ASPIDA affair with that of Dreyfus in France in the year 1894. *"The ASPIDA case is but an aspect of the current Greek political problem. It is a symptom of the deep political crisis, of the deep conflict that is under way in Greece.[...] it discloses the ease with which a sector as important to the country as the Army may be shaken to its foundations, may have its morale destroyed, in the service of some tactical political advantage. It disclosed the ease with which the King (in his letters to the Prime Minister) not only concludes that there has been a conspiracy against the State, before any evidence had been brought to-bear on the matter, but also the ease with which he charges the Prime Minister and his immediate colleagues for being involved in it. It discloses the extent to which military justice in Greece is but a tool in the hands of the Right. It discloses the utter disregard for human dignity [...] and it discloses finally the ease with which the Establishment that dominates Greek political, social and economic life can use the smear, the slander technique, and finally the state machinery to combat a politician when it cannot defeat him in the political arena."*[4]

Then Andreas spoke about the fact that since its independence in 1832 Greece had always had a protective power, in the beginning Great Britain and then the US. During the Civil War the US had completely controlled the political life of Greece. This was true even in the following years. But now Andreas insinuated that the Americans still controlled the political life and this in two ways, by the Embassy, the CIA and the military mission: *"Greece, as a developing nation, a nation barely emerging from a semicolonial status, is extremely sensitive*

1 Linardatos, *op. cit.*, V, p. 406f; Papandreou, *Democracy on Gunpoint*, p. 208f; *FRUS 1964-1968*, XVI, p. 556.
2 Meynaud, *Abschaffung der Demokratie*, p. 50; Linardatos, *op. cit.*, V, p. 413.
3 *Archiv der Gegenwart*, p. 12.897.
4 M. Papandreou, *Nightmare in Athens,*, p. 129.

about its national independence, its freedom to chart its own international political course, its right to pursue freely its own national interest without placing in quandry its allied relationships. We do not raise the question concerning the participation of Greece in the NATO alliance. But at the same time we demand that Greece be recognized as an independent nation, which pursuing its own particular interests has chosen to be a member of the Western Alliance. Greece refuses the status of a poor relative, of a satellite. It insists on ist right while executing its obligations as an ally, to determine ist own course." Two representatives of the US-Embassy left the rooms after these critical remarks. Later they published a declaration stating that they had done this because their country had been criticised.[1]

But by this behaviour they intensified the impression which Andreas had denounced i.e. that Greece wasstill a client state of the Americans. The reaction of the press was enormous: The right press was irritated by Andreas' nationalist explosion and by his criticism of the *xenos paragontas* (foreign factor) because the conservative politicians acted always according to the principle *"ti thelei o xenos paragontas"* (What does the foreign factor wish)? They could not imagine acting against the will of the protective power. The newspapers of the middle critcized the inacceptable behaviour of the American diplomats and the left press felt in their prejudices confirmed. Embarrassing, however, was that many foreign newspapers reported the case also.[2]

Andreas Papandreou's claims were absolutely true if one judged them on European standards. Not one of the NATO-Allies of the Americans would have thought of informing the American Ambassador or the CIA Resident about internal political developments or even to consult them in regard to political decisions. But in Greece other rules of the game existed. Greece was a second class ally in which the US Ambassador had played the role of a proconsul during the civil war and after. The CIA was not put on leash. In the years after the end of the civil war the Americans had reduced the direct control but the behaviour practised before that time, the anticipatory obedience, remained active among the conservative ruling class, as already mentioned. Andreas Papandreou was socialized in the US and saw the clientelistic dependence of Greece with critical eyes of a former US citizen though the Greek-American relations of that time were almost liberal. The quality of the interference had been reduce to such a degree that it only still existed with Greek eyes.

On 17 March Ambassador Talbot, the official in charge of Greece at the State Department, H. Daniel Brewster and the member of the Embassy, John G. Day visited G. Papandreou in his house in the Athenian suburb of Kastri. Papandreou excused himself for the verbal attacks by his son and emphasized that the foreign policy ideas of the EK had not changed, but then he made critical remarks: *"In the past, particularly during the period of the late Ambassador Peurifoy, there was open intervention by the US, but in recent times, especially since the arrival of Ambassador Talbot, there has been no such interference. (Ambassador Labouisse once mentioned to him that CIA in Greece was not completely under his control)."* He intended to mention this in the forthcoming UPI-interview, which he did indeed. Openly he admitted that he had his fingers in the pie when Paraskevopoulos was appointed. He had promised to the King that he would support Paraskevopoulos and accept the new election law that was basis on a a simple proportional system even if this discriminated his own party. However, he wanted to go back to normalcy. Then Papandreou spoke about the "junta": *[He] expressed grave concern over the current activities of the 'junta'. In response to the Ambassador's question, he named Garoufalias, Pipinellis, and (retired) General Dovas as members of*

1 *Ibidem*, p. 130.
2 *Ibidem*, p. 131.

the junta. It also includes other retired generals and deputies who fear elections. The 'president' of the junta [...] is probably Queen Frederika." He was afraid that this clique intended to created conditions or establish a dictatorship by arresting Andreas as soon as parliament was dissolved; something which would trigger unrests to a great degree.

He had rccommended to the King via Bitsios to grant an amnesty un regard to the ASPIDA affair. This would cause an outcry among the media but this would not last long. Then Papandreou became almost prophetic. A dictatorship *"would be a disaster not only for Greece but also for the monarchy. King Constantine would soon find that he was no longer master of the situation and that on the contrary, he was a captive of the dictator, just as the King became a captive of John Metaxas."* The King should not take the slogans of Andreas seriously, only deeds and not words counted and as yet he was in charge of assessing the course of the EK. He hoped that Talbot would take the question up with the King.[1]

On 20 March in a speech in parliament Papandreou recommended the 28 May as election day. The next day Kanellopoulos agreed to this proposal, i.e. both sides adhered to the agreement of December.[2] On 23 March Papandreou and Kanellopoulos agreed that they fully trusted the Paraskevopoulos Government. While the moderate and liberal forces of ERE acquainted themselves with the idea that the elections should take place in May or at least accepted it. Yet the idea that elections would take place in May provoked panic elsewhere. On 24 March Ambassador Talbot reported on their activities. The right-wing group wanted to topple the Paraskevopoulos Government and postpone the elections by installing a new government. Members of this government would be ex-prime minister Panagiotis Pipinelis, the editor of *Eleftheros Kosmos* Savvas Konstantopoulos, ex-minister of defence Petros Garoufalias, former minister of security Christos Apostolakos, the former ERE deputy Nikolaos, of this junta Farmakis and Queen Frideriki. Probably the aide de camp of the King, Arnaoutis belonged to this group as well as the chief of the general staff Spandidakis, who in case of a crisis planned take over power (operation Ierax). The civilians among those mentioned gave thought how the present government could be overthrown and the elections postponed. They discussed if Andreas Papandreou should be arrested after the dissolution of parliament in order to provoke unrest or whether they could prompt the gendarmerie and the TEA to interfere in the election in favour of ERE which certainly would raise protest. They even mentioned Markezinis as new Prime Minister.[3]

The King's position was of particular importance. Allegedly he had been very satisfied with the solution Paraskevopoulos and new electionsm because then he could no longer be made responsible for his behaviour in 1965. But he was angry that G. Papandreou could not control his son more thoroughly: *"The King has begun to have second thoughts on wisdom of holding elections in May and of permitting EK [Enosis Kentrou- Centre Union], and, particularly, Andreas Papandreou to emerge as leading political force. King has undoubtedly been under strong pressure from rightists, including possibly his mother."*

But then Talbot talked about the military: *"In our view, a plan probably does exist for certain actions by military in event of a dictatorship, but there is no evidence that army leader-*

1 *FRUS 1964-1968*, XVI, pp. 555-557.

2 Meynaud, *Abschaffung der Demokratie*, p. 51.

3 *FRUS 1964-1968*, XVI, pp. 560-562. During a conversation with on 30 March Andreas Papandreou mentioned further names: ther ERE-deputy K. Maniadakis, the generals Spyros Mourikis, Berakis and Kolias, the lawyers Konstantinos Kollias, Chatziskos, Moustakis, Sokratis Sokratidis (attorney in the ASPIDA case), militasy attorney colonel Papapoulos and the retired general Verros. Papachelas, *op. cit.*, p. 287. These statements should be taken cum grano salis, because general Verros had already died. Indeed TEA had begun to spread nationalist propaganda in the villages of Northern Greece and together with the Gendarmerie terrorize dissenters. Rousseas, *op. cit.*, p. 50.

ship is actually plotting to create conditions leading to deviation from Constitution. On contrary, we hold to opinion that military would not seek ndependently to impose a dictatorship, but would support a dictatorship if King decided in favor of such regime." Regarding the establishment of a dictatorship the King and the other poitical leaders were told that this was considered extremely dangerous. He had the impression that the King wanted to avoid a dictatorship. The local CIA leadership agreed with this.[1]

Until 27 March the Paraskevopoulos Government had done its duty in compliance with the agreement of Papandreou and Kanellopoulos and there had been no major disturbances. On this day the Prime Minister called together the defence council in a special session. It was decided that the chief of the general staff, General Tsolakos, and the chief of the gendarmerie N. Panagiotakopoulos should retire. The first had angered the Right by his announcements during the ASPIDA trial and the latter had been too neutral. Allegedly Ex-Queen Frideriki had been in favour of the dismissal.[2] With this act Paraskevopoulos went beyond his competences because traditionally an interim-government did not have the right to take so far reaching decisions in regard to appointments. Papandreou recognized the intention behind all this but reacted only reluctantly. He would not withdraw the confidence in the government only to keep the elections on 28 May from becoming moot. *"We do not wish to offer the junta, which exists, conspires, and bides its time, the pretext that it needs."* Indeed Paraskevopoulos under the pressure of the Right seems to have thought whether the elections could be postponed for four months.[3]

On 29 March the crisis deepened as the parliament discussed the new election law. The Centre Union (EK) had accepted that the elections based on the simple proportional representation system would take place. Now a group of EK deputies proposed an addition according to which the immunity of the deputies should remain intact until the results of the new election was clear. The purpose of this addition was to prevent the arrest of Andreas Papandreou. Two deputies of ERE had proposed a similar modification of the law in the legal commission of the parliament in order to avoid investigation against member of the party. The parliament sat until late in the evening but no agreement was achieved - on the contrary - out of party tactical reasons they were at odds with each other. The deputies of the EK insisted on their proposal and the ERE deputies rejected it equally obstinately. Kanellopoulos was of the impression that Papandreou tried to torpedo their agreement and decided to object .A short time before midnight it was clear that the resignation of the Paraskevopoulos Government was a question of hours only.[4]

On 30 March Talbot had a conversation with the King: *"He represented himself as deadly serious in concluding that he cannot afford to risk the destruction of free Greece by permitting Andreas Papandreou to come to power. From that conclusion, if he should hold to it, there naturally could low decisions ranging on the extreme. At least for now the King's thinking has been narrowed to the question of whether he can stop Andreas by constitutional (or relatively constitutional) means or will be forced outside the Constitution into an extra-parliamentary government."* The King knew that the American Government totally rejected such solutions but now he wanted a clear raction to the present situation. He asked for a quick reply from Washington.[5] On 31 March he demanded for detailed instructions.[6]

---

1 *Ibidem*.
2 Linardatos, *op. cit.*, V, p. 415.
3 *Ibidem*; A. Papandreou, *Democracy at Gunpoint*, p. 210.
4 Kanellopoulos, *op. cit.*, p. 138f; Linardatos, *op. cit.*, V, p. 417f.
5 *FRUS 1964-1968*, XVI, pp. 562-564.
6 *Ibidem*, p. 567 Footnote 2.

On the same day on the advice of Kanellopoulos. Prime Minister Paraskevopoulos declared his resignation which was accepted by the King. The following two days the King talked with the leaders of the two parties. Constantine wanted to form a government of national unity and thus postpone the elections with the agreement of all. Of course the King did not mention this but received the party leaders to individual talks. Papandeou as leaer of the biggest party was received at first. He proposed to the King the dissolution of parliament, a renewed formation of an interim-government and elections within 15 days. Furthermore the King should proclaim an amnesty for all who had participated in the ASPIDA affair. If the King aimed at the formation of a responsible government he would be obliged to ask him, Papandreou, to form it, after all the EK was the biggest party. Should he ask the ERE to form the Government he would violate the Constitution and deviate from his position as neutral monarch who stood above the parties and would become a party leader. This would bring about new attacks against him.[1]

Papandreou repeated his demands in front the parliamentary group of his party and stressed that he would not aim at a popular government together with EDA. It was obvious that Papandreou tried to return to the December agreement and had the impression that the King was searching for a democratic way out of the crisis[2]

On 1 and 2 April the talks between the King and the party leaders continued. According to Andreas Papandreou the US diplomat Anschuetz advised to form a government of national unity together with ERE and to postpone the elections, else a dictatorship was threatening.[3] On Sunday, 2 April the King invited the party leaders to a kind of crown council session in the morning of 3 April to discuss the situation. Papandreou easily understood that the King together with the conservative politicians wanted to put pressure on him in order to form a government of national unity and to postpone the elections. Therefore Papandreou refused his participation in this session, but declared that he was ready to talk with the King alone. In the evening news the radio announced that the King had called together the crown council in order to discuss the formation of a government of national unity, Papandreou however, had refused his participation, and therefore the session had been cancelled. On 3 April the King ordered Kanellopoulos to form a government.

1 Rousseas, *op. cit.*, p. 60; A, Papandreou, *Democracy at Gunpoint*, p. 213f.
2 Linardatos, *op. cit.*, V, p. 419.
3 A. Papandreou, *Democracy at Gunpoint*, p. 215.

THE PUTSCH ON APRIL 21, 1967

The Kanellopoulos Government

The quickly formed government of Kanellopoulos comprised of both wings of ERE, Kanellopoulos had even managed to include even a member of the big junta (Pipinelis) for which Karamanlis congratulated him from his self imposed exile in Paris. In a radio message Kanellopoulos announced that the King had given him the power to dissolve parliament but nevertheless he would try to get a majority in a vote of confidence.[1] In order to achieve this Kanellopoulos tried to lure the smaller parties by promising them that the election law which had not yet passed by parliament but was favouring the smaller parties would pass soon if they voted for him. But it soon became clear that not even by this means Kanellopoulos would win a majority because in its actual form the law would not find a majority.

Papandreou condemned the formation of the Kanellopoulos Government as yet another coup by the King who had made himself leader of ERE. Then he appealed to the democratic world to fight against this scheme. In the elections a new Greece would be create and democracy would win a resounding victory. The US Embassy arrived in their analysis at a similar result. The decision of the King to entrust Kanellopoulos with the forming a government was probably the biggest mistake he had made so far: *"By granting mandate to Kanellopoulos, King has openly committed himself to ERE which probably has support of between 35% to 40% of population. This is obviously narrow ground on which to base his future. [...] Not only has King provoked EDA and EK, both moderate and Andreas Papandreou's supporters, but he also deeply embittered Progressives and FDK [FIDIK] deputies who feel they have been left in lurch after they came to King's rescue in July 1965. They have now unhappy choice of either voting for ERE Govt or going to elections under an electoral system which is to their disadvantage. Stephanopoulos has bitterly remarked to us that FDK and probably Tsirimokos and Progressives will abstain if Kanellopoulos Govt conducts elections."*[2] The US analyst did not even exclude an election boycott if Papandreou gained the impression that the elections might be falsified.

The ERE leadership had considered the right to dissolve parliament as a sufficient pressurising medium to win the small parties to support the government and being in power they were able to distribute rousfetia in order to attract voters, but "hard-core ERE ministers, on the other hand, would be willing to proceed to elections only if they were certain of ERE's achieving first place. [...] Therefore, we fear that ERE will soon realize that 45 days is not enough time to change situation appreciably and that effort will be made to find a pretext to postpone elections, if necessary, through a deviation from constitution." All party leaders distrusted each other and the future was sinister. The formation of a government of national unity might offer a way out of this dilemma.[3]

On 3 April Dean Rusk had replied to Talbot's questions of the week before. Since Talbot's detailed questions of 31 March were not published the detailed contents cannot be presented nevertheless it is possible to state that Rusk was decidedly against a dictatorship. *"We would be inclined to warn more strongly against possible constitutional deviation. Depth of Greek feeling against such a move should be more carefully weighed by King. [...] As*

1 Spyros Linardatos, Apo ton emfylio sti chounta, V, p. 420f. There is a list of all cabinet members. Panagiotis Kanellopoulos, *Istorika dokimia, I, Pos efthasame stin 21i Apriliou 1967* (Athens, 1979)., p. 14

2 FRUS 1964-1968, XVI, p. 569. Boycotting elections was a typical means of protest in Greek politics if it was clear that the elections would be manipulated. This form of protest sometimes had catastrophic consequence e.g. when the Leftists and Liberals boycotted the elections of 1946 and the Right gained a free hand.

3 *Ibidem*, p. 569f.

matter of principle, of course, US would be opposed to extraparliamentary move. You should stress point that US reaction to such move cannot be determined in advance but would depend on circumstances at time."[1] The latter remark was ambiguous, of course.

On 9 April Talbot passed on Dean Rusk's reply to the King. The King could not expect any support in case of an erection of a dictatorship: .*"I [...] noted our traditional opposition to dictatorial solutions to constitutional crises. They are wrong in principle and rarely work yet create many new difficulties."* The reply of the King showed his real anxieties and in which categories he though: *"He anticipated that a Papandreou government would move rapidly to retire or transfer officers loyal to the King and move Papandreou adherents into positions of trust, thus effectively ending the King's control of the armed forces. This would destroy his ability too keep Greece free and attached to West. He asked whether this is what United States wanted."* He expected that the crisis would begin when Kanellopoulos would ask for a vote of confidence and obtained no majority and would have to dissolve parliament. As soon as Andreas was arrested the question would arise whether the election should be postponed and Greece to be governed for some time, at least, without parliamentary agreement. If the first crisis would be overcome the next would follow in May when it became clear that ERE would lose the elections. It became clear that he saw the erection of a dictatorship as an alternative. Also in this case he would like to know whether the US were ready to defend Grece against an attack by the Eastern Block and keep Turkey from misusing the situation of Greece in Cyprus and to shield his country against a communist infiltration from the North. Talbot stressed that his Government rejected any dictatorial solution and would never make such a declaration. Turning to Washington Talbot stated that the King was in some kind of panic: *"He has concluded that only near miracle can save him from final choice of yielding his country to Papandreou, or establishing a dictatorship before or just after elections scheduled in May."*[2]

In the meantime background negotiations went on to overcome the crisis. Kanellopoulos made efforts to find a parliamentary majority for his vote of confidence. This, however, failed as G. Papandreou again managedto pull some apostates to his side by promising them seats in parliament. The King yet again tried with the help of some go-betweens to check the possibilities of an all-party government but did not receive a positive echo. During the conversation of Talbot and G. Papandreou on 13 April the latter stated that the King had made a capital mistake when he let Kanellopoulos form the Government. He was now King of the ERE. If parliament was dissolved and the ERE-Government held new elections then he and the whole Centre Union (EK) would run an election campaign with anti-monarchy slogans. Should the King establish a dictatorship this would lead to a new civil war. The only way out was to form a interim-government which would organize fair and honest elections. In order to control the neutrality of such a government, ministers without portfolio could be included, one from ERE and one from EK. He categorically rejected the idea of an all party government as the King wanted it.[3] On 14 April Kanellopoulos dissolved parliament and announced new elections for 28 May.[4]

A few days later Talbot sent another alarming message. Polarisation grew stronger: *"With the King and one party (ERE) now aligned against rest of political field, traditional instruments of power - Palace, armed forces, conservative political and economic interests - find themselves ranged against all centrists as well as leftist elements, undoubtedly representing*

1 *FRUS 1964-1968*, XVI, p. 567f.
2 *Ibidem*, pp. 570-572.
3 *Ibidem*, pp. 572-574.
4 Kanellopoulos, *op. cit.*, p. 174.

majority of population, who in turn act increasingly frustrated, angry, anti-monarchical and probably ant-Alliance." If elections were to take place Papandreou would be victorious. Against this all conservative forces fought: *"Fearing such consequences of adverse election results next month, coteries in Palace, armed forces and ERE are evidently building up steam for 'constitutional deviation', meaning dictatorship. They would hope to set things straight by period of firm rule and control of radicals."* If after the dissolution of parliament the chances of the Right in election did not improve the present Government would be changed into a emergency government supported by the armed forces and the King. *"Dictatorship can be avoided if at all only by very heavy American pressures on Palace, armed forces and rightist politicians. [...] King and Kanellopoulos have told me Greece 'will not' be delivered to Andreas Papandreou. Nonetheless, we must consider this possibility if we are to oppose dictatorship."* He, (Talbot), himself was of the opinion that Greece would survive Andreas Papandreou, though he has Nasserist tendencies. The best, however, would be if Karamanlis returned and Andreas left the scene.[1]

On 20 April 1967 Foreign Secretary Rusk replied. In Greece there were two critical issues at stake. First, Andreas Papandreou whose arrest in the context of the ASPIDA affair would lead mass demonstrations and measures of repression by the Government which in turn could lead the establishment of a dictatorship. Secondly, the King's fear of Andreas Papandreou who might deprive him of his power position by taking over control of the armed forces and the secret services. Talbot was told to advise Andreas to remain moderate and submit the following proposal to him: *"We would propose compromise based on iron-clad assurances from both sides. Our formula would envision assurance from King to G. Papandreou that Andreas Papandreouwould not be arrested, in return for following two concessions from Papandreou, on assumption he wins May 28 elections: (1) that he appoint only persons of 'mutual confidence' to sensitive positions of foreign affairs and Defense and (2) that he not carry out widespread shakeup in armed forces leadership. [...] You should attempt to induce George Papandreou to put such a compromise formula forward to Palace on his own. If he will not see King but asks youto help, you could serve as 'honest broker' and convey compromise proposal to King. [...] Would appreciate your comments urgently as to wisdom [of] foregoing proposal. Please include your thoughts re dangers, charges US meddling in internal situation. Also comment on possibility [of] approach being made through CAS [= CIA] or unofficial channel. Take no action in absence [of] further instructions."* Rusk's proposals went back to ideas G. Papandeou had developed some time before. Whether they would have been suitable to overcome the crisis must remain an open question because events overran it.

On 20 April 1967 a routine session of the highest military council under the presidency of the chief of the general staff, General Spandidakis, took place in the Ministry of Defence. In the early morning there had been a warning that a putsch was impending. Spandidakis ordered General Panagiotis Panouras to discuss this topic with - of all things - with Brigadier Pattakos. He himself discussed the matter with Colonel G. Papadopoulos. However, any measures were not taken because Spandidakis did not take the warning seriously. The session of the military council went off without a hitch. During a break General Lieutenant Odysseas Angelis suggested that the forthcoming crisis should be discussed in the context of the opening of the election campaign when G. Papandreou would stay in Thessaloniki two days later. Spandidakis agreed and ordered Angelis to call together some officer comrades for an exchange of ideas after the end of the session of the council.

1 *FRUS 1964-1968*, XVI, pp. 574-577.

Following the session the commanders of the three army corps (Kollias, Manettas, Zoitakis), the commander of Attika and the islands (Papadatos) and Spandidakis as well as Angelis met. When Spandidaakis wanted to know from his comrades, what they thought about a military action (Ierax) Kollias, Manettas and Christos Papadatos rejected it as a matter of principal except the King gave the green light. Angelis, Zoitakis and Spandidakis were in favour of an action, Zoitakis even without the agreement of the King. The majority agreed that they should talk about it to the King and Spandidakis was ordered to ask for an audience. But none of them saw any need for speed.

Quite in contrast the colonels hurried up. Four day after the dissolution of parliament, i.e. on 18 April, they decided to carry out their putsch on 22 April. When they heard from the Generals Spandidakis and Panourgias of the anonymous call and were informed by Zoitakis about the decisions of the generals they decided to bring the date of their putsch forward and hit in the night of the 21 April. At 2 o'clock in the morning the tanks rolled through the town and the putsch went on on the basis of the Promithefs plan with the clock-work precision; and in the morning of April 21, 1967 Greece was a dictatorship.

"No one outside the conspiracy seems to have had an inkling of the threat. The King had gone to bed late in his country house at Tatoi. The American Ambassador, Phillips Talbot, was asleep at home. Senior officers of the CIA and JUSMAGG appear to have suspected nothing out of the ordinary. The Greek Council of Ministers had met in the evening of the 20th, after which Kanellopoulos went back to his flat on the lower slopes of Lykavittos (Lycabettus). Andreas Papandreou spoke at a meeting of Democratic Clubs that evening, and returned to his house in the suburb of Psychiko - somewhat unusually, because he lived in fear of attack and frequently slept at the homes of various friends. General Papadatos, who commanded all the troops in Athens and Attica, had other engagements after Spandidakis' conference. Returning home on foot in the early hours of Friday morning, he was amazed to see tanks moving through the streets, without any orders known to himself."[1] If this description by Woodhouse is true, then what is behind the narratives spread around Greece that the CIA was behind the putsch of April 21, 1967?

Military Coup or the CIA in the Background

This was the title of one of the most informative books on the events in Greece by Stephen Rousseas in which it was eleborately 'proved' that the CIA had been behind it.[2] The book published by Wagenbach in Berlin is less apodictic but also adheres to the opinion that the putsch was the work of the CIA.[3] Andreas Papandreou reinforced this impression in his memoirs of that time: The putsch of April 21, 1967 was the work of the CIA.[4] In the historical consciousness of the Greeks the belief is present to this day that the coup of April 21, 1967 was the work of the CIA. The basis of this conviction ir formed by more or less fantastic conspiracy theories which all have one thing in common namely the absence of hard evidence. Even I was impressed and only while working on this article on the basis of reliable sources I recognized that Stephen Rousseas had been taken in by wrong information and that there had been no CIA involvement. C. M. Woodhouse formulated this accurately: *"Almost*

---

1 C. M. Woodhouse, *The Rise and the Fall of the Greek Colonels* (New York: Franklin Watts, 1985), p. 23.

2 Stephen Rousseas, *Militärputsch in Griechenland oder im Hintergrund der CIA* (Reinbek: Rowohlt, 1968), pp. 71-92. The English edition has this title: Stephen Rousseas, *The Death of a Democracy, Greece and the American Conscience* (New York: Grove Press, 1968).

3 The French edition bears this title: Jean Meynaud, *Rapport sur l'abolition de la démocratie en Grèce* (Montréal: Nouvelle Frontière, 1972).

4 A. Papandreou, *Democracy at Gunpoint: the Greek Front* (New York: Doubleday, 1970), pp. 226-236.

certainly there was no CIA plot either, though Greek mythology still insists that there was. [...] The Greeks are inclined to believe that everything which happens to them is due to foreign influences. But the Colonels needed no such external stimulus. They saw themselves as divinely chosen saviours of the nation after years of conspiring and experimenting, they took the dissolution of parliament on 15 April as the signal for action."[1] Woodhouse was right of course, but he also did not present hard core evidence. The first who presented verifiable proof was Laurence Stern in 1977. But his book *The Wrong Horse. The Politics of Intervention and the Failure of American Diplomacy* was banned by court and therefore was not taken notice of.[2]

Laurence Stern quotes a civil servant of the State Department who then worked in the US Embassy in Athens: *"We were looking at the wrong coup. [...] We were caught off guard."*[3] Indeed the Americans were informed about both conspiracy groups but in differing degrees. As we have seen in this article the CIA in Athens was very well informed about the big junta. Its military leader, general chief of staff Spandidakis informed the Americans about his plans (Ierax II). But this group of conspirators would act only when a putsch was considered necessary and the decision would be taken by the King. Since the aide de camp of the King (Arnaoutis) and his chief advisor (Bitsios) belonged to this circle and were in contact with the American Embassy the Americans were not only informed but could influence the developments. Additionally the King was in constant contact with the US Embassy and Ambassador Talbot had told him incessantly until the very last moment that Washington wouldn't support a dictatorship. Though specific right wing politicians and the clique around Frideriki a clock-work settled the King incessantly insecure but influenced by the US Embassy he procrastinated and postponed a decision. He would have given green light to the putsch if the takeover of power by the Papandreous would have become concrete but even this is speculation. In reality the King was a typical 'cunctator' who was afraid of taking decisions.

In contrast to the big junta direct information on the small junta ceased in December 1966 with the report on the session of the "revolutionary council" and finally in January 1967 when this group allegedly met again.[4] In the beginning of February an experienced analyst of the CIA centre by the name of Charilaos Lagoudakis was astonished that the information sources all of a sudden fell dry. On 6 February he sent a memorandum to his superior and to Brewster in the State Department in which he summarized the information about this group and suggested that they should try to get more information in Athens.[5] Since the Embassy and the CIA did not reply until April 21, as Stern assumed, that in Athens a group of extremely right-wing Greco-Americans on the CIA-team were interested in covering up,[6] In reality the CIA team was unable to distinguish the big from the small junta, as the report of the CIA resident of 9 March contained information about the Papadopoulos clique. On that day the Chief of the General Staff Spandidakis reported to the CIA chief in Athens about the planning of *Ierax II*, about the fact that certain officers (among them Papadopoulos) had been alerted and that 35 officers had been transferred to Athens.[7] As Linardatos reports Spandidakis allegedly ordered

1 Woodhouse, *Rise and Fall*, p. 20. JUSMAGG (Joint United States Military Assistance Group in Greece) stemmed from the time of the Greek Civil War and was coordinating the common war efforts.
2 Stern's book is neither in the Library of Congress nore in the British Library.
3 Laurence Stern, *The Wrong Horse. The Politics of Intervention and the Failure of American Diplomacy* (New York: Times Book, 1977), p. 41.
4 Stern, *op. cit.*, p. 43.
5 *Ibidem.*
6 *Ibidem*, p. 44.
7 *FRUS 1964-1968*, XVI, p. 552f.

Papadopoulos and Makarezos to prepare for ertain tasks of *Ierax II.*[1] They, however, misused the order to adapt the plan Promithefs to their plans. In view of this personal mixture it is astonishing that the local CIA could not recognize the difference. The small junta had become invisible behind the big one. Nothing changed when the former ERE deputy Nikolaos Farmakis gloated to Anschuetz about his knowledge of the preparations of the putsch by the small junta. The US diplomat did not take this information serious and saw no reason for action.[2] In the eyes of the CIA agents in Athens the activities of the small junta were a part of the big junta's preparations for a possible putsch of the King. As they knew that neither the generals nor the King would attack without recourse, they did not see any necessity to raise alarm. Thus one can come to the conclusion that the American diplomacy and the American secret services were well informed about the plans of the King and of the big junta nevertheless indulged in treacherous security. They simply had not noticed the preparations of the small junta. It may be assumed that if the had understood what was going on they would have reacted as decisively against this scheme as against the putsch plans by the King and the big junta.

To this day the Greek public believes that the Americans organized the putsch. This can be explained by a typical Greek phenomenon. The Greeks had encountered two types of interferences during the time of the civil war and in the following years which Theodore Couloumbis characterized as structural and manipulative: *"Structural interference is perhaps the easiest variant to study empirically. Here we must look for observable and measurable dependencies between small nations and the large nations which penetrate them. These dependencies can be subdivided further into military, political, economic, and cultural types. [...] Manipulative interference denotes the degree to which external powers are seeking to manipulate (i.e. change) the domestic and foreign policies of Greece in order to serve their own interests. It often involves an attempt to alter significantly the composition of a government. Manipulative interference can take place either through the use of military force (intervention) or through diplomatic, economic and other channels of influence."*[3]

In addition to this interference Couloumbis sees a perceived interference: *"Perceived interference is harder to assess. It is not dependent upon the actual degree of structural and manipulative interference, but upon the degree of supposed or believed foreign penetration of the Greek political system. There is also usually a time lag in perceived interference. A state which enjoys a high degree of influence in another state may continue to be held responsible for what goes on in the target state long after it actual influence has waned."*[4] The Greeks became aware of the structural and manipulative interventions in the past only through the appearance of the Centre Union (EK) in the early 1960s and the change of the political climate this caused. Andreas Papandreou was one of the first who denounced the past intervention in his speeches but he assumed that these interventions continued and thus he arrived at the "perceived" intervention.[5] This assumption shapes the conspirative historical interpretation of the Greeks to this very day.

---

1 Linardatos, *op. cit.*, p. 407.

2 Stern, *op. cit.*, p. 45.

3 Theodore Couloumbis, J. A. Petropoulos, H. J. Psomiades, *Foreign Interference in Greek Politics* (New York: Pella, 1976), p. 147f.

4 *Ibidem*, p. 148.

5 Typially: Andreas Papandreou, "Greece: An American Problem" *The Massachusetts Review*, 12:4 (1971), pp. 655-671.

The First Junta Government

The putsch of the small junta came as a great surprise. Shortly after 2 o'clock a.m. of April 21, 1967 Pattakos' tanks left the tank school in the outskirts of Athens and occupied all strategically important positions of the city. Light tanks surrounded the royal residence in Tatoi, cooperating infantry units arrested members of Government and the leaders of the opposition as well as loyal higher officers among them Major Arnaoutis. In the first hours efforts to stop the putsch failed because the chief of the General Staff had joined the putschists and they had interrupted all telephone lines. The High Commander of the Navy, Admiral Engolfopoulos refused any cooperation with the putchists and was promptly arrested; the Chief of the Air Force, General Antonakos, procrastinated. Spandidakis was even ready to send the code word *Promithefs* to the strongest military force of Greece, to the IIIrd Army Corps in Thessaloniki, thus ensuring the success of the putsch.[1]

At 3 a.m. US-Ambassador Talbot was informed that Kanellopoulos had been arrested. He went to the Embassy and informed the State Department. Then he tried to call his people together and ordered them to find out what had happened. A little after4 a.m. the American Military Attaché rang up the King and found him in panic: He had no prcise information. There had been arrests and he added: *"They are headed this way for me. Get word to Sixth Fleet. Get word to Washington and have them send your army in."*[2] Talbot passed this information on to Washington and recommended to the Government to be very cautious with issuing any declaration until the situation had become clear in Greece. Even the radio station, "the Voice of America" should not broadcast any comment.[3] In Washington the councillor of the President, Walter Rostow, advised President Johnson only to express his regret that democracy had been suspended.[4]

At 6 o'clock the three major putschists delivered a letter by Spandidakis to the Americans stating his support of the putschists. As ordered by the King Spandidakis arrived at Tatoi at about 8.30 a.m. He explained his behaviour by stating he had done so for monarchy and fatherland. Constantine decided to go to the Pentagon, the Greek Ministry of Defence, and put on his uniform and drove there together with Spandidakis. On the way he suggested that Spandidakis should take over the office of the Prime Minister but the latter refused this.The Attorny General Konstantinos Kollias should become the new Prime Minister. When the King arrived at the ministry he was enthusiastically welcomed by a group of officers..

During his conversation with the putschist trio (Papadopoulos, Pattakos, Makarezos) he demanded that Arnaoutis should be released. This was done immediately. Then he wanted to talk to the generals present in the Pentagon as a group and individually. This was also accepted. The putschists were rather sure and indeed only one general spoke against it. Later the King tried to persuade the trio to give up, but in vain, because the three felt confident and stubbornly kept to their position.

Generously they permitted the conversation between King and Kanellopoulos who was later arrested in the Pentagon. When Kanellopoulos understood that the King had come to an arrangement with the putschists he told him that he was no longer the King. When the King told him he would appoint Kollias Prime Minister Kanellopoulos replied that he regarded himself as retired. During the ensuing conversation the question was only who would become Prime Minister, Kollias or Spandidakis who was favoured by the colonels. Finally they agreed

1 Woodhouse, *Rise and Fall*, p. 25ff.
2 *FRUS 1964-1968,* XVI, p. 580 footnote 2; Papachelas, *op. cit.*, pp. 315-317.
3 Papachelas, *op. cit.*, p. 318.
4 *Ibidem*, p. 319; *FRUS 1964-1968*, XVI, p. 580 footnote 3. Very detailed: Cyrus L. Sulzberger, *An Age of Mediocrity. Memoirs and Diaries: 1963-1972* (New York: Macmillan, 1973), p. 338ff.

that Kollias would become Prime Minister and Spanddakis his deputy. Kollias who knew nothing of his luck was brought in and told about his new office. Makarezos became Minister of Coordination, Pattakos Minister of the Interior and Papadopoulos Minister in the office of the Prime Minister. Oikonomou Gouras remained Foreign Minister. Spanidakis beame in personal union Minister of Defence. At 17,15 p.m. the new government was inaugurated by the palace priest because the Archbishop Chrysostomos refused so pretending to be too old and sick.[1]

Subsequently Constantine went to his Athens residence in the Irodou Attikou street where he received Ambassador Talbot. The latter reported their conversation to Washington: *"King Constantine, blazingly angry, has just told me that neither he nor General officers control Greek army tonight. 'Incredibly stupid ultra-rightwing bastards, having gained control of tanks, have brought disaster to Greece,' he said. [...] According to King, government which he swore in tonight was forced upon him after five-hour rough session with coup leaders during which he had wrung sole concession that it be headed by civilian. King believes Spandidakis generally aware of plan and easily agreed to go along with three officers who mounted coup. King said he had contemplated shooting perpetrators when they came to Palace to be sworn in tonight, but concluded this would be worthless gesture as his Palace then surrounded by tanks loyal to them. King is unsure of next developments. He asked how long it would take helicopters to reach Tatoi to evacuate his family if needed. He also asked whether any possibility U.S. Marines could be landed in Greece if necessary to help him and Generals reassert their control over armed forces. He expressed view Greek troops would not fire at U.S. Marines. King also asked if I could make strongest demarche to his new government to insist that it not only maintain order and protect civilians who have been arrested but also strictly follow orders of King. He proposed that I say 'U.S. will hold King responsible for actions of this government and government responsible to King.'"*[2]

Talbot could offer the King little concrete help without first consulting Washington except in one case: He knew that a shipload with American war material was approaching the harbour of Piraeus. As the delivery of these weapons to the new regime might have been interpreted as kind of recognition he determined that the transport was diverted to Turkey.[3]

Shortly after te meeting with the King Talbot met Spandidakis and Nikolaos Farmakis which had been promoted to his advisor. Spandidakis organized a meeting with Prime Minister Kollias in which participated also. Kollias justified the putsch with an alleged Communist danger using the word extensively: *"By Communist [...] he meant not only those who belong to extreme left but also those who 'sympathize' with them. In latter category he undoubtedly was thinking of Andreas."* If the military had not reacted, so Kollias, a second Vietnam would have come into being. When Talbot asked what would happen to the arrested persons Spandidakis assured him that all former ERE minister would be released that very evening. G. Papandreou would be released also but not Andreas. No one arrested would have to suffer. Talbot criticized that weapons delivered by the Americans had been used for the putsch. He expected that the Government would keep order and return to normal as quickly as possible. Talbot expressed the hope that the army would soon again obey the generals and that the Government would listen to the King. Kollias and Spandidakis agreed and assured that they were on friendly terms with Nato. Besides that, as soon as normal conditions returned they intended to hold elections. Talbot received the impression that Kollias was just a

1 Woodhouse, *Rise and Fall*, p. 26f.
2 *FRUS 1964-1968*, XVI, p. 582f.
3 Woodhouse, *Rise and Fall*, p. 28.

puppet of the military, the question however was of which clique?[1] The State Department replied that it was possible to evacuate the royal family within 36 hours by helicopter should it become necessary. But a military intervention was excluded. Talbot was ordered to inform the King to that effect.[2]

Later in the evening of April 21 when the telephone lines worked again Eleni Vlachou rang up the King and wanted to know whether he had indeed made Kollias chief of government. The King admitted that he had been forced to face everything alone. She advised him to keep his distance to the putschists and avoid having taken pictures with them under all circumstances. She got the impression that he had accepted her advice. But a few days later the first photos appeared showing Constantine surrounded by his new government.[3] Obviously the King did not understand that he compromised himself by such actions and undermined the position of the monarchy.

In the early morning hours of April 22,Talbot sent this recommendation to the State Department this: *"(1) That for present we continue fairly starchy posture toward new Greek Government but still stay in touch with it and not burn bridges by threatening cutoff of aid and other drastic measures unless government's performance in next few days is rough and rotten. (2) That I attempt to stay in closest possible communication with King and that we rapidly canvass steps which could strengthen his hand, since King likely can prove principal focus for restoring normalcy. While I do not now expect situation to require emergency evacuation of Royal family, urgent response to King's request on helicopters would be practically and psychologically valuable. (3) That our public and press posture reveal our regret and our distaste for process of changing governments by military coups but also reflect a certain slowness to pass moral judgments since there remain so many gaps in our understanding of what has happened and why."*[4]

On 23 April Foreign secretary Rusk replied: The King had to remain in Greece except his life was endangered. His position in regard to the military was stronger than he assumed, because the putschists needed him and thus could enforce them to make concessions. This would strengthen his position in the public. They were ready to help the royal family in regard to an evacuation but it would make more sense if they remained on Greek soil. *"Finally, while we recognize that decision as to capitulation vs. resistance must be made by King alone, it is our view that if he capitulates he will have lost all opportunity for leadership. This does not mean that he may not have to compromise on some issues while showing his own stamp on the situation as he forces others to compromise, we would hope in as visible a manner as possible."* These proposals were correct but they asked too much of the 27 years old King who was simply inexperienced and did not have the intelligence and stability to steer such a course. Furthermore he could not find the clever advisors he needed among his entourage.

The presidential advisor Rostow was against any public reactions by the President at that time. But later, in his memoirs he regarded the silence which Rusk had kept as unsuitable. It was damaging the picture of the Administration in the eyes of the American intellectuals and Liberals.[5] On 23 April Talbot sent another analysis: The putschists controlled the situation by means of the army. The chances of a counter-coup were zero and even the King had accepted this: *"Coup is revolutionary. Its central core - Papadopoulos, described as the top theoreti-*

1 *FRUS 1964-1968*, XVI, p. 584f
2 *Ibidem,* p. 584 footnote 2.
3 Woodhouse, *Rise and Fall*, p. 29.
4 *FRUS 1964-1968*, XVI, p. 585f.
5 *Ibidem*, p. 586f.

cian; Pattakos, the top executive; and Makarezos - are limited, politically inexperience, tough-minded, no-nonsense types setting out to 'purify' Greek political, social and economic life. [...] They declare themselves thousand percent pro-American and are urgently seeking any hint of American understanding of what they're doing. With or without it, they know they must succeed or lose their heads." Andreas Papandreou had contributed to the putsch with his radical strange attacks on the Greek political system and on the army. *"Because they exceed bounds of Greek political tolerance and therefore induced deepest distrust in rightist quarters especially the army, Andreas lost chance to move Greece in directions he favored."* Talbot stated that the transfer of the 6th Fleet towards Greece had made the regime insecure. Finally he asked for instructions. The State Department informed him that the American military relief shipments would be stopped. *"In sum, we should follow a policy of watchful waiting, and an attitude of coolness towards new govt while encouraging King vigorously to support move towards more viable government."*[1]

On 24 April the State Department recommended a more distanced attitude towards the regime. One should leave it to the King to press for a liberalization.[2] On 25 April Talbot sent another situation report. The King had insisted during the first session of the cabinet that constituent committee should be inserted in order to show to its allies that Greece intended to return to a constitutional government soon. Talbot said that the Embassy would keep its distance towards the Greek Government. Constantine informed the Ambassador that the junta had demanded that Arnaoutis left the country and thus he did no longer have any advisor but he would try to strengthen his position opposite the junta.[3] During a conversation between Talbot and Pattakos on 28 April the latter promised the appointment of a constitutional commission. Nothing would happen to the internees in the meantime. Then he spoke about military logistics. Until 26 April 6,500 people had been arrested. Of these 1,701 had been released. Of the remaining ones, 1,558 had been transferred to the island of Giaros. And 1,727 were on their way there. 2,152 were still in prison on the mainland. The prisoners were divided in three categories, the first of which would be reeducated to turn them into good citizens. The Communists belonged to the group of the ineducable. Finally he stressed his wish to closely cooperate with the US.[4]

On 2 May 1967 Dean Rusk answered from Washington. He had the impression that the King moved back from the regime too fast. He was afraid that *"pressures within Greece for us to enter into normal relationship with regime result in our moving in that direction without having gained anything in return. We feel we must not permit our leverage to be dissipated thus."* The promises of the regime to return to normalcy soon were welcome but the US would appreciate more details. Then Rusk mentioned the American dilemma: *"We have been pondering whether we should to pin regime down to a definite blueprint of political steps in direction of normalcy and if so what this blueprint should be and how soon we should put it forward. The price would probably have to be the relaxation of our restrictions on military aid and the commencement of normal relations with the GOG, with the resultant disadvantages for the US image. [...] It has also been suggested here that we might use our present leverage to try to push the GOG further in the direction of a Cyprus solution, perhaps by pressing for agreement on a sovereign Turkish base on the island, or perhaps on the transfer of*

1 *Ibidem*, pp. 586-589 und footnote 3.
2 *Ibidem*, p. 590
3 *Ibidem*, pp. 591-593.
4 *Ibidem*, pp. 594-597.

Grivas. We doubt we have enough leverage to move the GOG very far on Cyprus, even should we decide to accept the disadvantages inherent in trying."[1]

Deam Rusk's apprehensions were realistic and Talbot's demands resembled a diplomatic high wire act which was partly recognized during the following months. The Arab-Israeli war in the beginning of June1967 (the Six Days War) ruined this act: *"The greatest stroke of luck for the junta was the outbreak, within two months of their coup, of the six-day war in the Middle East between Israel and Egypt. US facilities in Greece and Turkey then became essential for the defence of Israel as well as for NATO. Without any formal announcement, the ban on heavy weapons was progressively lifted. A further consequence was that it became urgent to settle the problem of Cyprus. When the US Administration hinted that negotiations should be renewed between Greece and Turkey, the junta responded satisfactorily."*[2]

In 2009 the US historian Miller came to the following conclusion: *"In the end, the United States got exactly the solution it had wanted to avoid. U.S. officials neither encouraged nor supported the coup of April 1967. Once it happened, they found themselves dealing with a brutal, repressive, and incompetent regime whose leaders wrapped themselves in the mantle of NATO and pointedly told their American interlocutors: 'we are your allies whether you like us or not'."*[3] You can only agree with this statement.

---

1 *Ibidem*, p. 598.
2 Woodhouse, *Rise and Fall*, p. 41.
3 James Edward Miller, *The United States and the Making of Modern Greece. History and Power, 1950-1974* (Chapel Hill: UP North Carolina, 2009), p. 135.

INDEX OF NAMES

On the next pages are information on the series of

PELEUS

PELEUS
Studien zur Archäologie und Geschichte Griechenlands und Zyperns bis Nr. 72
hrsg. von Heinz A. Richter und Reinhard Stupperich,

Vol. 1 **Ingrid Krauskopf**
Heroen, Götter und Dämonen auf etruskischen Skarabäen. (1995) 145 Seiten, 4 Taf., brosch., € 14,90

Vol. 2 **Heinz A. Richter**
Griechenland im Zweiten Weltkrieg 1939-1941 (2011) 456 Seiten, 41 Taf., brosch., ISBN 978-3-447-06410-1, € 49, (2. Auflage)

Vol. 3 **Volker H. Heenes**
Die griechischen Vasen der Sammlung Erbach. (1998) 90 Seiten, 41 Taf., brosch., € 25,50

Vol. 4 **E. Chrysos, D. Letsios, H. A. Richter, R. Stupperich (eds.)**
Griechenland und das Meer. Beiträge eines Symposions in Frankfurt im Dezember 1996. (1999) 222 Seiten mit 94 Abb., 8°, geb., ISBN 3-933925-03-7, € 24,50

Vol. 5 **Joachim G. Joachim**
Ioannis Metaxas. The Formative Years 1871-1922. (2000) 367 pages, 15 photos, 2 maps, 8°, hard cover, ISBN 3-933925-11-8, € 32,20

Vol. 6 **Michael Wedde**
Towards a Hermeneutics of Aegean Bronze Age Ship Imagery. (2000) 356 pages, 58 plates., hard cover, ISBN 3-933925-09-6, € 46,00

Vol. 7 **Özdemir A. Özgür**
Cyprus in my Life: Testimony of a Turkish-Cypriot Diplomat. (2001) 176 pages, 29 photos, 8°, hard cover, ISBN 3-933925-18-5, € 24,50

Vol. 8 **Karl Giebeler, Reinhard Stupperich, Heinz A. Richter (eds.)**
Versöhnung ohne Wahrheit? Deutsche Kriegsverbrechen in Griechenland im 2. Weltkrieg. Konferenzband der gleichnamigen Tagung der evangelischen Akademie Bad Boll. (2001) 98 Seiten, 8°, geb., ISBN 3-933925-16-9, € 19,90

Vol. 9 **Claude Nicolet**
United States Policy Towards Cyprus 1954-1974. Removing the Greek-Turkish Bone of Contention. (2001) 500 Seiten mit Abb., 8°, geb., ISBN 3-933925-20-7, € 42,90

Vol. 10 **Ingeborg Huber**
Die Ikonographie der Trauer in der griechischen Kunst. (2001) 271 Seiten, 24 Abb., 8°, geb., ISBN 3-933925-19-3, € 34,80

Vol. 11 **Alexander Papageorgiou-Venetas**
Eduard Schaubert 1804-1860. Der städtebauliche Nachlaß zur Planung der Städte Athen und Piräus. 192 Seiten, . 80 sw Abb., 4 Farbtaf., geb., ISBN 3-933925-21-5, € 39,90

Vol. 12 **Hermann Frank Meyer**
Von Wien nach Kalavryta. Die blutige Spur der 117. Jäger-Division durch Serbien und Griechenland. (2002) 556 Seiten, 193 Abb., 43 Kartenskizzen und Faksimiles, 1 farbige Faltkarte, 8°, geb. ISBN 3-933925-22-3, € 49,00

Vol. 13 **Andreas Stergiou**
Im Spagat zwischen Solidarität und Realpolitik: Die Beziehungen zwischen der DDR und Griechenland und das Verhältnis der SED zur KKE. (2001) 200 Seiten, 27 Abb., 8°, geb., ISBN 3-933925-17-7, € 32,70

Vol. 14 **John Charalambous, Alicia Chrysostomou, Denis Judd, Heinz A. Richter, Reinhard Stupperich (eds.)**
40 Years on from Independence. Proceedings of a Conference in the University of North London on 16-17 November 2000. (2002) 200 pages, 8°, hard cover, ISBN 3-933925-30-4, € 29,00

Vol. 15 **Ioanna Spiliopoulou-Donderer**
Kaiserzeitliche Grabaltäre Niedermakedoniens. Untersuchungen zur Sepulkralskulptur einer Kunstlandschaft im Spannungsfeld zwischen Ost und West. (2002) 277 Seiten, 62 Abb., 8°, geb., ISBN 3-933925-32-0, € 37,50

Vol. 16 **Emanuel Turczynski**
Sozial- und Kulturgeschichte Griechenlands im 19. Jahrhundert. Von der Hinwendung zu Europa bis zu den ersten Olympischen Spielen der Neuzeit. (2003). 586 Seiten, 3 Karten, 70 Abb., 8°, geb., ISBN 3-933925-34-7, € 45,90

Vol. 18 **Michael Attalides**
Cyprus. Nationalism and International Politics **(1979).** Reprint 2003. 226 pages., 8°, hard cover., ISBN 3-933925-35-5, € 35,00

Vol. 19 **Hubert Faustmann & Nicos Peristianis (eds.)**

Britain and Cyprus. Colonialism and Post-Colonialism 1878–2006. 656 pages, 30 photos, 8°, hard cover, ISBN 3-933925-36-3, € 49

Vol. 20 **Robert Stupperich**
Die griechisch-orthodoxe Kirche und ihr Verhältnis zu den Kirchen in Rußland und in Westeuropa. (2003). 256 Seiten mit 70 Abb., 8°, geb., ISBN 3-933925-37-1, € 32,50

Vol. 21 **Alexander Papageorgiou-Venetas**
Friedrich Stauffert. Städte und Landschaften in Griechenland zur Zeit König Ottos. (2008) 280 Seinten, über 70 Abb. 8°, geb., ISBN 978-3-941336-24-3, € 42,00

Vol. 22 **Vassilis K. Fouskas and Heinz A. Richter (eds.)**
Cyprus and Europe. The long way back. (2003) 212 pages., 8°, hard cover, ISBN 3-933925-41-X-3, € 32,50

Vol. 23 **Elena Pogiatzi**
Die Grabreliefs auf Zypern von der archaischen bis zur römischen Zeit. (2003) 322 Seiten mit 70 Tafeln, 8°, geb., ISBN 3-933925-42-8, € 44.50

Vol. 24 **Nicolas D. Macris (ed.)**
The 1960 Treaties on Cyprus and Selected Subsequent Acts. (2003). 212 pages., 3 maps, 8°, hard cover, ISBN 3-933925-53-3, € 32,50

Vol. 26 **Peter Loizos**
The Greek Gift: Politics in a Cypriot Village. (reprint of the 1975 edition). (2004). 344 pages. 8°, hard cover, ISBN 3-933925-55-X, € 36.50

Vol. 27 **James Ker-Lindsay**
Britain and the Cyprus Crisis 1963-1964 (2004). 143 pages. 8°, hard cover, ISBN 3-933925-58-4, € 24,50

Vol. 28 **Reinhard Stupperich (ed.)**
NOVA GRAECIA. Festschrift für Heinz Richter (2004). 260 Seiten, 8°, geb. ISBN 3-933925-63-0, € 32

Vol. 29 **Heinz A. Richter**
Geschichte der Insel Zypern* Band 1: *1878-1949 (2004) 560 Seiten, 8°, geb., 5 Karten, 1 farbige Faltkarte, 95 Abbildungen, ISBN 3-933925-64-9 € 42.50

Vol. 30 **Moshe Ha-Elion**
The Straits of Hell. The Chronicle of a Salonikan Jew in the Nazi Extermination Camps Auschwitz, Mauthausen, Melk, Ebensee (2005) 120 pages, 8°, hard cover, ISBN 3-933925-70 € 30, 21.50

Vol. 31 **Sevgül Uludağ**
Cyprus: The Untold Stories (2005) 120 pages, 8°, hard cover, ISBN 3-933925-72-X, € 21.50

Vol. 32 **Makarios Drousiotis**
Cyprus 1974: Greek Coup and Turkish Invasion (2006) 274 pages, 61 illustrations, 8°, hard cover, ISBN 3-933925-76-2, 38 €

Vol. 33 **Alexander Jossifidis**
Die Slawophonen Griechen Makedoniens (2006) 290 Seiten, 8°, geb., ISBN 3-933925-73-8, € 38,00

Vol. 34 **Sozos-Christos Theodoulou**
Bases militaires en droit international: le cas de Chypre (2006) 146 pages, 8°, hard cover, ISBN 3-933925-83-5, € 28,00

Vol. 35 **Heinz A. Richter**
Geschichte der Insel Zypern 1950-1959 (2006) 665 Seiten mit über 100 Abbildungen, 32 Phototafeln und einer herausnehmbaren farbigen Faltkarte (41x34 cm), 8°, geb. ISBN 3-933925-79-7, € 49,00

Vol. 36 **Ina M. Minner**
Ewig ein Fremder im fremden Lande. Luwig Ross (1806-1859) und Griechenland. Biographie (2006) 436 Seiten mit 73 Abbildungen, 8°, geb., ISBN 3-933925-82-7, € 42,50

Vol. 37 **Heinz A. Richter**
Geschichte der Insel Zypern 1959-1965 (2007) 644 Seiten mit über 100 Abbildungen sowie und eine herausnehmbare Faltkarte (41x34 cm), 8°, geb. ISBN 3-938646-12-5, € 49,00

Vol. 38 **Tim Potier**
A functional Cyprus settlement: the constitutional dimension (2007) 765 pages, 8°, hard cover ISBN 3-938646-20-9, € 49,00

Vol. 39 **Vaios Kalogrias**
Makedonien 1941-1944: Okkupation, Widerstand und Kollaboration (2008) 383 Seiten Text, 1 Karte, 4 Tafeln, 8°, geb., ISBN 978-3-938646-25-0 , 42 €

Vol. 40 **Maria Xagorari-Gleißner**
Meter Theon. Die Göttermutter bei den Griechen (2008) 175 Seiten 14 Tafeln. 8°, geb., hard cover, ISBN 978-3-938646-26-7 , € 32

Vol. 41 **HeinzRichter**
Geschichte der Insel Zypern 1965-1977 (2009) zusammen 808 Seiten, über 110 Abbildungen, 8 sw Karten, 8°, geb., ISBN 978-3-938646-33-5 , € 65

Band 42 **Wolfgang Decker**
Die Wiederbelebung der Olympischen Spiele (2008) 200 Seiten Text, 43 Abbildungen, 8°, geb., ISBN 978-3-938646-36-6, € 30

Band 43 **Glafkos Clerides**
Negotiating for Cyprus 1993-2003 (2008) 192 pages, 39 b/w photos, 8°, hard cover, ISBN 978-3-938646-37-3, € 30

Band 44 **Alfons Kitzinger**
Διχως σπαθια και βολια. Josef Schwind: Bilder aus Griechenland 1942 – 1944 (2009) 140 Seiten, 160 schwarz/weiss Fotos, 8°, geb., ISBN 978-3-938646-41-0, € 32.-

Band 45 **Mihailo St. Popovic**
Mara Brankovic: Eine Frau zwischen dem christlichen und dem islamischen Kulturkreis im 15. Jahrh. (2010) 238 Seiten, 15 Abbildungen, 5 Karten, 8°, geb., ISBN 978-3-938646-49-6, € 32.-

Band 46 **Hans-Martin Kirchner**
Friedrich Thiersch. Ein liberaler Kulturpolitiker und Philhellene in Bayern (2010) 289 Seiten, 5 Abbildungen, 8°, geb., ISBN 978-3-938646-50-2, € 35.-

Band 47 **Mustafa Bulba**
Geometrische Keramik Kariens
(2010) 222 Seiten Text, 55 Tafeln mit 370 Abbildungen, 8°, geb., ISBN 978-3-938646-42-7, € 35.-

Band 48 **Lucie Bonato et Maryse Emery**
Louis Dumesnil de Maricourt. Un consul pour la France (1805-1865) Naples, Messine, Séville, Stettin, Port Maurice Newcastle, Moscou, Larnaca
(2010) 308 pages, 10 pictures, 8°, hard cover, ISBN 978-3-938646-51-9, € 35.-

Band 49 **Heinz A. Richter**
Kurze Geschichte des modernen Zypern 1878-2009
(2010) 272 Seiten Text, über 100 Fotos auf 56 Tafeln, 1 Faltkarte, 8°, geb., ISBN 978-3-938646-53-3, € 35.-

Band 50 **Heinz A. Richter**
A Concise History of Modern Cyprus 1878-2009
(2010) 232 text pages, over 100 photos on 56 plates, 1 folded map, 8°, hard cover, ISBN 978-3--938646-53-3, € 35.-

Band 51 **Maria Deoudi**
Die thrakische Jägerin. Römische Steindenkmäler aus Macedonia und Thracia
(2010) 165 Seiten Text, 36 Tafeln, 8°, geb., ISBN 978-3-938646-54-0, € 35.-

Band 52 **Gerhard Weber**
Hellmuth Felmy. Stationen einer militärischen Karriere
(2010) 332 Seiten, 8 Tafeln, 8°, hard cover, ISBN 978-3-447-06299-2, € 45.-

Band 53 **G. R. Wright**
Cypriot Connections: An Archaeological Chronicle
(2010) 214 pages text, 13 plates and 122 pictures in Text, A4, hard cover, ISBN 978-3-447-06301-2, . € 39.90

Band 54 **Heinz A. Richter**
Operation Merkur. Die Eroberung der Insel Kreta im Mai 1941(2011) 320 Seiten Text, 80 Tafeln, 22 Karten, 1 Faltkarte, 8°, geb., ISBN 978-3-447-06423-1, € 49.-

Band 55 **John Sakkas,**
Britain and the Greek Civil War 1944-1949 (2013) 17x24, 150 pages, 10 plates with photos, hard cover, ISBN 978-3-447--06718-8 , € 30.-

Band 56 **Alexander Papageorgiou-Venetas,**
In Focus: Athens. Im Brennpunkt: Athen (2012)232 S. 147 Abbildungen, Format A4, geb., ISBN 3-447-06721-8 EAN: 978-3-447-06721-8, € 44,00

Band 57 **Ekrem Akurgal,**
Erinnerungen eines Archäologen (2013) 224 Seiten, gebunden, 32 Seiten Textabbildungen, 30 Seiten Zusatztafeln, ISBN 3-447-06875-2 EAN: 9783447068758, ca. € 35

Band 58 **Thorsten Kruse,**
Bonn - Nikosia - Ostberlin. Innerdeutsche Fehden auf fremdem Boden 1960-1972 (2013)17x24, 400 Seiten, 67 Fotos auf 32 Tafeln, hard cover, ISBN 978-3-447-06766-9 EAN: 9783447067669, € 49.-

Band 59 **Heinz A. Richter,**
Griechenland 1940-1950. Die Zeit der Bürgerkriege (2012) 17x24, ca. 550 Seiten, 20 Karten, 1 herausnehmbare Faltkarte, 150 Fotos auf 64 Tafeln, hard cover, € 49.-, ISBN 978-3-447-06704-1 EAN: 9783447067041,

Band 60 **Heinz A. Richter,**
Griechenland 1950-1974. Zwischen Demokratie und Diktatur (2013) 600 Seiten, 125 Fotos, Hardcover, gebunden, € 49, ISBN 978-3-447-06908-3

Band 61 **Mihailo Popovic,**
Historische Geographie und Digital Humanities. Eine Fallstudie zum spätbyzantinischen und osmanischen Makedonien (2013) ca. 300 Seiten, 33 Abbildungen, 44 Karten, 8°, hard cover, ISBN 978-3-938646-49-6, € 32.-

Band 62 **Joachim Franz, Rosmarie Günther und Reinhard Stupperich (Hrsg.)**
„Ein Wald von Statuen" Kolloquium zum 20jährigen Bestehen der Antikensaal-Galerie in Mannheim und zur Begründung der Kurpfälzer Abguss-Sammlung vor 300 Jahren 300 Seiten, zahlreiche Abbildungen, Hardcover, gebunden, ISBN 978-3-447-10302-2, € 37.-

Band 63 **Harald Gilbert,**
Das besetzte Kreta 1941-1945 (2015) 404 Seiten, 47 sw und 8 farbige Abbildungen, 1 Landkarte, Hardcover, gebunden, € 49, ISBN 978-3-447-10186-8

Band 64 **Harry Cliadakis** (ed. Heinz Richter)
Fascism in Greece (2014) 147 pages, 34 photos, hard cover, threadbound, ISBN 978-3-447-10188-2, € 39.-

Band 65,1 **Heinz A. Richter**
Krieg im Südosten I, Gallipoli 1915 (2014) 340 Seiten, 120 Fotos, 17 Karten, 1 Faltkarte, gebunden, € 42, ISBN 978-3-447-10118-9

Band 65,2 ***Krieg im Südosten II, Makedonien 1915-1918*** (2014) 250 Seiten, 91 Fotos, 4 Karten, gebunden, € 35, ISBN 978-3-447-10249-0

Band 66 ***Von Mainz nach Kreta im Winter 1942-43. Das Reisetagebuch des "Künstlersoldaten" Rudo Schwarz.*** (2015) 150 Seiten, 91 Seiten mit Reproduktionen des Tagebuchs und von Skizzen, 51 Fotos, Hardcover, gebunden, ISBN 978-3-447-10304-6, € 32.- (ed. Heinz Richter)

Band 67,1 **Heinz A. Richter, *Geschichte Griechenlands im 20. Jahrhundert,*** *Band 1: 1900-1939,* (2015) 350 Seiten, 4 Karten, Hardcover, gebunden, 40 Euro, ISBN 978-3-447-10396-5

Band 67,2 **Heinz A. Richter, *Geschichte Griechenlands im 20. Jahrhundert,*** *Band 2: 1939-2004,* (2015) 467 Seiten, 9 Karten, Hardcover, gebunden, 49Euro, ISBN 978-3-447-10398-5

Band 68 **Heinz A. Richter *Griechenland 1915-1917 im Spiegel russischer Akten*** (2016) 118 Seiten, Hardcover, 28 Euro, 2015 ISBN 978-3-447-10612-2

Band 69 **Heinz A. Richter *Griechenland 1945-46. Die britische Intervention*** (2016) 456 Seiten, 39 Fotos, gebunden, 49 Euro, ISBN 978-3-447-10533-0

Band 70 **Heinz A. Richter** (ed.), *Griechenland 1942-43. Erinnerungen von Elisabeth und Konstantinos Logothetopoulos* (2015) 320 Seiten, 3 Abbildungen, Hardcover, 28 Euro, ISBN 978-3-447-10460-9

Band 71 **Johannes Fouquet** und **Lydia Gaitanou**, ***Im Schatten der Alten? Ideal und Lebenswirklichkeit im römischen Griechenland*** (2016) 193 Seiten, zahlreiche Karten und Fotos, gebunden, 40 Euro, ISBN 978-3-447-10450-0

Band 72 **Heinz A. Richter *Der griechisch-türkische Krieg 1919-1922*** (2016) 222 Seiten, 132 Fotos, 18 Karten, 1 Faltkarte, gebunden, 30 Euro, ISBN 978-3-447-10656-6

Band 73 **Heinz A. Richter *The Greek-Turkish War 1919-1922*** (2016) 211 pages, 132 photos, 18 maps, 1 folded map, hardcover, 30 Euro, ISBN 978-3-447-10671-9

Band 74 **Heinz A. Richter, *Mythen und Legenden in der griechischen Zeitgeschichte*** (2016) 116 Seiten, 19,80 Euro, ISBN 978-3-447-10703-7

Band 76 **Heinz A. Richter**, ***Hellas und Zypern in meinem Leben. Erinnerungen eines Zeithistorikers*** (2017), 236 Seiten, 56 Tafeln mit 128 Fotos, 30 Euro, ISBN 978-3-447-10846-1

Band 77 **Heinz A. Richter**, ***Geschichte der griechischen Linken***, 560 Seiten, 99 Fotos, gebunden, 50 Euro, 2017; ISBN 978-3-447-10846-1

Band 78 **Harald Gilbert**, ***Der Krieg in der Ägäis 1943-1944***, 340 Seiten Text, 32 Seiten Fotos, 16-24 Seiten Karten im Text, Hardcover, xx Euro, (2017); ISBN 978-3-447-10913-0

Band 79 **Heinz A. Richter**, ***Geschichte der zypriotischen Linken***, 248 Seiten, 16 Tafeln mit 47 Fotos, gebunden, 30 Euro, ISBN 978-3-447-10867-6

Band 80 **Heinz A. Richter**, ***Die türkischen Meerengen in der internationalen Politik 1900-1917***, 300 Seiten, 32 Tafeln mit 77 Fotos, 7 Karten, 1 herausnehmbare Faltkarte, gebunden, 40 Euro, ISBN 978-3--447-10915-4

Band 81 **Vaios Kalogrias**, ***Die Sicherheitsbataillone 1943/44. Hitlers griechische Armee***. xxx Seiten, xx Tafeln mit xx Fotos, xx Karten, gebunden, ca. xx Euro, erscheint im Herbst 2019; ISBN 978-3-447-10917-8

Band 82 **Caroline M. Fischer, *Das Land der Griechen ... gefunden. Mein Leben im griechischen Alltag seit 1979. Erinnerungen,*** *Gedanken, Impressionen.* xxx Seiten, xx Tafeln mit xx Fotos, xx Karten, gebunden, ca. xx Euro, ISBN 978-3-447-10951-2

Band 83 **H. Richter - S. Dordanas - V. Kalogrias, *Ernst von Falkenhausen. Tagebuch des deutschen Militärattachés in Athen 1914 - 1916*** xxx Seiten, xx Tafeln mit xx Fotos, xx Karten, gebunden, ca. xx Euro,; ISBN 978-3-447-10952-9

Band 84 **Heinz A. Richter,** ***Das Osmanische Reich im Ersten Weltkrieg bis zum Friedensschluss 1924,*** 274 Seiten, 32 Tafeln mit 103 Fotos, 32 Karten, 1 herausnehmbare Faltkarte, gebunden, 40 Euro, ISBN 978-3-447-11038-9

Band 85 **Heinz A. Richter,** ***The Ottoman Empire in WWI until the Peace in 1923*** 256 pages, 32 plates with over 100 photos, 32 maps, 1 folded map, hard cover, 40 Euro, ISBN 978-3-447-11045-7

Band 86 **Heinz A. Richter,** ***Die Griechen im Osmanischen Reich 1913-1923. Ihre Verfolgung und Vertreibung*** **198** Seiten, 32 Tafeln mit über 60 Fotos, 6 Karten, 1 herausnehmbar Faltkarte, hard cover, 40 Euro, ISBN 978-3-447-11131-7

Band 87 **Heinz A. Richter**, ***The Greeks in the Ottoman Empire 1913-1923. Their Persecution and Expulsion*** 188 pages, 32 plates with over 60 photos, 6 maps, one folded map in the back, hard cover, 40 Euro, ISBN 978-3-447-11150-8

Band 88 **Heinz A. Richter** (ed.), *Aspekte neugriechischer Geschichte* 132 Seiten, viele Fotos, hard cover, 30 Euro, ISBN 978-3-447-11132-4

Band 89 **Heinz A. Richter,** ***Modern Greek Myths*** 120 pages, hard cover, 19,80 Euro, ISBN 978-3-447--11165-2

Band 90 **Heinz A. Richter**, ***German-Greek Relation 1940-1960 and the Merten Affair*** 108 pages text, 28 photos on 12 pages, hard cover, 20; ISBN 978-3-447-11177-5

Band 91 **Heinz A. Richter,** ***Greece 1936-1946 Events and People*** 192 pages, numerous photos in the text, hard cover, 35 Euro, ISBN 978-3-447-11241-3

Band 92 **Heinz A. Richter**, **Greece 1947-1967 From Civil War to the Putsch on April 21, 1967** 190 pages, hard cover, 30 Euro,ISBN 978-3-447-11255-0